Denis La Plume

MONEY:
What You Don't Know
… and that you absolutely should.

Money: What you Don't Know
Denis La Plume Editions
September 2017
denis@denislaplume.com

Acknowledgements:

to my wife, her ideas and support,

to my colleagues, who will recognize themselves,

to the Ğ1 community,

to the reviewers who gave very precious advice.

Table of Contents

Preamble...7
1. **History of Money**..10
   1.1 Barter or Debt?...10
   1.2 The Egyptian Exception..13
   1.3 Currencies of Kingdoms and Empires...............................15
   1.4 Counterfeiting..18
   1.5 The Goldsmiths...19
2. **Today's Money**..22
   2.1 The National Central Banks...22
   2.2 Federal and Supranational Central Banks........................26
   2.3 "Debt Money"..29
   2.4 The Problem of the Interest...31
3. **Speculation**..35
   3.1 The Stock Markets..35
   3.2 Shadow Banking...39
   3.3 Curves Analysis..42
   3.4 Some Orders of Magnitude..43
4. **The Euro**...47
   4.1 The ECB and the Euro..47
   4.2 Quantitative Easing..50
   4.3 The Impact of the European Monetary Policy.................52
   4.4 The Problems of the Single Currency...............................53
   4.5 Disparities Within the Eurozone.......................................55
   4.6 The CFA Franc..60
5. **Debt and Balanced Budgets**...63
   5.1 Public Debt..63
   5.2 Public Services..65
   5.3 The Problem of the Interest...67
   5.4 Tax Evasion...70
   5.5 Work vs. Dividends..73
   5.6 The "Tickle-Down Theory"...75
6. **Money and the World Economy**..79
   6.1 USD Domination...79
   6.2 The Special Drawing Rights (SDR)...................................81
   6.3 Globalization and Free Trade..83
   6.4 General Criticism of Free-Trade.......................................84
   6.5 Free Trade Treaties in Practice...86

6.6	Who Benefits from Free-Trade?..	88
7.	**The Independence of Nations...**	**91**
7.1	Why We Really Need Regulations...	91
7.2	International Organizations..	94
7.3	National Debts..	96
7.4	Privatizations and National External Debt.................................	97
7.5	Counter-Powers?..	99
7.6	World Finances and the States...	100
8.	**A World in Crisis..**	**103**
8.1	The 2008 Subprimes Crisis..	103
8.2	Europe and the European Banks..	105
8.3	Crisis, Cash and Gold..	106
8.4	How Can We Improve the System?...	109
9.	**Alternatives in the World..**	**115**
9.1	Silvio Gesell's "Freiwirtschaft" (Free Economy).....................	115
9.2	The Swiss WIR..	118
9.3	The LETS and Local Complementary Currencies....................	119
9.4	The Universal Exchange Garden...	121
9.5	The "Community Exchange System" and the "Sardex"..........	122
9.6	In-Game Currencies...	123
9.7	M-Pesa..	124
9.8	Get Rid of Money Altogether?..	125
10.	**Bitcoin and the Blockchain..**	**127**
10.1	What Is At Stake?..	127
10.2	The Creation of Bitcoin...	128
10.3	Bitcoin's Peer-To-Peer Network..	129
10.4	The Blockchain..	131
10.5	Forks, Blockchain and Democracy..	134
10.6	Addresses and Transactions...	137
10.7	Bitcoin Mining...	139
10.8	Advantages of Bitcoin...	139
11.	**Cryptocurrencies in Practice...**	**142**
11.1	Bitcoin's Monetary Creation..	142
11.2	Who Owns Bitcoins?...	145
11.3	Bitcoin and Scalability...	146
11.4	Other Technical Problems of Bitcoin..	149
11.5	Social Problems of Bitcoin..	151
11.6	Altcoins..	154
	Overview: The Flaws of Existing Systems............................	**162**
12.	**The Relative Theory of Money..**	**166**
12.1	What is "Value"?...	166
12.2	Value and Cognitive Biases...	168

12.3	The Importance of the Frame of Reference.................171
12.4	"Value", "Pay" and "Work"......................................174
12.5	The Four Economic Freedoms...................................176

13. Free Currencies..179
13.1	The Human as a Frame of Reference........................179
13.2	The Universal Dividend..180
13.3	Absolute Money Supply Growth...............................183
13.4	Monetary Mass Stability in the Relative Scale..........184
13.5	Attraction Towards the Average...............................186
13.6	A "Communist" Currency?.......................................187
13.7	Free Currencies and Universal Basic Income............189

14. An Implementation for Free Currencies......................194
14.1	Duniter / Ğ1...194
14.2	The Web Of Trust...195
14.3	Why Ğ1 and Bitcoin are very Different....................196
14.4	One Fear: Savings..197
14.5	What about Multinational Corporations?..................199
14.6	Discrimination..201
14.7	Other Criticisms...202
14.8	What Next?..203

Note on Conflicts of Interest..207
Glossary...210
Addendum..216
References...217

Preamble

To reach the truth, you need to get rid once in your life of all the opinions you have received, and rebuild the whole system of your knowledge.

– René Descartes

In this book, we will analyze money, in every of its aspects, to understand how it works and the important implications it has in our lives. We will address various subjects such as the history of money, who creates it, what are its impacts during a crisis, the current economic and financial system and its problems worldwide, the different types of money that exist, cryptocurrencies, and many other things, including some cognitive biases that sometimes make our brain go nuts. All this will also lead us to think about the notions of "value" and "work", which are intimately linked with money, since they are at the core of the economy. This is a summary that aims to be as little technical as possible, but we will sometimes need to get into some details without which it is not possible to understand the global view.

All this information seems essential to understand the world in which we live, and to consider calmly our future by having the main comprehension keys in our hands in order to make the right decisions. The purpose of this book is not to convince anyone of anything, since my personal philosophy is that everyone has to make his own opinions by himself. But to form an opinion, we must open our mind, detach ourself from the prejudices that surround us, take in new ideas, discover new models, and it is the main purpose of this book. The current financial system is often presented as the only possible model. But with this book, you will understand that there are many options when it comes to monetary systems. So at the end of your reading, you will have grasped the current system's advantages and disadvantages, and seen many other options, each with their pros and cons.

We use money every day, yet we usually ask very few questions: we have a bank account, we pay with a credit card, we withdraw "money" from the ATM, and that's it. When we get a loan, we try to negotiate the best interest rate from the banker even if we know that we don't weight much in the negotiation[1]. The only thing we care about is how much we will pay every month and for how many years. This is where our reflections on money usually end.

Furthermore, we think that all this is complicated, that it is reserved for an elite of experts, and that we can not understand it. But we don't have any guarantees that the so-called "experts", to whom we have totally delegated the management of money without a second thought, do not fool us thanks to our ignorance. Or even that, in good faith, they may be totally mistaken in their decisions. After all, Janet Yellen, who is no less than the current Chairwoman of the Federal Reserve, admitted about the 2008 subprimes crisis: "I did not see and did not appreciate what the risks were with securitization, the credit ratings agencies, the shadow banking system, the S.I.V.'s — I didn't see any of that coming until it happened."[2].

In fact, "all that" is quite simple, there is no need to be an economist, you just have to search a little to learn and understand the mechanisms that govern our monetary system. While digging further and further, we usually go from one surprise to another, and we see that the existing system looks like a very fragile idol with feet of clay. In the meantime, we realize that there are hundreds of different ways to manage the economy and money, and that alternatives are possible. Economists generally use complex words to explain other words that in turn sound even more complex, but are sometimes not complicated at all. At the end of this book, you will find a glossary which explains some of these terms and acronyms in the most simple way.

While surfing the Internet on this subject, you will find many sites around conspiracy theories, often with approximations or even blatant lies, but here we will stick to verifiable facts. What I am presenting here is mostly from reliable and mainstream media[i]. I also use Wikipedia as a reliable source, since it cannot be accused of spreading fake news: they remove anything that might be on the fringe. Most of the time, beyond the few references given within this book, I invite you to double-check everything I am putting forward by doing your own research, as I present here only outlines and summaries. We are intelligent beings, and I consider that it is not difficult to type a few keywords in a search engine to get more details on the information you need, while keeping your own critical mind.

Still, bear in mind that this is the summary of years of investigation, reading of blogs, articles and books, and it took me months to put everything together and compile this book. When it comes to economics, there are many schools of thought that often contradict each other, and we will not study them here. I am more interested in analyzing facts and presenting a global vision of money and economy than giving the details of such and such controversial economic doctrine.

Indeed, the subject is really crucial in the sense that we, the ordinary people, must reclaim the concept of money, for it is at the heart of our lives. And the advantage is that we can act on our own, with a bottom-up approach, starting at the individual level, without the need to totally rebuild our political and social institutions.

I have added some "free thoughts" during the writing, not always to be taken literally or even seriously...

Finally, note that this book is mainly centered around Europe and takes many examples from the current situation of the European Union, and especially France. Bear in mind that, regarding money, France is very similar to many countries, and that, wherever you live, the problems of the French system are most likely the same in your own country as well. In any case, we will also go through the global economic and financial situation worldwide.

---

[i] Some references (around 10%) are in French as the book was initially written in French and sometimes takes examples from events occurring in France, but I have searched equivalent references in English when they were available. Some news are also covered in English but on websites whose credibility can be questioned, so I preferred not to use them.

Chapter 1
History of Money

It's important to navigate through history to understand the birth and origin of money, what problems our ancestors faced, and how they solved them.

1.1 Barter or Debt?

At the very beginning, mankind evolved in small tribes, and everything was shared among all members of the tribe. There weren't any exchanges *per se*. Everyone was participating in the tribe's life without counting who was doing what. Everything was "common good".

To explain how we invented money, we all have in mind this story that our ancestors were bartering, that is exchanging one good for another, but as it was not practical, they eventually came up with money. But it's actually a big myth. An anthropologist, David Graeber[3], explains that it never worked this way. It is easy to understand that barter itself can not function except perhaps marginally. "Uh, would you give me 1,000 pounds of apples for my cow?" It is clear that bartering is not only limited, it simply cannot be used practically in exchanges in general, even on a small scale.

Besides, barter cannot solve the problem of the three producers, as it is described in the Relative Theory of Money, by Stéphane Laborde. If A wants B's product, and B wants C's product, and C wants A's product, then these three individuals cannot operate by bartering. And yet this is a potentially very common case because we do not value the same things: the baker may not like vegetables, the butcher may not like bread, the grocer may not like meat. In that case, if they want to exchange their products, they cannot trade through barter, they have to find another way than bilateral exchanges:

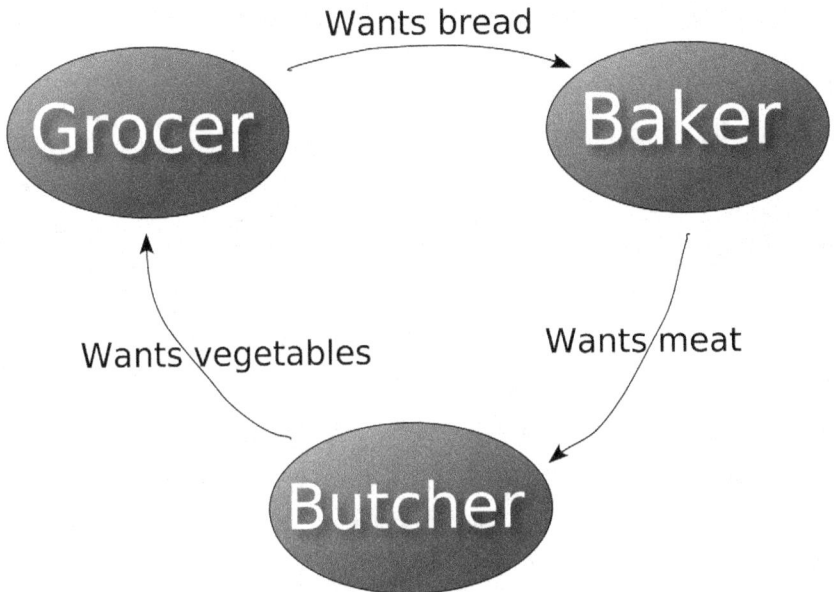

1. *The three producers' problem, where they cannot simply exchange their products using bilateral barter*

David Graeber explains that in order to survive, since the dawn of time, regardless of physical currency, people count and keep in mind their debts towards others, to pay them back at least in part in the future.

At first glance, you could say that the danger of such a system of debts, especially if it is simply kept orally, is that someone may cheat, have debts towards everyone else, and never pay back or give anything to others. But in a community of a limited size, these "parasites" are spotted very quickly. The risk of being excluded, either by being driven out of the tribe, or even physically eliminated, is real, it still happens in some remote tribes. Human beings have a major fear: to be socially isolated, since being part of a group was their only chance of survival.

One of the disadvantages of this system is that, since the economy naturally produces consumption loops due to the problem of the three producers, the accounting of debts can quickly become complex.

David Graeber explains that in the Middle Ages, in some English villages, physical money was not sufficient for every day exchanges. So the villagers kept in mind the debts they had towards each other rather than paying them right away with coins, because of the lack of money. To solve the problem caused by the debt loops, meetings were held periodically to examine the debts of all the villagers, to cancel these loops and thus cancel out a large part of the debts. If the fish seller owed five monetary units to the butcher, who himself owed five to the carpenter, who in turn owed five to the fish seller, then everyone was even and those debts were immediately canceled. The remaining small debts were mostly settled on the spot, generally paid in kind, so that everyone would start from scratch for a new cycle.

Then, because memory can be deceitful and oral contracts are unreliable, especially when the first cities emerged, whose scale exceeded the small group "where everyone knows each other", it was necessary to count in writing who possessed what, and who owed what to whom. The first known accounting dates back to the Sumerians, who recorded the stocks on clay tablets 5,000 years ago.

To exchange, to fix the debt recognition system other than in people's heads, which gets difficult when you are part of a larger group, they had to find something that everyone wanted to exchange, not perishable and whose value did not fluctuate too much.

For example, you can not take a tomato as a unit of universal exchange. To begin with, it rots too fast, and very soon it has to be eaten. Moreover, even still today the value of tomatoes varies according to the seasons, so if you think about an ancient civilization that did not have fridges, the value of a tomato could vary very significantly during the year. During the tomato harvest period, everyone has some, a tomato is not worth much. But in the middle of winter, it becomes a rare and very expensive resource. So this resource can not be used as a reference for trade, its value varies too much and too fast over time.

Finally, our ancestors thought that they had to choose a resource that wasn't too abundant, and not too easy to produce either. Otherwise, some people would start producing massive quantities of it and become rich. Thus, among the different currency systems worldwide in history, we find for instance that they used shellfish with particular shapes as money. Some even used whale teeth in certain archipelagos. The Aztec Empire's main currency was based on cocoa beans, because they were very difficult to produce at the time.

1.2 The Egyptian Exception

In this context, Ancient Egypt is an exception. This multi-millennial civilization did not use money in the form of coins as we know them. The earliest known Egyptian coins appeared around the 4th century BC, almost three centuries after the appearance of the first known coins in the world, and only because Egypt was ruled by a Greek Dynasty at the time. As Egyptians believed that gold was the flesh of the gods and silver their bones, it is not surprising that they were reluctant to forge coins which would have been in everyone's hands, even the poorest[4]. But this means that for nearly three millennia, a civilization as complex and evolved as Ancient Egypt could prosper, trade, defy its rivals, without using coins as we know them today.

To trade objects of significant value, the Egyptians relied on the equivalent in value of a certain weight of gold. Thus, a house worth 10 "shat" could be bought by giving in exchange goods, cloth, bed and other, equivalent to a value of 10 "shat"[5]. This is actually similar to barter, with a gold standard serving as a reference for the individual value of each object.

But for daily exchanges of smaller scale, they used another system. The economist Bernard Lietaer[6] explains that, in addition to their standards based on gold and silver weights, they used commodities as a currency unit, especially wheat, which was abundant. Some of the wheat was of course consumed along the way. They had enormous reserves of wheat, which was growing easily thanks to the providence of the Nile's yearly floods. In fact, Ancient Egypt is being considered the granary of the ancient world by today's anthropologists and archaeologists. Egypt was a major exporter of cereals at the time. Moreover, they knew how to preserve wheat for long periods of time, making it possible to use it as a currency. On the other hand, storing wheat came at a cost: if you stored 10 bags, you would only get 9 bags back after a certain amount of time, due to conservation costs. Thus, the value of a given bag of wheat was depreciated over time due to its storage and natural degradation, and this "money" was created by farmers, who formed the main part of the population. On the other hand, the price of wheat bags varied very little, as the quantity of wheat in circulation was quite constant over time, thanks to conservation systems.

2. Weighing Wheat in Ancient Egypt. Source: Wikipedia.

So, instead of relying on the scarcity of a commodity, on the contrary, they based their money system on the eternal abundance of cereals, while having a relatively constant "money supply" over time through storage. Could this have played a decisive role in the extraordinary longevity and prosperity of ancient Egypt? We must of course put things into perspective and avoid idolizing their society as a whole: a large part of the harvests were "confiscated" through taxes, Pharaoh knew very well how to establish his own wealth...

1.3 Currencies of Kingdoms and Empires

Unlike the Egyptians, most civilizations, and even until the last century, turned to rare resources: gold and precious metals that were available to them like bronze, copper, and so on. They had already solved what they perceived as a problem: conservation. The other incentive is that these coins were used to pay the armies, which often evolved far from their motherland, and it was necessary to find something compact and transportable to pay the soldiers.

Coins appeared simultaneously in different parts of the planet, and were produced in different ways: minted in Greece, stamped in India, and cast in China. Their face value most often corresponded to the value of the metal used to make the coin, as it was still recently the case with silver and gold coins. It is interesting to note that coins appeared a long time after the first recorded debts (remember the Sumerian tablets, which appeared more than 2,500 years before coins). Another interesting fact is that the value of coins based on precious metals was often too high to allow for daily transactions, let alone buying a loaf of bread[7].

One problem of indexing money on the value of metals is that their value fluctuates over time. This happened especially when a new mine was discovered for each of these metals: as a mine was discovered, there was suddenly more metal in the economy, or people simply speculated that the metal would be more abundant, leading to lowering its value. In turn, the currency based on that metal would also lose its value. One historical evidenced of this is the sharp depreciation of gold and silver following the massive importation of these metals from South America by the Spanish and Portuguese[8].

> As a side note, the one who was informed before anyone else of the discovery of a new gold mine had a decisive advantage over the one who suddenly discovered that his gold coins had been depreciated on the market without understanding the core reason...

On the other hand, when all the mines of the kingdom had been drained, it was no longer possible to issue money, which was also problematic and consequently increased the price of the metal. In such cases, the population started storing their coins rather than spending them, leading to deflation. This happened for instance in China starting in the sixteenth century, when the Chinese had to import huge amounts of silver from abroad to cover their needs.

As can be seen, metals, since the appearance of the first coins known in the 6th century BC, have been closely linked to money. In French, the word "silver", "argent", is a synonym of "money". In English, gold is found in many expressions related to money: "to be worth its weight in gold", "gold digger", "to be sitting on a gold mine", "golden parachute". The "golden calf" in the Old Testament is a symbol of idleness, for when you have gold you can afford not to work any more. In the New Testament and the Talmud, Mammon, linked to the "treasure", to "money" in Hebrew, is a divinity, one of the princes of Hell, and intimately connected with wealth.

Back to the implication of the use of precious metals to create money, we must bear in mind that the issue of money has always been the privilege of the Kings, they had that monopoly. Moreover, sovereigns and states have also an important privilege: the one of taxation, which enables them to impose a currency on their subjects who are forced to pay their taxes in that currency.

Try to pay your taxes with bananas, I'm not sure this will go very well... but the Egyptians paid a portion of their taxes in wheat, which was consistent with the use of wheat as a currency.

There is only one exception to the monopoly of the state on monetary creation: crises. During crises, there is often a shortage of money in circulation (called a "liquidity crisis"), while people always need to exchange goods and services in order to survive. In these cases, the state begins to tolerate parallel currencies which always emerge, and which are then called "emergency money" or "notgeld", to avoid any popular revolutionary urges. In the 1920s in France, because of the crisis happening in the same way than in America, the state authorized numerous associations and even some individuals like bar tenders, to print money[9].

It is strongly discouraged to create notgeld outside of crises periods...

Throughout history, sovereigns also had in mind social peace within their people. We generally ignore that in ancient times, the general cancellation of debts was common, particularly debts due to the king or the "state". This took place regularly for over a thousand years in Mesopotamia and then in Egypt[10]. The term "jubilee" is associated precisely with these periodic cancellations of debts.

Today, the cancellation of a debt is a complete taboo: we believe that we have to repay our debts, otherwise it would be unfair. And above all, the so-called cancellations of debts in modern times always come with a total enslavement of the debtor to the creditor. We have a recent example of this, with the sale of Greece's public goods and services to financiers, we will examine this in more detail later. In the old days, they canceled a debt without any compensation, which is very difficult to understand for us because we have been conditioned to think that we must systematically pay off our debts!

We have spoken here mostly about coins, as for banknotes, the first ones appeared in 7th century China[11]. At the beginning, every banknote had its counterpart in valuables kept in Buddhist temples. But the state soon started printing banknotes without any guarantees, which created uncontrolled inflation, and eventually destroyed the credibility of that form of money.

I will let the reader compare that situation with the current economic state of the world when reading the rest of this book...

Banknotes and coins are called "fiat money", we will see later that it is not the only kind of money that currently exists.

Another problem with state money is when it is too easy to copy. In the 17th century, French soldiers officially got paid with "playing cards cut in quarters", believe it or not[12]. Soon enough, people were cutting their playing cards into pieces...

1.4 Counterfeiting

Counterfeiters, by creating illegal money, have been the nightmare of all powers, since the appearance of coins in antiquity. The penalties for counterfeiters were very high and today they would be considered as totally discouraging. To give just one example, in the Middle Ages, counterfeiters of all kinds were merely boiled alive before being hanged in public.

It becomes interesting when you learn that counterfeit money was most often produced by official money makers. There are even examples of princes who have also made counterfeit money to get rich at the expense of the king. The first known counterfeiter is Diogenes the Cynic, a Greek philosopher. His father was a banker, and he got involved as a young man in counterfeit money, to the point that he was forced to go into exile.

It left such a mark on him that he spent the rest of his life as a vagrant philosopher, advocating poverty.

As the coins were often worth the value of the metal itself, counterfeiters often used techniques to replace the original metal by something else. One of the techniques is to use an alloy, a mix of metals, that resembles the original metal. For instance you could use brass in place of gold, or what is called "billon", which is a silver alloy and which perfectly resembles silver, but which contains only a smaller percentage of the precious metal.

One other disadvantage of having coins made of precious metal is the so-called "coin debasement", which involves removing some of the metal from the coins in the most discreet way possible. This can be done by scraping the outer parts of the coin. The "cropped" coin is lighter, but in the meantime, the cheater has recovered some precious metal. Unless facing someone very suspicious, the trick would go unnoticed. This is why some coins have notches on the circumference, to fight against this practice since cropping such a coin would be immediately spotted. Another technique is by shaking many coins in a bag, and collecting the dust worn off.

One other trick is to make the coin with another cheap metal, and cover it with the precious metal, so that the visible part of the coin looks perfect. To detect these counterfeit coins, weighing can be used because each metal has a different weight. But the forgers are clever, for example, some gold coins currently found on the market are coated with gold with a core made of tungsten. Tungsten and gold have a very similar density ($19.3 \text{ g} / \text{cm}^3$), so you cannot spot these forgeries by simply weighting the coins. Beware of fakes, even if they are rare, whether it is for gold or silver coins. Other tests such as the attraction of a magnet or the sound made by the coin are used to detect fakes.

Other forging techniques have even involved, for example, altering existing coins to make them look like other, more valuable coins that looked like them. The imagination of counterfeiters is limitless!

Counterfeiting was also used as a war tool. For instance, Britain used it during the War of Independence in the US. It was later a victim of it during the Second World War when Nazi Germany forced prisoners to create fake British Pounds, and the Pound was seriously devalued at the end of the war, because of the large mass of counterfeit currency in circulation[13].

Karma does come back around...

1.5 The Goldsmiths

The goldsmiths hold a very special position regarding money.

Some have been counterfeiters, but this is not what I want to talk about.

I want to speak about the IOUs, promissory notes, where one certifies that he owes something to someone else.

The Sumerians, as we have already mentioned, already kept records of who owned what, and who owed what to others, on clay tablets.

In the Middle-Ages in the Middle East, banks were holding precious goods for rich merchants in exchange for IOUs[i], called "Shakk", which

---
i   IOU = I Owe You. A paper that certifies that one person owes a certain amount of value to another.

gave the word "cheque". In Europe, the "bill of exchange" was developed to try and standardize a new way of dealing with debt[14]. This new system based on debt created chaos all over Europe[15] as the different kingdoms often defaulted and didn't pay their debts back. It also brought Renaissance Florence to its knees[16].

Besides, the goldsmiths, due to their profession, have always had reserves of gold, associated with the adequate security. As a result, rich people who needed a safe place to store their gold, entrusted it to the local goldsmith rather than keeping it under their bed. The goldsmiths were given large stocks of gold, and for each piece of gold stored in their vaults, they gave a certificate in exchange, guaranteeing that the owner of the gold could recover it when he needed it.

These certificates were nominative at first, then became impersonal, and thus became an new means of exchange. Instead of paying with the local currency, it became possible to pay with one of these certificates. A person who received such a certificate could go and retrieve the corresponding gold at the goldsmiths. Expanding the practice further, goldsmiths agreed with each other to accept certificates from other goldsmiths throughout Europe. Certificates became a kind of "parallel currency", resulting from the recognition of debts, and were therefore a form of monetary creation. The goldsmiths invented the current "Debt Currency" system, but of course on a tiny scale compared to what it has become today.

At that point, they realized that they always had some reserve in their vaults, and not everyone came at the same time to recover their gold. They realized that they did not necessarily need to have all the gold in stock. It was enough for them to have only a sufficient amount to satisfy only the needs of the proportion of their customers who generally came to claim their gold. They had invented the system of "fractional reserves", which will be discussed later.

It is not by chance that the Rothschilds were goldsmiths.

Summary:

Our ancestors faced the problem of exchanges, especially the one of the Three Producers. They solved it by counting and memorizing their debts, and finally by creating money in the form of coins, most of the time made with rare metals. The first banknotes appear in China around the 7th century to avoid carrying heavy and cumbersome metals.

Banknotes and coins are called "fiat money", which is created and controlled exclusively by the sovereign or the state. Counterfeiters, sometimes officials, were severely punished.

Ancient Egypt was an exception, with its "wheat money", a currency that decayed with time and was constantly created in abundance by the whole population.

Debt cancellations (associated with Jubilees) were common practice in Ancient Times.

Starting in the Middle-Ages, from China to Europe, paper money as promissory notes develop and is generalized by the goldsmiths in Europe.

Chapter 2
Today's Money

We have seen so far the way our ancestors have dealt with the different problems they met when they wanted to do some exchanges. It is now time to fast-forward to modern times to understand how and why the current system was built.

2.1 The National Central Banks

The principle of a National Central Bank dates from the late 17th century with the creation of the Bank of England. At the time, private banks create their own money, it is common for kings to borrow from them, especially to finance wars. But their authority allows them to easily default and not pay back. Bankers are constantly afraid they will never see there precious money again, which creates a climate of mistrust towards the sovereign. We already have seen this in the previous chapter with the many defaults of Spain, and the bankruptcy of powerful cities such as Venice or Florence, mostly due to the unreasonable use of "paper money" which is backed by nothing.

In 1672, the English King Charles II declares a period of non-repayment of the royal debts of one year, causing an incredible chaos. This happens while the country is at war with the Netherlands, and the financiers refuse to lend more money to the king to finance the ongoing war. Twenty-two years later, King William III decides to create the Bank of England to avoid any further default. The Central Bank system was born. It most often comes along with the monopoly of the production of money by the Central Bank. In other words, no private bank is allowed to create money anymore. However, the Bank of England was still a part of the government at that time.

In France, Napoleon creates in 1800 the Bank of France, of which he becomes a shareholder, with the help of his financial friends, mostly French and Swiss bankers. It is created thanks to the state's own treasury, which our happy bunch of friends take for themselves[17]. The basic idea, in addition to become immediately rich, was that the Bank of France, both independent and dependent of the State, could create and destroy fiat currency at will, depending on the needs of the state. But above all, it implied a monopoly on monetary creation, as it happened with every other Central Bank. Most of the other European countries have also created their own central bank during the nineteenth century. We are going to talk here about "national banks", because they operate within a country.

While this system of central banks addressed the problem of paying back the debt, it still suffered from another flaw: the central bank could still create money at will. Any state invests continuously in the country's infrastructure and the salaries of civil servants. When starting a new project, it becomes very tempting to create as much money as needed to finance it. Similarly, if the accounts of the state are empty, why not create some money to fill them up? There is even no need to "manage" your budget: just create money!

This means that there is more and more money in the country, since the state creates some all the time. The problem is that when there is no control, the monetary supply, which is the total amount of money in circulation in the economy, grows without any bounds. But more money in the economy means that prices start rising[i]. This leads first to growing inflation, and then to hyperinflation. Prices inevitably skyrocket which causes problems for the population as a whole. But more than that, it discredits the currency worldwide and in turn ruins the nation's credibility on the world economic scale.

To avoid this problem of hyperinflation caused by the uncontrolled growth of the money supply, most countries in the nineteenth century

---

i If everyone in the population has 1.000 coins in their pocket, they may be ready to pay a loaf of bread 10 coins. But if they all have only 100 coins in their pockets, they will be ready to pay only 1 coin for the same loaf. So the total amount of money circulating has a direct influence on the prices.

turned to the "gold standard". Basically, they created coins made of gold, or used notes or coupons that were directly exchangeable with gold held physically in the vaults of the banks. This ensured that every penny was "backed by something" and that the money supply was never going to grow in an uncontrolled way.

However, economists quickly understood that this model suffers from a serious problem: it favors deflation, that is, the contraction of the money supply in relation to the real economy. As the rare resource (gold) on which the currency is indexed is limited, it is not possible to create new money when the economy needs it.

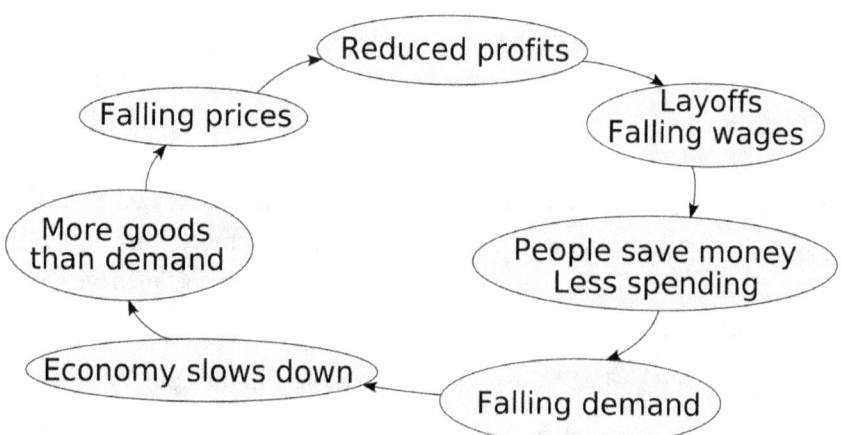

3. The deflation spiral. People hoard money and spend less => falling demand => the economy slows down => but because existing goods are still on the market, they are more abundant than the demand => prices fall => companies make less profit => companies reduce their investments and proceed with layouts => people spend less since they anticipate future falling of prices.

So, if countries produce more and more resources but the money supply does not grow at least in the same proportions, there is deflation because there is not enough money to cover the needs for the exchanges. Prices fall.

Additionally, the gold-indexed currency encourages the population to accumulate and stockpile this precious resource. What would you do if you knew that prices are going down and you own a gold coin? You would keep it as long as possible, especially for large expenses. This means that there are less and less coins circulating in the economy, as everyone holds to them. But if there is less money around, then your gold coin is getting even more valuable, which pushes you to hold it even further. This situation creates a "deflation spiral" which inevitably leads to an economic crisis due to a "liquidity crisis", where there isn't enough money as everyone holds to their coins instead of spending them. As we have seen, money is the "lubricant" of the economy. With less and less money, the economy slows down and eventually stops, This deflation spiral is the main nightmare of economists, much more than inflation[18].

The first world war totally disrupts the existing economies, which struggle after the war to get back to the gold standard, with very little success. Besides, and to follow the economic booms in the 1920, financiers switch to speculative systems, which create bubbles. These bubbles burst in 1929, and the decade of crisis that follows leads the world into WWII.

Once bitten, twice shy...

After the failure of coming out from the gold standard between the two wars, it is back in business with the Bretton Woods system in 1944: each USD[i] is directly exchangeable for gold, and this time at an international scale. But starting in 1971, this system is shaken. The rigidity of the gold standard as observed in the 19th century hits its limits again. The Americans have printed more money than their gold reserves to satisfy the growing demand of the world, and this doesn't go unnoticed.

The Germans finally kill the system by leaving it. Many countries follow, leading to a massive demand to convert Dollars into gold in 1971. Nixon, The American President, doesn't want to totally lose the gold reserve of the US and decides to freeze the system and suspend the conversion of the USD to gold[19]. This causes the collapse of the system in

---
i   I will use "USD" or "Dollar" for "Dollar of the United States of America" in the rest of this book.

the next few years, and this will be the trigger for the "oil crisis" of the 1970s[20]. It is actually not the first time the US breaks the Gold Standard. In April 1933, Roosevelt also decided that the Gold Standard. Following his decision, the ounce of gold went from 20.67\$ to 35\$[21].

As we have just seen, the control of the amount of money in circulation, called the money mass or monetary supply, seems to be key to manage the economy and avoid crises. The role of central banks is exactly that: controlling the money supply.

To summarize, Central Banks today are "banks for commercial banks". Once a central bank is created in a country, nobody is allowed to create money anymore. Kings, Emperors, Presidents, Prime Ministers, Commercial (private) banks, everyone has to borrow from the Central Bank if they want fiat money. The central bank is responsible for all monetary policies. As they are independent from the state, it is assumed that no ruler will ever have the possibility of not paying back his debt anymore. Additionally, the independence of central bankers becomes a safeguard against artificial hyperinflation caused by the states.

One of the obvious challenges is that it is necessary for the leaders of central banks to be able to judge the "needs of the economy" at a given moment, which raises the inevitable question of conflicts of interest: if they are not strictly controlled, the "judges" can then estimate the needs for money depending on their own personal needs rather than the needs of the general population.

2.2 Federal and Supranational Central Banks

The United States had its first Central Bank since the independence in 1795. The Central Banks System was then abolished by Andrew Jackson in the 1830s. Then, following the American crisis of 1907, the system of Central Banks called "Federal Reserve System", abbreviated to "Fed", was introduced in 1913 in somewhat unclear circumstances on Christmas Eve while most congressmen were enjoying their holidays at home.

First, its appellation is strange and confusing. Indeed, the Fed does not strictly have a "reserve", the term indicates that it is a bank that has control over monetary policy: issuance of money and control of interest rates. Then, it is not a "Federal" entity because it does not depend on the American state, in violation of the US Constitution: it is originally a privately owned bank, with a private board of directors composed mostly of Wall Street bankers, and which didn't answer to the President or Congress of the United States.

A very interesting book about its creation and influence, although dating back to the 1950s, is the book "The Secrets of the Federal Reserve" by Eustace Mullins[22]. In addition to the history of the Federal Reserve, he presents the destruction of the network of small American banks during the Farm crisis in the 1920s, and conflicts of interest of the Fed governors during the crisis of 1929, as well as many conflicts of interest in the world of finance.

Since then, the Fed has gradually lost its "totally private" status, it is generally described as an "independent institution within the government". But to quote Wikipedia, "its monetary policy decisions do not have to be approved by the President or anyone else in the executive or legislative branches of government"[23]. Its governors are appointed by the President of the United States, their term of office is renewable for 14 years. The privileges of the Fed remain very large but some voices start requesting more transparency in its operations since the 2008 subprimes crisis.

The situation is not much better in Europe[24]. The European Central Bank, known by its abbreviation ECB, first called "European Monetary System" and then "European Monetary Institute", is headed by members of various National Central Banks of Europe. I will call "National Banks", the different Central Banks of every member states. According to Wikipedia, the administrators of the ECB are appointed "from among persons of recognized standing and professional experience in monetary or banking matters by common accord of the governments of the Member States at the level of Heads of State or Government, on a recommendation from the Council, after it has consulted the European Parliament and the Governing Council of the ECB". In short, the heads of the member states trust people who are in conflicts of interest to present "good" candidates to them, and accept them without much examination. That's for the ECB.

On the other hand, National Banks of every member country of the EU, even if they are headed by senior officials from each country of the Union, are no longer accountable to their respective countries. Instead, they are under the direct tutelage of the ECB.

Besides, the article 130 of the Lisbon treaty specifies very clearly that no country or government should try to interfere with the doings and decisions of the ECB: it is a sovereign entity[25].

To summarize this situation, the ECB, which is a totally independent entity from governments, therefore controls National Banks, whose members become governors of the ECB. We realize that there is a very vicious circle in which the ECB and the National Banks are interdependent and are not subject to any external scrutiny: they control themselves totally independently. Moreover, the current President of the ECB is in full conflict of interest[26], which doesn't come as a surprise since we now know how the Presidents of the ECB are nominated.

I would really like to be appointed director of my own bank by my wife, and then make my own private loans at my own fixed interest rates...

The ECB is, in fact, only dispatching orders, asking the various European National Banks to print money whenever it wants to, it does not print anything. Thus, for instance the Bank of France prints Euros, and these Euros immediately become an 8% credit on the ECB. The remainder is given in proportion to the "importance" of the different countries in the Union. In reality, Euros are valued in a totally different way depending on the countries of the Union, due to the economic health and inflation of each country, which is very different from one to another.

Above all the Central Banks of the world, there is the Bank for International Settlements, the BIS, whose headquarters are in Basel, Switzerland. It is called the "Central Bank of Central Banks", and is hosting meetings of the various directors of the world's Central Banks. No one escapes this "Centralized Central Banking System", even China or Russia, except a few countries like North Korea or Libya before the fall of Muammar Gaddafi[27].

The BIS is relatively transparent on its analyses of the state of finance and world trade, but it is totally opaque regarding the decisions and meetings of its members[28]. This is strange as there can be no state secrets in these meetings that would require high confidentiality levels. The members are directors of the Central Banks from different countries who exchange information among themselves. Obviously, they wouldn't disclose any sensitive information about their respective countries to their competitors, so the lack of transparency towards the general public is quite intriguing. In addition, its members benefit from a full diplomatic immunity guaranteed by the Swiss state, which inevitably encourages corruption.

To make a caricatural summary, the whole system is made of Central Banks that are not controlled by any state, and are supervised by the BIS, a fully diplomatic immune institution that is very opaque in its operations.

2.3 "Debt Money"

Credit has always existed, very often accompanied by interest. The three monotheistic religions, perceiving the downward slide associated with high interest rates, unanimously condemn loans with interest, at least in principle. While Jews and Christians have made concessions, Muslims, on the other hand, follow it to the letter, and develop "Islamic banks". These banks lend money without interest. Consequently, they are seriously involved in the projects they finance in order to secure the repayment of the loans. They also receive a portion of the profits when there are some. This is the principle of dividends, which is very different from interest. Dividends are about sharing profits, while an interest is some kind of "insurance" in case of a default of the borrower.

Since the Bretton Woods system has collapsed, "Debt Money" has taken an unprecedented magnitude in modern economy. Any entity, private or public, that needs money, is forced to borrow it from banks, who in turn, borrow from Central Banks.

First of all, the lending systems in the world are quite varied. In France, when repaying a loan from a bank, the borrower repays both interest and principal, very often at fixed rates. In the United States, loans are often at variable rates, which can have unfortunate consequences when interest rates rise, as we will see when analyzing the subprimes crisis. In Switzerland and Sweden, there is a system in which the borrower reimburses only interest, with very long term loans, sometimes more than a hundred years[29]. We can also compare this with "buying" real estate in Great Britain, where the "purchase" of real estate is in fact most of the time a "leasehold", so the "owner" actually has to "buy back his property" when the lease expires. This is totally different from French law, for instance, where you own a land for life when you buy it, and you can even transfer it to your children.

Let's examine what happens when a bank delivers a loan, whether it's a central, national or private bank, and whatever system it is using from the above examples. When the contract is signed, the bank adds the money to the borrower's account, and writes in its own accounts that "M. or Mrs. X" owes the bank that amount of money, with the added interest. Some new money gets created from nowhere, only due to the contract signed between the bank and the borrower. A computer adds a line in the accounts, and that's it! When the loan is paid back in full some time later, the bank keeps the interest for itself in its own account, but destroys the "principal", which is the amount that was originally borrowed. It thus destroys that money that was temporarily created, for the needs of the loan. This mechanism seems very strange at first, but this is how the current system actually works.

This system is supposed to balance the economy, by creating money when the economy needs it and to those who need it, and by destroying that money when it is no longer needed. We will see how this very Utopian version of the system is very far from what happens in reality.

We can already note that, in this perspective, cooperative credit systems that lend existing money cannot be competitive compared to banks, since they need to really have the principal in their accounts when lending the money, while banks can create money from the void, whenever they wish.

In this respect, one can question the need for an "interest" since the bank takes no risk as the borrowed money is created from a simple click on a mouse button of a computer, but I probably have a sharp tongue here...

To avoid banks making boundless loans, there is a limit to the credits they can grant. Every bank needs to have in their vaults a percentage of the total money they have lent. The value of this percentage is decided by the administrators of the BIS behind closed doors. They regularly publish the "Basel Accords", the last one being "Basel III"[30], which sets the necessary percentage at around 7% of the total credits, which hasn't changed much since the first "Basel I" accord.

In 2010 and 2011, after the subprimes crisis in 2008, these Basel III agreements were signed, to be originally implemented in 2015, and now extended to 2019.

Of course, the mainstream media have thoroughly covered this event for us to participate in the decision... it is very reassuring to know that our banker friends are taking care of us in such a discreet manner!

In concrete terms, this means that when a bank issues loans for 100 units of a currency, it only needs to have 7 units of that currency in its vaults. This is called the "Fractional Reserve System". They just need to have a "Fraction" of what they lend in their "Reserves". This reminds us of the system invented by the goldsmiths, but at a much wider scale.

2.4 The Problem of the Interest

With this system, the monetary mass in circulation can vary sharply depending on the loans that are granted. Moreover, this system also has a very major problem: the interest that is kept by the banks when the loans are paid back. This aspect can be easily understood with a simple caricatural example: the island of the shipwrecked sailors[31].

Let's imagine 10 shipwrecked survivors stuck on an island, who all produce some value by their work, and face the three producers' problem. One day, an eleventh castaway comes to the island, and offers to be their banker. He offers to loan them each 100 coins, and asks them to each give back 110 at the end of the year, due to the interest. It is obvious that, as there are only 1,000 coins in total on the island, it is impossible for all the survivors to give back a total of 1,100 coins at the end of the year. And the more of them will pay back their loans with interest, the more others will be in big financial trouble. Also remember that, as a loan is paid back in full, the banker destroys 100 and keeps 10 in his pockets.

Globally, to be able to deal with the situation, our survivors all have to make new larger loans to be able to reimburse more at the end of the next year. And so on every year. Until the banker starts asking for guarantees and mortgage since the loans get bigger and bigger with time. You may argue that this is a simple caricature, and that many people in real life pay back their loans. But this example is representative of the economy as a whole, and perfectly matches the growing debts of all main nations of the world. If one state pays its debt in full, it is doing so at the expense of other states.

This spiral of debt creates the need for more and bigger loans, and is one of the main reasons for the "economic growth" that is observed and asked by economists. Without growth, no bigger credits can be granted, and the whole system collapses.

Another problem related to this system of debt-money is that it intensifies the crises, and creates cycles that induce more crises. Indeed, during an economic boom, banks grant loans without much trouble to everyone, as we will see when we study the subprimes crisis. This create bubble effects, since a lot of money is created in the economy thanks to the many loans that are granted by the banks. When these bubbles burst one day or another, or when the symptoms of a crisis are on the horizon, the banks suddenly stop lending money to protect themselves from bankruptcy. This in turn reduces the monetary mass, causes deflation, and increases the effects of the coming crisis in a spiral of failing loans and banks.

Finally, the main challenge is that this debt-money gives all the power to the banks. They are the ones who decide how much money should be created, and who should benefit from it, besides themselves of course.

Banks can borrow from Central Banks with very short term "loans", and at extremely low rates. The current rate for a bank making a 2 months loan to the ECB is currently at... 0%[32]. However, when you want a loan to buy a house, you obviously don't get a loan at a 0% interest rate. The current rates in France for 20 years loans are currently about 1.30 to 1.75% per year, which is very low. Well, that's what you think.

The trick of the banks to attract you is that they always talk about the interest rate "per year". They don't want to scare you off, they need your money. You may think that, at a 1.5% interest rate for a $100,000 loan, you will give $1,500 of interest back to the bank. Well, that's true if this is only a 1 year loan. But for a 20 years loan, they still speak about "1.5% interest rate", but it is still a yearly rate. What does this change? If you get a $100,000 credit from a bank at a fixed 1.5% interest rate on 20 years (which is very low, it is actually much higher in the US), you will pay back $115,810.90[33]. That's $15,810.90 of interest, which means a 15,8% total interest rate. And that is still very low, since current interest rates are low.

As we have already pointed out, "interests" are actually a kind of insurance to cover some costs if you can't pay back your loan at some point. Of course, if you don't pay back, banks seize whatever possible from you to try and still recover that money (which was created from nothing, but still needs to be paid back with your house if necessary). But in addition to that, banks force you to subscribe to an insurance, which they generally "generously" provide. In France, the current rates for the insurance are around 0.36% on average. But that means that for the exact same $100,000 loan, you will actually pay $23,010.90 in interest and insurance, that's a 23% rate, noting like our initial 1.5%. Remember that these sums are kept by the banks when you pay back your debt. For a loan at a 4.5% interest, which has been a "normal" rate some years ago, a 25 years credit results in more than 70% of interest, which is quite something else.

But then, if they have so much income for so little risk, why do banks fail? The main reason is that they create money based on nothing. Remember, they have 7, and they owe you 100. The second reason is that they have to give back dividends to their investors[34]. Which means that some of the money they "keep" actually goes to their stockholders. And finally, the most important is that... they gamble with that money![35]

Summary:

When creating money which is not backed by anything, States always tend to create more and more of it for themselves, which leads to hyperinflation.

The gold standard has been used to avoid such uncontrolled production of currency by the states. But it leads to deflation, which is still a bigger danger than inflation. Deflation implies that money becomes more valuable than goods, which encourages speculation and accumulating money rather than spending it, which creates even more deflation. It causes a contraction of the monetary mass in circulation which provokes crises.

Central Banks were created to regulate monetary creation and interest rates on loans. They are not controlled by the States, and are independent entities. The BIS, an intriguingly secretive institution, is giving directives to all Central Banks.

When a bank grants a loan, it creates the principal from nothing, which is "Debt Money". When the loan is repaid in full, it destroys the principal and keeps the interest. This creates a spiral of debt to repay ever increasing interest, which in turn creates the need for "economic growth". Under the Basel III agreements by the BIS, banks are required to have around 7% of the money they lend in their vaults (Fractional Reserves).

The Debt-Money system is giving banks the considerable power of deciding who and which projects should be allowed to be awarded money. This system also intensifies and even provokes crises cycles.

Chapter 3
Speculation

3.1 The Stock Markets

Speculation on money is not new[36], but during the last century speculation has been reaching an unprecedented magnitude. Since the 1920s, bankers have been speculating on loans. In other words, they "sell" to each other the loans they have granted, of course without informing the borrowers. Speculation is in use in the whole economic sphere. Any goods, services, companies, and even humans[37], can be speculated upon. In this paradigm, everything is based on belief, faith and rumors. When it comes to speculating on already speculated assets which are called "derivatives", investors are totally disconnected from reality. In 2003, the billionaire Warren Buffet warned us and said: "derivatives are weapons of mass destruction". This "disconnection from reality" allowed Bernard Madoff, a "trustworthy-like" investor and president of the NASDAQ in the 1990s, to fool his customers for 48 years, until the fraud was uncovered following the subprimes crisis.

Along with speculation come new laws, typically to forbid what is called "Insider Trading". Indeed, as everything is now about how much information one has on the economic health of a company, or the future demand on such or such goods or service, the person who obtains confidential information before others has a critical advantage.

For instance, imagine that you have had access to a company's balance sheet a few hours before it is released to the press because of your position in that company, or because you're the CEO's daughter and you saw the papers on your father's desk. You notice it announces a complete disaster for the future of this company, which is almost bankrupt. You rush to sell your shares of this company before anyone else learns the bad news. This is called "insider trading". There are many cases in which this can happen. You may have heard that a huge gold deposit has been found that will lower the price of gold. Or that a company is going to buy another one. Or maybe that a revolutionary scientific discovery by a company will multiply its stock value by magnitudes nobody can even dream of.

So, laws are put in place to condemn anyone who would be caught doing "insider trading". But how can we really verify who has been able to get some confidential information, which is by definition unofficial and obviously kept secret? It is easy to realize the practical limits of such laws, especially as it is possible to make very complex arrangements in which any manipulation can be hidden.

Another aspect of the stock market is that, since the 1990s, increasingly complex computer programs have invaded the markets, which use "microtransactions" performed within milliseconds or even microseconds. They have been disrupting the global stock market significantly for more than 10 years. In May 2010, the major US stock indexes fell by more than 9% in a few minutes, largely due to high-frequency transactions, for a total of several trillions of Dollars (yes, thousands of billions...). And this is obviously not a good reason to stop the madness. Nowadays, based on estimates, 75-85% of transactions are made by computer algorithms on the New York Stock Exchange[38].

Humans, better brace yourselves!

One of the main problems of speculative markets is that all actors have access to the same information at the same time. In order not to be accused of spreading conspiracy theories, I will not even talk about that minority who have the information in advance and who can anticipate the trends. Most speculators play it by the ear, and as they follow the same signals, they react like herd of sheep following the latest trend.

They typically follow the advices of "Rating Agencies". These agencies, which are private organizations, give notes to states, large corporations, stock markets, just as a school teacher gives grades to his students. These agencies are therefore very powerful, and run the show for the companies, but also for the countries, they act like sheepdogs for the herd. They are very profitable, and are paid by the very companies they have to rate. So if you need a rating, you knock on their door, ask them to rate your company and pay them for this service. This obviously raises problems of conflicts of interest[39]. Their ratings are far from objective or even justified, as will be seen from their role in the subprimes crisis.

Because of this, speculators can crash the stock of a specific value very easily and in a very short time. Even "safe bets", such as the British Pound itself, which experienced a "flash crash" in Asia following stock market panics in 2016[40]. In 2014, "emerging currencies" (India, Russia, Turkey...) were the victims of a massive movement of big investors, causing their prices to plummet[41]. Another recent example is the collapse of the Chinese market in 2015[42].

It looks like there isn't a single year when speculators don't "break" some toy lately!

Behind each stock index of the market, there are humans. Every raise and crash of the price of rice or wheat on the market affects real people from one end of the world to the other, who sell or buy goods that are necessary for their survival. Life is thus totally dehumanized, in the hands of "traders" who have in mind only short-term profits and algorithms programmed only for instant monetary gain, regardless of the impacts in the real life of billions of people[43].

Another effect of a company being on the stock market is that its only goal is to attract and please its stockholders. And stockholders are after immediate profit. They don't care much about long-term profits, which are riskier. One very classic way of pleasing investors is to proceed with a layoff. Why is that? It sounds totally crazy to get rid of people you have trained to do their job, who know the ins and outs of the work they are doing, and who are productive by definition. But for shareholders, this has an immediate effect: the company will have to pay less wages in the short term, which means higher immediate profits, which in turn generates more dividends. And when this drives the company to fail on the long term, investors have sold their stocks long before that and moved on to another company. In the meantime, employees find themselves jobless.

Another symbol of the "market" is billionaire George Soros, known as "the man who broke the Bank of England". Back in 1992, speculating on the British Pound, George Soros puts the Bank of England on its knees, and gains one and a half billion pounds sterling of profit. Speculators do not care about human beings, their sole and only goal is to make more and more profit.

> *I don't judge them. They are merely using the system as it is. We cannot ask every single person on this Earth to be a Buddha*[i].

Besides that, banks also don't always play fair. On the international scene, scandals involving banks agreeing with each other to manipulate the markets are widespread. The two most famous scandals are the Forex[44] and Libor[45] scandals, which even made it to the mainstream media, but didn't get much attention anyway. The main idea is to change the actual interest rates in order to obtain short term profits. So yes, indeed, banks are not playing fair and do any tricks, including illegal ones, to make more money. And in these two scandals in which billions were made illegally by banks, only two traders (who are mere subordinates) in total (yes, one trader each, just to say that "someone has been condemned") have been prosecuted. The big fishes have escaped any judgment, even if some of them have resigned to keep appearances up.

Hedge funds are also big players that can terrorize the markets. In 2010, the Wall Street Journal reports a dinner in which some of the heads of the biggest hedge funds bet that the Euro would fall to parity with the USD, when at the time one Euro was valued at $1.51[46]. Among them, George Soros, who then published some scare-mongering article in the Financial Times to help faith a little[47]. The fact is that, while gambling on the stock market is regulated, gambling with currencies is not. Therefore, speculators have real fun with currencies. But this brings us to other markets that are unregulated as well.

---

[i] "Buddha" is actually a title, which means "enlightened". So Siddhārtha Gautama was given the title "The Buddha", since he is considered as an exceptional being, but anyone reaching enlightenment as described by Buddhists can become a Buddha.

3.2 Shadow Banking

So far, we have seen only speculation and "official" markets, including some cheating. But there are also unofficial and unregulated markets, which are rarely subject to mainstream news, but which do exist and are acknowledged by officials. These are called the "dark pools". This name sounds very evil, but they only designate speculative platforms that exist outside the regular stock markets. What is the difference?

A stock exchange is actually made up of two parts: sellers and buyers, who publish sale and purchase offers. For example, a seller may offer to sell 10 units of a product at a price x. A buyer offers to buy 10 units of the same product at a price y. As long as the buyer has a lower purchase price than the seller, no transaction can take place. If a buyer comes and makes a public offer to buy at the same price than the seller, then the exchange carries out the transaction: the buyer buys from the seller the 10 units of the product at the matching price. Thus, at a particular instant, we obtain a sort of balance between the offers of sale and purchase which fixes a price for the object that is exchanged. In the meantime, the stock exchange owner takes a commission on the transaction for its running costs. In this system, everything is done publicly. So everyone knows the public selling and buying offers at all times, along with the average purchase price for that particular good in the last minutes, in order to be able to follow the global trends, downwards or upwards.

Dark pools, on the other hand, operate with "over-the-counter" transactions. To caricature the way it works, while all others publish offers to buy and sell, the "over the counter" buyer and seller meet face to face in a dark corner of the room, and directly negotiate a price for their own transaction. They therefore do not go through any intermediary, and their transaction is not negotiated in any public stock exchange[48]. A Reuters study indicates that since the 2008 crisis, dark pool transactions have gone from 16% to 40% in the United States[49].

There are two "advantages" that are put forward for this system. The first advantage concerns only those who carry out transactions: they remain anonymous, instead of making public bids. The second advertised advantage is to avoid disturbing the markets by avoiding the "waves" of panic of the regular stock market.

It seems to me, on the contrary, that these "black markets" add some extra opacity to a system that is already in a bad shape. To believe that a transaction made "under the table" will not disrupt the markets is quite Utopian. And this exacerbates conflicts of interest and insider trading risks even more.

In fact, these transactions outside the stock markets are raising more and more concerns, Reuters even said they "may be more harmful than high-frequency trading"[50]!

We finally come to what are called "shadow financing", also modestly called "market-based financing". This is again not a matter of conspiracy theory, but actual and documented players in world finance, which are not banks[51]. These include hedge funds and asset managers. The giant BlackRock, for example, manages by itself 5,400 billion Euros worth of assets for its customers[52] (more than double the GDP of France!). As you can see in the following graph, a Bloomberg study clearly shows how they are growing compared to "traditional" markets:

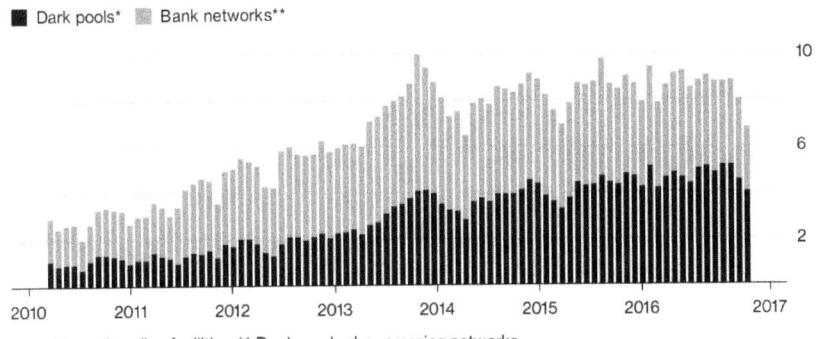

4. *This clearly shows how Dark Pools gain trading volume at the expense of traditional trading platforms. Source : A Bloomberg study*[53]

All these players in the "shadow market" are not subject to the regulations that apply to banks, and are totally beyond the control of the central banks. This shadow finance is made possible by the extremely low rates of Central Banks. These "non-bankers" can borrow at zero or extremely low interest rates and then invest in whatever they want, often in schemes that are too risky or ever forbidden by regulations for regular banks[54]. This is worrying regulators, like Mario Draghi, the president of the BCE[55].

It looks like the EU finally tries to slow down the rise of these shadowy traders, by passing a new regulation that will lower the volumes that can be traded through dark pools. However, now that these dark pools have taken so much influence, I am concerned that the regulators are coming in too late. In 2014, some bankers from Luxembourg said the following about the efforts of the European Commission to regulate Dark Pools: "It is an attempt that even Hercules wouldn't try out on his good days."[56] I'll let you meditate on that comment for a minute given the "mistakes" the regulators have made in the past. In fact, the new regulation was finally supposed to be effective early 2017, but has been postponed to 2018[57].

Traders are quite anxious about the effect of such regulation if huge parts of the market suddenly migrate from dark pools back to "regular" trading platforms. One problem is that it will cost a lot of money to banks that have invested huge amounts of money in dark pools and some are worried that some banks may have a hard time surviving the change[58]. Another one is about high-frequency trading. There is no such possible thing on dark pools, as traders negotiate directly their transactions and no robots can take their place. So if big portions of transactions switch back to regular trading platforms, this will suddenly give back a lot of power to high-frequency trading, with all its side-effects[59]. That regulation also attempts to regulate high-frequency trading, and as you can see, this is a huge project that will totally shake up the whole financial system. The strange thing is that, although these new regulations look like it is indeed the "thirteenth labor of Hercules" that will have huge implications, very few media have reported anything about it.

Now it's all about whether the number 13 is a good or bad omen in this case...

There are many other concerns with speculation. For instance leverage methods help speculators multiply their gains but make all this even riskier, but I will let the eager reader learn by himself these details since it gets a little technical[60].

As we have seen, interest rates are one of the key aspects of speculation. These interest rates, set by the central banks, have a direct effect on the economy and on the markets. One of the obvious impacts is on the real estate market: when rates are very low, as in recent years, many people can borrow to banks, real estate prices go up since there are more buyers. But if rates go up, fewer people can get loans, and mechanically real estate prices fall. This is what happened during the subprimes crisis in the US, which will be studied later in part 8.1. The same effect can be observed in shadow finance and speculative markets: central banks can no longer raise their interest rates without taking the risk of causing a huge collapse of dominoes. And yet, rates can not remain at 0% forever. This is why regulators are ready to take heavy measures, because they are trapped.

3.3 Curves Analysis

Let's talk for a minute about the analyses of very serious economists who study the curves of the markets and create mathematical models from them. We find this type of analysis everywhere today. So of course, I do not deny that there are cycles, nor that a speculative bubble always follows the same pattern. But until now, none of these mathematical models could predict the Wall Street crash in 1987, the Dot-Com bubble in 2000, the subprimes bubble in 2008, or even the Bitcoin bubble in 2013. It is easy to analyze past curves. I can also predict yesterday's weather using the data from the previous day. But if these mathematical models cannot predict future crises, they are useless. Science, the real one, is used to predict the future according to present conditions. We sometimes know that a bubble will break out one day or another. But no one knows exactly when.

Moreover, a very serious experiment and study of the Wall Street Journal shows that financial advisors on the stock exchange do not perform better than random picking[61].

And the reason for this powerlessness is very simple. These curves correspond to reactions of human groups following rumors and events that are happening in the real world. And while statistical models of trader robots manage to "scrape" a few cents over milliseconds, they are unable to know the longer-term trend. As with climate and weather models, financial mathematical models lack the small details, the little rumor at the coffee machine that will trigger THE sale which will bring down all the dominoes one after the other. That's the butterfly effect that also makes your weather forecast so unreliable on the long term.

However, the one who strolls the corridors and who hears the rumors before anyone else certainly has more prediction capacities...

Let's take a recent example of a real life event that affected the market value of an asset. On September 4, 2017, China announces that ICOs, which are fund-raising for new cryptocurrencies, are banned from the Chinese territory. In less than a day, the value of Bitcoin loses 15% compared to the USD[62]. Whoever knew in advance the Chinese declaration was lucky. However, the sudden fall of the value of Bitcoin could not be predicted by "statistical models" or any other mathematical models. The scenario runs again a week later, when the Chinese announce that all Bitcoin exchanges are banned from their territory. Again, Bitcoin plummets to $3,000 to go back to $4,000 a few days later.

3.4 Some Orders of Magnitude

We have seen that some money is created by central banks through national banks, and a large part is created by loans and is called "Debt Money". This is not entirely transparent, because although some figures are published, they are not all published. Moreover, their analysis is particularly complex, especially since each central bank has its own accounting system. On the other hand, central banks do not always act appropriately during crises, and private banks only think about saving their own skin. And this shouldn't come as a surprise, it is the law of the market.

To put all this in perspective, here are a few numbers on the current world money in circulation, in billions of USD[63]:

- 5,000 fiat money (physical money, paper money and coins), including 1,000 Euro and 1,500 USD,
- world global debt is around 200,000, of which 60,000 is public debt by States, which is 40 times the amount of fiat money,
- the public debt of France is 2,000, a little above its GDP, an unprecedented record and growing,
- the US public debt is around 20,000, also above its GDP,
- derivatives speculated on the markets are around 630,000 in the low estimate (these are of course very difficult to estimate), and the high end estimate is around 1,500,000[64].

To visualize these numbers, here is a little graph that represents the share of "Fiat Money" compared to "Debt Money" and "Derivatives":

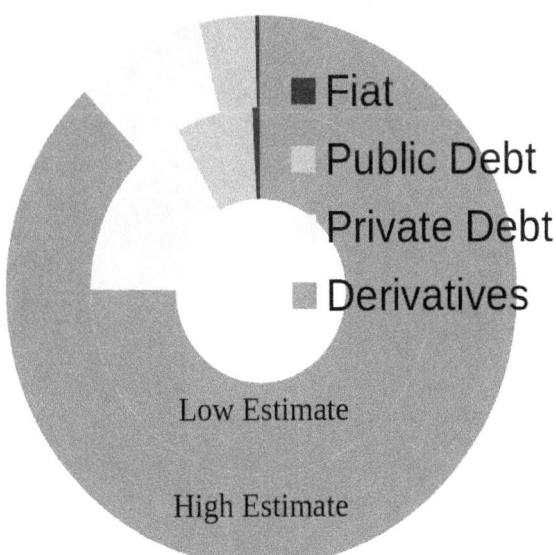

5. *Proportion of different types of money in circulation in the economy. This graph is compiled using the numbers given previously. The inner circle represents the low estimate of derivatives, and the outer circle is the high estimate.*

As you can see, speculation takes up the biggest part of the pie. The problem is that in the economy there is absolutely no difference between a "speculated" USD or Euro and a fiat coin or banknote. The two are mixed in the mass of money that circulates. We can therefore understand that speculation has a quantitatively important and very real effect in the economy.

This also answers the question: "but if banks need to have 7% of what they lend in their accounts, debt-money shouldn't be more than 14 times the amount of fiat money, but it is 40 times!" Because you can never know where a specific Euro comes from for instance, banks can actually consider "debt-money" in their vaults as new Fractional Reserves. So the 7% limit is actually not on "fiat money", and is quite useless.

Summary:

Currently, physically created money (fiat money) represents only a small portion of the currency that circulates through speculation.

Speculation represents almost 90% of monetary circulation worldwide. A large part of global speculation is carried out by unregulated "shadow bankers", who take proportional risks to the short term profit they dream of.

Most speculation on regular trading platforms is now done through High-Frequency Transactions by "trading robots" ("High Frequency" being around the microsecond).

The European Commission is making a desperate move to regulate dark pools as well as High-Frequency Trading, which will heavily transform the financial world in 2018, if the regulations become really effective as planned.

Human speculators themselves are disconnected from reality and base their actions only on short to medium term profits, depending on rumors and ratings from rating agencies, like a herd of sheep following the sheepdogs. This causes effects of waves in panic, which regularly disrupt the stock exchanges worldwide. But the values of stocks, especially those of raw materials, have a direct influence on the life of the populations.

Chapter 4
The Euro

We now have a good idea of the different types of money that exist. It is time to examine an important economic zone: Europe. We will start studying the interactions between money and the economy of this very interesting area of the world.

4.1 The ECB and the Euro

Before the Euro, the European institutions had created the ECU, a "basket of currencies". A basket of currencies is a currency whose value is fixed by a weighted sum of various currencies. The exchange rate of this type of currency varies according to the different currencies from which it is made of. This was a first step to try and normalize the different currencies in the Eurozone before introducing the Euro.

The ECB was created to supervise all National Central Banks of all countries of Europe, and as we have already seen, it is a fully sovereign entity. Well, sovereign in the sense that it doesn't answer to anyone. Besides, its presidents are "people with banking expertise", in other words, bankers. So there are obviously strong conflicts of interests with banks.

Let's examine the mission of the ECB as stated on its website, which drives its policies[65]:

"Our mission is to serve the people of Europe by safeguarding the value of the Euro and maintaining price stability."

Thus, like most central banks in the world today, the ECB has a main mission: to fight inflation. This seems to be a good idea at first glance, but it is less so when we find out about the "Phillips curve". This was discovered by an American economist, and shows that the lower the inflation in a country, the higher the unemployment. And this becomes exponential when inflation is very low. Here is the typical example taught in Economy classes:

6. Phillips curve establishing the relation between inflation and unemployment rates. Source : an online economy blog[66]

This curve has been studied by many economists in different ways around the globe, and it seems that it is a close match to reality. When you have in mind the current catastrophic state of unemployment in Europe, it seems quite strange to "fight against inflation".

In this regard, it would seem logical that the ECB would avoid creating too much money. But when we check the curves of the Euro monetary mass, it looks like it has been growing steadily in the last 20 years, as we see in figure 7. This graph starts in 1999 and ends in 2017. It shows the fiat money supply M0, which is the actual coins and banknotes that are circulating in the economy. This money supply has quadrupled in 15 years and doubled in 10 years!

When looking at the M0 monetary supply, we see that our friends at the ECB are having fun creating and destroying money at will, especially since the 2008 crisis:

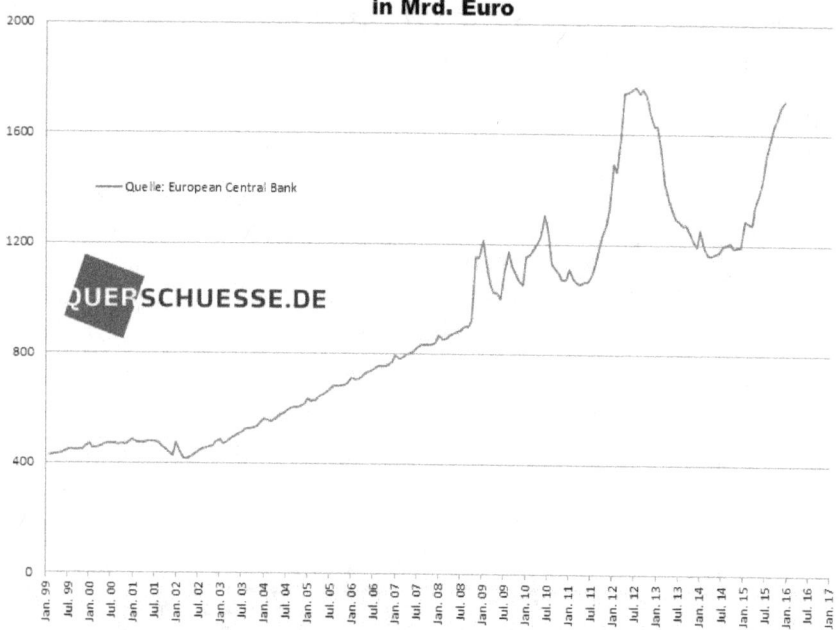

7. Monetary mass in Euros, M0 (fiat money only). Source: querschuesse.de[67]

How come my salary hasn't been multiplied by 4 in the meantime???

Not surprisingly, this curve (which is quite difficult to find, the ECB is absolutely not transparent on this!) follows the same trend than other curves which are more easy to find: the ones for other monetary indicators, M1, M2 and M3 as seen in figure 8. It shows in blue, the bottom curve, the money supply M1, which according to the ECB represents fiat currency in circulation to which is added the balances of current accounts (basically, the money you have in your current bank account). The other two curves in orange, M2 which includes short-term savings, and yellow, M3, which includes short and medium-term investment and savings products, generally follow the same trend. However, we can see that while before 2008 the savings were raising, they have been decreasing since then in proportion to the mass M1. In green, we see the variations of the total mass M3. The contraction of M3 due to the 2008 crisis is very clear, while M1 in blue has steadily increased.

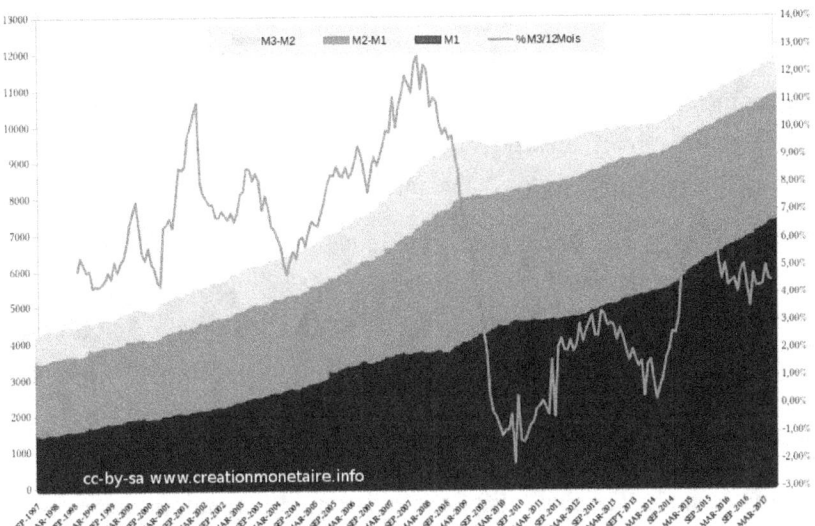

8. *Monetary mass in Euros, M1 (bottom blue mass), M2 (middle in orange) and M3 (top in yellow), as well as the variation of M3 (green line) from 1997 to 2017. Source : www.creationmonetaire.info*

So the ECB is actually creating lots of money, but the impact is not as strong as you could expect, especially on inflation, and I will explain why later in this chapter. But first, let's examine how the ECB is actually creating money.

4.2 Quantitative Easing

During the last few years, the ECB has been using a technique that injects liquidity into the economy (in other words, it is creating money). It does this by buying securities, particularly government bonds, in exchange for hard currency. This is called "Quantitative Easing"[68]. You may hear people saying that the ECB is "buying debt", which is a misuse of language. The currency created by the ECB of course doesn't benefit the indebted States, but it goes directly to their creditors. In other words, people who had government bonds that would be paid tomorrow get their money today instead.

Let's take an example to explain this technique. Let's imagine that Emmanuel has bought some government bonds. He has given some of his money to the State when he bought them, and the State has promised to give him back his money, plus interest, in a few years. This is when the ECB comes in, and offers Emmanuel to buy him his bonds right now, in exchange for money, instead of waiting. This way, Emmanuel has now some new money that he can spend and add into the economy.

We see that by using this technique, the debt of the states gets transferred from private hands... to the ECB. When the ECB wanted to use this technique, it has been challenged legally by some[69], since Central Banks are normally not supposed to directly hold the debts of states. Besides, the first to benefit from this are the ones who were rich enough to buy bonds in the first place.

Why is the ECB doing this? Economists are not blind: they see that the economy is totally at a halt. Besides, they are terrified by the shadow of deflation, which seems to float above Europe. But they have very few means of action.

The first way central banks can do something is by playing with interest rates, which by encouraging people to take more or less credits can have an impact on the amount of debt-money in circulation. Low rates push people to take more credits, and debt-money flows into the economy. Higher rates send a signal to wait for lower rates to make credits, which naturally contracts the available amount of debt-money. As we have seen in the previous chapter, debt-money plays a great role in today's economy, so interest rates are an extremely important parameter.

But the rates are already so low that this mechanism is no longer usable. Recently, France even made a bunch of loans at negative interest rates[70]. Things seem to be upside down. Who would lend money only to receive less in return? Just think for a second. You have a lot of money and you have several choices: leave it in the bank, lend it to France that will repay you a little less, or lend it to a company or a country that may never pay you back. Of course, the last choice doesn't sound so great. And the first choice, leaving your money in the bank at a zero interest rate is making you actually lose money because of inflation. So you choose to lend to France over a few years, even if it is at a small negative rate. So the interest rates system is already at its maximum, the ECB can not go further in the negative rates.

What is left for the Central Banks to try and jump-start the economy? Quantitative Easing, which injects fresh money into the economy and so encourages to spend more money.

But despite the steady increase of the money supply, official inflation in the European Union over 10 years is around 2% per year, hardly more than 25% in 10 years. This is a quarter of the increase in the money supply (remember, the money supply M1 doubled in the last 10 years and M0 quadrupled in the last 15 years). How can we explain the difference between the 25% inflation and the 100% increase of the money supply?

4.3 The Impact of the European Monetary Policy

First of all, we must remember that the share of money created by Quantitative Easing is in the tiny piece in the pie of the currencies circulating in the economy. So it is just a drop of water in the ocean as shown in figure 5. The ECB could multiply the fiat money supply by 10, the effect would not necessarily be so visible.

However, the increase of this mass implies that the banks have potentially more reserves and that they can therefore make more loans (remember the 7% fractional reserves). But it so happens that the banks, instead of making more credits with their growing reserves, keep the money in their vaults "for the coming bad days". But remember that Quantitative Easing is only giving money to people who were ready to wait for a long time before getting their money back, so they are obviously not so eager to spend it anyway. Besides, the extremely low interest rates set by the central banks also stop banks from making new credits, since they know that they will recover very little profit with almost 0% interest. Why take the risk of making a credit if you won't make much profit?

In a way, and due to these factors, inflation of the money supply is simply captured and absorbed by the banks, and does not really enter the real economy since it doesn't create more "Debt Money". But if the economy was suddenly revived by a miracle, there would be massive inflation, because banks could suddenly make loans at will and with more confidence: "debt money" would suddenly flow into the economy. Central Banks could then raise their interest rates safely, unless the "revival" was only temporary (as it happened in the subprimes crisis, as we will see later).

In fact, central bankers don't have much grip on the economy anymore. Here is a quote from Reuters[71]:

> Bank of England chief economist Andrew Haldane in a recent speech said central bankers may need to accept that their good old days – of adjusting interest rates to boost employment or contain inflation – may be gone for good.

4.4 The Problems of the Single Currency

The Euro certainly has some advantages. The banking system used to charge excessive fees to trade from one country to another[72]. But well, we have to reflect on the fact that it doesn't cost a dime to the banks to make an electronic transfer, and these fees were unjust in a monopoly situation. This by the way made it possible for companies such as Western Union to thrive. Anyway, in this context, yes for sure, the Euro is a great leap forward.

> It is a great satisfaction for a slave who is bound in chains to be relieved from his chains, even if he remains a slave.

We may also like to be able to go from one country to another without needing to change our coins and notes. Anyway the challenges the Euro offers to the Eurozone definitely out-weight its small advantages, as we will see.

One of the economic problems of the European Union is the "Strong Euro", which we often hear about without necessarily measuring or understanding its consequences. What is the problem? The Euro has been, since its creation, and with some variations, roughly valued at around one

USD. But the US Dollar is still the "Strong World Currency". What is the disadvantage of having a "strong" currency, while the term itself seems rather positive? The disadvantage is that a "strong" currency has an impact on imports and exports. When you have a "strong" currency, the products you export are expensive for foreign countries importing these products. At the opposite end, a "low" currency makes the products very cheap for foreigners. Typically, the Chinese have a weak currency policy. They are even accused by the whole world of cheating by playing on the value of their currency and making it as low as possible on purpose[73]. This clearly favors their exports. Thus, Chinese products are not only cheap because they are produced by cheap workers, but also because the Chinese Yuan is a weak currency. So foreigners, especially Europeans with their strong currency, can buy Chinese products at very low prices.

Well, in that case, why don't we just do the same with the Euro to boost our exports worldwide?

The problem is that one of the main European economic powers is Germany, and it is the main country that drives economic decisions in the Eurozone. Coincidentally, the ECB is located in... Frankfurt, Germany. But then, why do the Germans want a strong Euro, they also have to export abroad! The particularity of Germany is that its production is mainly composed of products with very high added value, associated with the German "quality and reliability" stamp. The German manufacturers often enjoy worldwide monopolies on their products, which the whole world fight over to buy. Thus, the Germans know that they will sell their production, whatever the price. So it makes perfect sense for them to want a strong Euro, so that their products sell at the highest price possible.

On the other hand, it is very bad for countries such as Spain, Portugal or Italy, whose production is mainly agricultural, and therefore of low added value. Their products face a fierce competition from countries outside Europe such as Morocco or Tunisia. It is then easy to understand that the strong Euro puts them in an unfavorable position, when exporting outside Europe. But it also does the same when exporting to other European countries. For instance, when a Spanish company exports fruit to Germany, the Spanish Euro is much stronger than the Moroccan Dirham for instance, and thus its prices are much higher than any Moroccan company also exporting to Germany.

The previous example shows that the strong Euro is not a problem when exporting outside of Europe. We already see that Europe is made of countries with very different competitiveness. The problem is that it is impossible to lower the value of a "German Euro" compared to a "Spanish Euro". So, the price of a German car is still competitive in Spain (because of the "German Quality" label on such a high added value product), but Spanish oranges are suffering from the competition of Moroccan oranges in Germany. By the way, all Germans don't benefit equally from this situation: for instance German milk producers are suffering very badly and protest regularly to get European subsidies. They can't sell their milk at a price that would cover the production costs due to our strong currency[74].

And rather than fixing the problem, we put quotas on milk production[75] and food production in general, while half of the world starves to death. What kind of logic is that?

4.5 Disparities Within the Eurozone

This leads us to have a look at the trade between the countries of the Eurozone. One system has been devised to be able to transfer Euros from one Central Bank to another, for instance from the Bank of Spain to the Bank of Germany and vice versa at a rate of exchange of 1 Spanish Euro for 1 German Euro. This system of electronic transfers is called the "Target 2" system, and it is very informative to check the balances of the different European banks. A simple glance at the figure 9 clearly shows the problem posed by the Euro.

This chart shows the balances of the various European National Banks: on top, positive balances with Germany that stands out clearly from the lot, and at the bottom the negative balances with Italy and Spain diving into darkness... Moreover, if we remember the quantitative easing of the ECB, 90% of the money that is injected into the European economy is reinvested in Germany, France, Luxembourg, the Netherlands and Finland[76]. These new funds, instead of benefiting those who need them most, are bounced back to the richest countries. Moreover, Germany itself suffers from the situation, as other ruined European countries can no longer buy German products, which has led to a slowdown of the German economy in some areas over several years, even if it recovered a little in 2016.

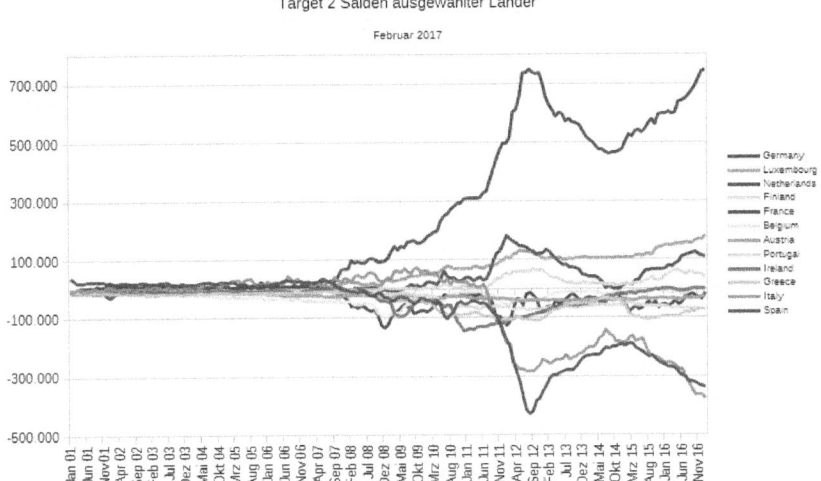

9. Balances of different European countries in the Target 2 System. Germany at the top, Italy and Spain at the bottom. Source : Wikipedia

In this context, it is easy for the Germans to require "equilibrium" of the national accounts at the European level, they are the only ones who can really achieve it... Recently, they started protesting about Italy in particular being too much negative in the Target system. The president of the Ifo, a very influential German Think Tank, said in a press release that the German state should intervene with the ECB to limit state deficits in the Target system[77].

If you are still not convinced, we can look at things from another angle, and turn to the studies published by the IMF, for instance the one for 2016[78]. At the end of the study, we find tables based on abbreviations that sound technical and complicated: "REER Gaps". In fact, this term means, by simplifying it a little: "the difference between a country's trade balance and the exchange rate of its currency". In other words, it is the difference between the competitiveness of a country worldwide and the strength of its currency in relation to other currencies. So a very negative value means that the currency is too "weak" compared to the country's economic power. On the other hand, a very high value means that the country has a currency that is too "strong". When we extract the European countries as presented in figure 10, the conclusion is obvious:

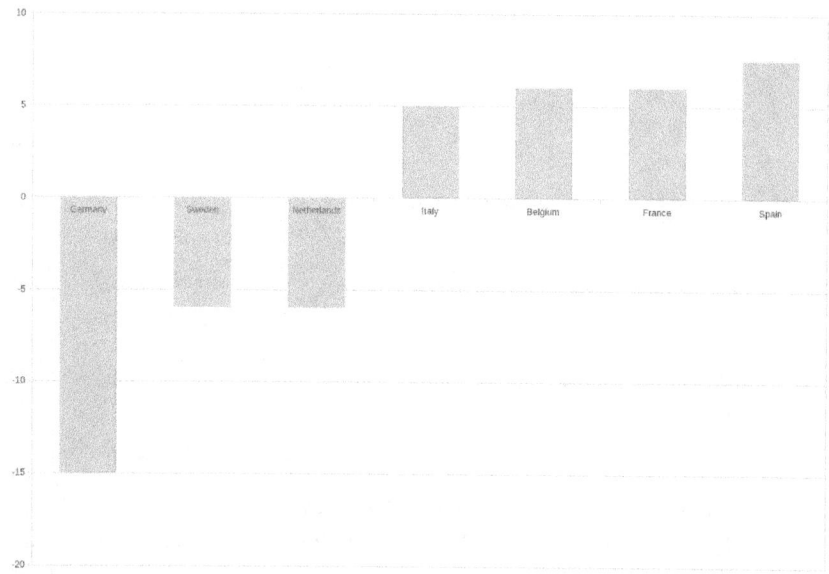

10. Difference between the trade balance and the exchange rate of the Euro for different European countries: from left to right, Germany, Sweden, Netherlands, Italy, Belgium, France, Spain. A positive value means that the currency is too strong for that country, and a negative value means that the currency is too weak for that country. Source : IMF 2016 report, data extracted and graphics home baked.

Just in case you still had some doubts, we can also have a look at the minimum wages through Europe, as shown in figure 11 whose data comes directly from Eurostat[79]. While Bulgaria's minimum is less than 250 Euros, Luxembourg is at 2,000 Euros.

How can you safely have such differences within a zone where there is "free circulation" of goods and people? And this is even as Bulgaria has seen a 110% increase in the minimum wage in the last 10 years.

By the way, you remember that the Euro monetary mass has doubled in the last 10 years, right? What happened to the equivalent doubling of salaries in most countries throughout Europe? The highest raise in the group 3 is Luxembourg with less than a 30% raise, still nothing compared to the 100% growth of the Euro monetary mass. This tells us that we have potentially lost more than 70% of our purchasing power, and still this is going unnoticed.

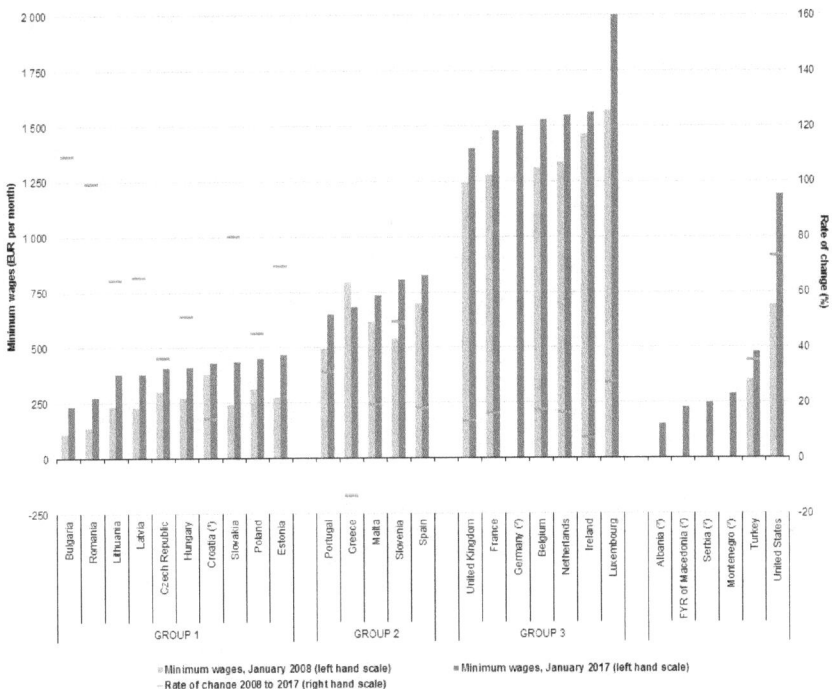

11. *Minimum wages within the European Union. From left to right, the "poorest" countries to the "richest". The last group on the right is a mix of world countries (the US being at the far right) to compare with the Eurozone. Source: Eurostat*

Finally, to conclude on the problem of the single currency, we often forget that Greece, if it had been using the Drachma instead of the Euro, could have devalued its currency during the crisis in order to stimulate its exports. It would have given it a chance to restart its economy, and may also have helped reduce its debt. Iceland did this after the 2008 crisis and recovered quite well from a catastrophic situation, as we will see later. But as Greece was bound to the Euro, it was not in a position to make this choice, and that proved to be fatal. You may have noticed that Greece is the only European country in which the minimum wage actually decreased in the last 10 years. What a waste!

You might call me anti-European. It is on the contrary because I like the European States that I think we should get rid of the burden which the Euro has become. Right now, it is only creating tensions between the South and the North of Europe, rather than promoting peace. Germany hates Greece and its debt, and blames Italy and others for having negative balances in the Target System. On the other side, everyone accuses Germany of being the source of all evil. As I am writing this book, I read news about protests all over the south of Europe against tourism (mostly from Northern Europe). It looks like the "Pax Europaea" is crackling these days. Unfortunately, populations always put the blame on other populations instead of looking at the real sources of conflict[i]. In fact, the German people don't find themselves in a much better situation than in any other European country, some of their elderly even can't survive without working past 70 years old[80].

---

i   We, the people, have to beware of anything that drives us against other people, whatever the reason. In his "Nuremberg Diary", Gustave Gilbert, an American psychologist, quotes the following from an interview he had with Hermann Göring, who had been Hitler's right arm during the first part of WWII:

Göring: Why, of course, the people don't want war. Why would some poor slob on a farm want to risk his life in a war when the best that he can get out of it is to come back to his farm in one piece? Naturally, the common people don't want war; neither in Russia nor in England nor in America, nor for that matter in Germany. That is understood. But, after all, it is the leaders of the country who determine the policy and it is always a simple matter to drag the people along, whether it is a Democracy or a Fascist dictatorship or a Parliament or a Communist dictatorship.

Gilbert: There is one difference. In a Democracy, the people have some say in the matter through their elected representatives, and in the United States only Congress can declare wars.

Göring: Oh, that is all well and good, but, voice or no voice, the people can always be brought to the bidding of the leaders. That is easy. All you have to do is tell them they are being attacked and denounce the pacifists for lack of patriotism and exposing the country to danger. It works the same way in any country.

As far as the Euro is concerned, simply put aside any ideology based on nothing concrete and just look at what is happening in the real economy. Alan Greenspan himself, former president of the Fed, declared in an interview on CNBC, just after the Brexit vote that for Europe "the Euro is the immediate problem".

4.6 The CFA Franc

As a French, it would be unfair for me to speak about the problems caused by the Euro in the Eurozone without mentioning the CFA Franc[81], which is very rarely known by the French people themselves. It is of course very well known by our politicians, but they rarely speak about it, if ever.

They may think that they act "to safeguard French interests". But this is a very short term vision of the world. Even if you set aside Human Rights and other very "idealistic concepts", we may need to remember that poverty in the world turns back to the ones who caused it, be it by immigration, violence, or even terrorism.

This currency, partially indexed on the French Franc and then on the Euro[i], is still used in 2017 by 15 African countries. For anyone who thinks that colonization is long gone, "CFA" originally meant "French Colonies of Africa". Of course, to sound politically correct, the acronym has found itself some new names, such as "Financial Community (or Cooperation) of Africa", but I don't think anybody gets fooled by these new names.

The justification to keep this currency is that African countries "benefit from the Euro, which is a strong currency". But as we have seen in this chapter, a "strong currency" is not always an advantage, especially if your economy is based on exporting raw materials. In the case of the CFAF, this is no less than a tool to submit these African countries to the will of the European rulers. Indeed, the monetary decisions regarding the CFAF are taken... in Paris and Frankfurt. So when the Europeans decided in 1994 to proceed with a brutal devaluation of the CFAF by simply dividing its value by two, they immediately threw all these African countries into poverty[82].

---

i   It has suffered some devaluations so it is not exactly "fixed", as we will see.

Meanwhile, Europeans are very happy that this didn't lead to broad social unrest[83]...

> This is also clearly a message that "Africans cannot be credible on their own". Colonialist mentality, anyone? [84]

To try and defend the "benefits" of this currency, people often cite the case of Mali, which quit the CFA Franc zone in 1962, and "ran back to the CFAF after heavy economic catastrophes". The reality is of course a little more complex: a military dictatorship along with generalized corruption is certainly not the best context to gain your own financial freedom.

This currency is causing more and more controversy in Africa, and even cause unrest between African countries[85], as the Euro creates unrest in Europe.

Summary:

The ECB keeps inflation low. This is not necessarily a good thing when you know the "Phillips curve", which shows that low inflation leads to more unemployment. Nevertheless, the Euro money supply has doubled in 10 years due to the Quantitative Easing mechanisms used by the ECB.

Unfortunately, this increase in the money supply is "captured" mainly by the financiers from Northern Europe. Because they fear a future crisis, they keep this money in their vaults instead of reinvesting it in the economy in the places where it is most needed.

The Euro, as a single currency on a vast and heterogeneous economic zone, poses the problem of not allowing to adjust each country's currency according to national productivity and inflation. Meanwhile, there are major differences in the national economies throughout the EU. This causes an "aspiration" of European capital, largely towards Northern Europe, at the expense of Southern countries, which get poorer since the Euro is too strong for them. This in turn causes social unrest.

Besides, the CFA Franc, a relic of colonization, is still indexed on the Euro and used in 15 African countries, causing further problems there.

Chapter 5
Debt and Balanced Budgets

5.1 Public Debt

Public debt is a subject we must put in the spotlight for a moment. We will study the case of France here, since it is very representative of the debt problem that most nations face nowadays.

Many activists claim that the debt of France was caused by a law voted in 1973, that they even call the "Rothschild law of 1973". They believe that this law has "forced" France to stop creating its own currency, and borrow on the markets instead. It's a little more complicated than that.

> *Okay, it was kind of the first step, like this toe you dip into the water to check its temperature before you dive into the lake... but let us give back to Caesar what belongs to Caesar... or rather in this case we should give back to Nero what belongs to Nero...*

When the states used to create their own money, the public debt was composed of the loans contracted by the state in addition to this monetary creation. As many countries worldwide, France enjoyed an economic boom during the 30 years after WWII, called the 30 years post-war boom. During that period, the French Government made arrangements with its Treasury and the Bank of France to borrow at zero percent interest rates, in addition to having no penalties when its balance was negative. It also asked the Bank of France to create money whenever it needed some. As can be seen from the graph in figure 12, this created a significant inflation during this period, which shouldn't come to you as a surprise since more money in the economy generally creates inflation. This is totally in line with what we have observed so far in history: a state that is allowed to create its own monetary policies tends to create money at will to fund its expenses, which leads to inflation.

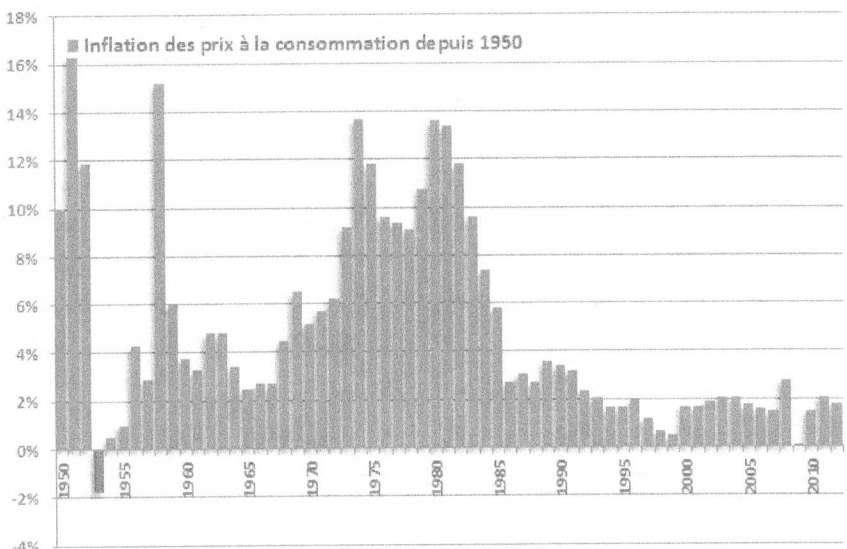

12. *Inflation in France since 1950. Source : Many French media show this graph.*[86]

In 1973, the "Pompidou-Giscard Law" ends these "arrangements", and forces the government to run any borrowing scheme and monetary decisions through Parliament, instead of doing whatever it pleases. In the early 1980s, under the impulse of the Parliament, the state began borrowing to the financial markets or commercial banks, and no longer created money, even if it could still have done so. This new policy had a very clear impact: inflation was "finally under control". Ten years later, the Treaty of Maastricht in 1993 actually forced the European States to borrow from the banks and the markets. But in fact, what did it really change? Simply put, instead of being financed at 0% interest rates by the Bank of France, the state had to borrow at interest rates fixed by the markets. So the main difference is that, from then on, when giving back money to its creditor, it also has to give back extra interest.

> *If you think about it, we could say that inflation did quite some good to the French during the 30 boom years, and on the other hand a reduced inflation for the last 30 years hasn't really done much good. Remember the Phillips Curve?*

As a short side note, some would say that the rising price of oil was the one that drove France and the world into an economic chaos. Although it did have some short term impact, the total energy importations for France are just over 2% of the GDP[87]. Besides, the trade balance of France hasn't changed that much in the 1970s compared to the previous decades, and has actually been even strongly positive in the 1990s[88]. Finally, France has been mostly "fueled", if I may say so, by nuclear energy in the last 30 years. So oil prices are not the only, if even the main, source of our current economic crisis for the last 40 years. Along with the impact of the collapse of the Bretton Woods system[89], there are also other sources, especially the changes in monetary policy, as we will see.

This historical "anecdote" invites us to reflect on the nature of a state and its management. Some argue that a state is not an company nor a household, implying that it is perfectly legitimate for a state to be in deficit. It is a very delicate position. For if it uses too much monetary creation to cover its deficit, it creates too much inflation, which is not necessarily a good thing when it is out of control and turns into hyperinflation. The state, as much as possible, should have "balanced" accounts. On the other hand, it needs to invest in infrastructure for the benefit of the country, and burdening it with interest is not an acceptable solution. Conversely, a little inflation does not do that much harm...

5.2 Public Services

I allow myself a little reflection on "public services" and the mission of a state. A private company has only one mission, "to make profits", but the state has other obligations. It must "provide services to the public" by financing and organizing activities such as education, health, justice, security, as well as making sure that its population does not die of hunger, which are all activities that can not be "lucrative" and cannot "make a profit". The way of thinking about the mission of a state is therefore totally different from the profitable business of a private company. In France, the "Macron Law" replaced railway lines by buses on the pretext that "trains lose money". It is obviously a wrong reason: yes, a "public service loses money". It is perfectly normal, as a public service it is financed by taxes!

On the other hand, the deterioration of this public service has a significant impact on the weakest, such as handicapped people. A bus does not offer the same services as a train, not to mention the travel time difference and the pollution it causes. Breaking news: some public services cost lots of money. Education is the primary source of deficit for the French state after the reimbursement of the public debt. We should probably banish public education altogether!

But of course, when the balance sheet of the state is threatened by the interest of loans contracted by the state and by tax evasion, which we will speak about later, politicians have to find a way to reduce spending at the expense of the population.

Back to monetary creation, we have already seen that fighting against inflation at all costs is not necessarily a good thing since it automatically creates unemployment. On the other hand the injection of liquidity thanks to money creation tends to revive the economy, which we can hardly complain about, even if it is not so efficient when interest rates are low as we are currently seeing in Europe.

By imposing the "Stability Pact" everywhere in Europe, the European Union is only suffocating the economies of countries that are already at a halt, while these countries need investments to revive their already worn out economies. It is quite similar to this old technique used by doctors in which they were taking high quantities of blood from the patient in order to cure him, or so they thought. The IMF itself in various reports believes that budget cuts are very detrimental to the economy and are not going into the right direction[90].

As for adding more "flexibility" in the laws that protect employees, especially against abusive layoffs, it is also counter-productive. The French government is currently "breaking" its labor laws under the pretext that they are the cause for unemployment. On the other hand, Germany has even more rigid laws but doesn't have as much unemployment problems as France has. In fact, it has been repeatedly shown that laws and unemployment are totally uncorrelated[91].

Finally, one of the "protective" roles of the state that is too often forgotten is to bail out banks when they go bankrupt. So when a bank makes a profit, it rushes to dispatch it to its shareholders instead of reinvesting it, potentially putting itself in a difficult situation in the future. But then, when this leads it to bankruptcy, it is the state's duty (and therefore with the people's taxes) to bail it out. One sentence summarizes this paradox: "banks have privatized profits and socialized losses".

> *Tricky question: when a state bails out a bank from which it has borrowed, should it repay the interest of the loans to this bank?*

We accept this system blindly, but there is a notable exception where things happened differently: Iceland. In 2008, hit by the global financial crisis, the main Icelandic banks go bankrupt and are nationalized. Their leaders are charged and condemned, the list of bankers who were sent to prison is quite impressive[92]. Furthermore, the Icelandic government asked the people what they thought should be done about the debts of these banks. These debts were mostly due to foreign investors, mainly in Great Britain and the Netherlands. The Icelandic people, to the world's amazement, refused by referendum to pay these debts. Just for the fun of it, the British Prime Minister put Iceland in the list of "terrorist" countries at the time, in order to seize the assets of its banks... The situation is still not really solved, but in the meantime, Iceland has emerged from the chaos in which it was, largely thanks to the devaluation of its currency, which boosted its exports. The whole story has also attracted tourists from all over the world, which also boosts the local economy. In January 2016, Iceland's unemployment is around 1,9%, and has stabilized at around 2,7% since then, still below all other OECD countries[93].

> *Countries of the world can only blush when faced with this number. Germany and China: 3.9. US and UK: 4.7. Russia 5.4. Canada: 6.9. France: 10. Turkey: 11.6. Spain: 18.7. Greece: 23.2.*

5.3 The Problem of the Interest

What is commonly referred to as the "sovereign debt" of the states is simply the public debt, that is, the loans contracted by the state. The French debt currently consists mainly of accumulated interest since France borrowed from banks and markets at non-zero interest rates in the 1980s. If we calculate the borrowings and repayments made by the French State since then, on the one hand by adding the interest, and on the other hand without including any interest, we obtain two totally different curves:

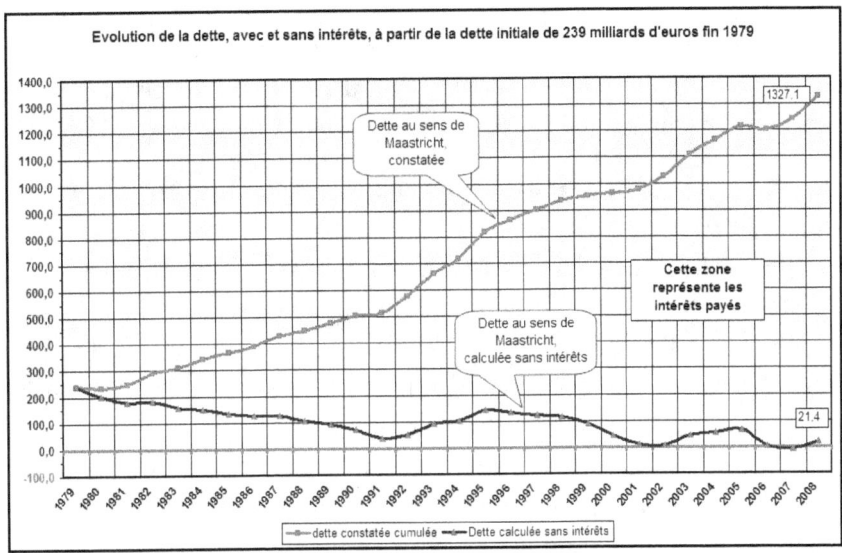

13. *Evolution of the debt of France from 1979 to 2008, calculated with the actual interest it has been paying (top red curve) and without interest if it had borrowed at a zero interest rate (bottom blue curve). Source : this graph can be found on numerous sites, including liberal ones[94]*

The top curve in red shows the actual debt between 1979 and 2008 as it is calculated using Maastricht rules, and we see that it is constantly increasing. In the meantime, the blue curve at the bottom represents the debt without any interest. We can conclude that if France had created its own currency and borrowed at a zero interest rate from the Bank of France instead of borrowing it on the markets with interest, it would have had virtually no debt in 2008. Indeed, 21 billion Euros is nothing compared to the more than 1,300 billion the same year due to the interest... French public debt is 2,000 billion Euros today. When looking at this graph, we can see that in the zero-interest scenario, the French state has been relatively well managed! It didn't even just remain at a reasonable level of debt, it has even succeeded to divide its debt by 10 between 1979 and 2008!

The analysis of these two curves leads us to a logical conclusion: by forcing the state to borrow at non-zero interest rates, we force the state not only to have a balanced budget, but we ask it to make a profit, as if it was a private business, in order to repay more than it borrowed, due to the interest! This is where the comparison between a state and a private company becomes meaningful: as we already have pointed out, the state is not supposed to make profits, especially if these profits are then distributed as interest to commercial banks!

The French governors, before thinking about borrowing on the markets with non-zero interest rates back in the 1970s, should have asked themselves how they would pay this extra interest. In the United States, the creators of the Fed have addressed that question at the time. Is it really a coincidence that the income tax was reinstated in the United States in 1913, the very year of the creation of the Federal Reserve? It is reasonable to assume that the craftsmen of the reform were not crazy and understood that it was necessary to increase the revenues of the state in order to pay the interest created by the change of the state's monetary system. The French were not so far-sighted.

One of the problems of the present debt, which as we have just seen consists mainly of interest, is that it now reaches such summits that we can reasonably say that it will never be fully repaid. It would take decades of massive profits for the state to repay it. And with the current economic situation, this is not likely to happen anytime soon. Because for now, the state is barely even able to repay just the interest.

One of the other problems of borrowing from banks is that, just like for private individuals, it makes the state vulnerable to the goodwill of bankers. Indeed, since the market is based on competition, bankers can choose whatever they consider to be most profitable for them, and therefore lend to whoever they want, whenever they want, and at the interest rate they think is best for them. Thus, while they willingly lend to France these days, and even as we have seen at negative rates, it is not the same for all countries. And what happens today to other countries could very well happen tomorrow to France.

As most speculators, the banks largely base their "trust" in a borrower based on the ratings of the Rating Agencies. By downgrading Greece's rating in 2010[95], they throw the country into a crisis, even though the Europeans were just finding solutions and agreements to the problems of Greece[96]. It is as if they actually accelerated things before the lucrative cake could be saved by European agreements... Anyway, following the downgrade, no bank wants to lend to Athens anymore, which causes the bankruptcy we know.

One last word on the Greek crisis. It has not been a "crisis" for everyone. If indeed the Greeks suffered dearly, the financiers, especially the German ones, took their share of the juicy cake: it is known today that they have earned 1.34 billion Euros thanks to the loans made to Greece[97]. Others have also benefited from this crisis, or even have been the actors of it. In 2010, many serious newspaper articles pointed to the bank Goldman Sachs, which would have helped Greece to cheat its balance sheet to look "acceptable" enough to enter the Eurozone[98]. Then, with the help of other banks and financial manipulation, the same people who had helped the Greeks accelerated his downfall.

5.4 Tax Evasion

Beyond monetary problems, Europe (and the rest of the world) is also struck by a plague that is becoming increasingly well known by the general public: tax evasion. It is a phenomenon that is not new but has become increasingly visible in the mainstream media in recent years. And we are not talking here of droplets of water in the ocean like an official who brings a money-loaded suitcase from time to time to Switzerland to "hide" a few banknotes[99].

What exactly is tax evasion? To simplify, large companies and very wealthy individuals hide their profits using sophisticated arrangements. In Europe, instead of declaring the profits in the country where they make them, they declare them in other countries such as Ireland or Luxembourg. These two countries have very reduced taxes rates, and also allow to redirect part of these profits to foreign countries outside Europe (tax havens). Thus, "escapees" do not pay the taxes they would have to pay if they simply declared their earnings where they got them. These arrangements are legalized by the European institutions and in turn allowed by the different countries of the European Union. In France alone, this results in a loss of no less than 80 billion Euros each year, probably actually much more[100]. For the whole of Europe, we are talking about 1,000 billion Euros a year of losses due to tax evasion[101], the equivalent of Spain's GDP!

A French whistle blower, Antoine Deltour, had the courage to reveal fiscal arrangements going through Luxembourg. But, far from being protected and praised by public authorities for having worked for the common good, he is in trial and in a very strenuous situation. In the meantime, Jean-Claude Juncker, the President of the European Commission, is still in office, despite being accused of blocking any EU initiatives to fight against tax evasion[102], and is in a big conflict of interest due to his past as former Prime Minister of Luxembourg.

Before him, another whistle blower, Stéphanie Gibaud, had exposed tax fraud going through a Swiss bank[103], enabling the French government to recover as much as 12 billion Euros, without even counting all the further fraud that has been stopped. Just as Antoine Deltour, she has also faced a lot of pressure (lost her job and can't find another one, is on minimal social benefit, and has been kicked out of her apartment...), and the least we can say is that this brave activist wasn't exactly helped by the government. At least we know on which side it stands.

Both these whistle blowers, along with Edward Snowden, have received from the European Parlement the Sakharov price, but this is merely symbolic.

All this does not include "tax avoidance". Tax "evasion" is "legal", but tax "avoidance" is in fact "illegal". For example, retail groups are notorious in France for not paying local land taxes[104]. They have such lobbying and pressure power on local elected representatives that until a measure is taken at the national level, the problem can never be solved. And this will not happen tomorrow, since their lobbyists are also very active in the government. In the meantime, this situation gives these groups significant competitive advantages over small local structures, which cannot avoid those very high taxes, and this is a clear case of abuse of dominant position.

All of this, whether it's tax evasion or avoidance, is just as much capital that is not reinvested in the local economy. It is estimated, but it is very difficult to quantify this since it is by definition concealed, that there is more than the equivalent of 600 billion French assets hidden in tax havens, which therefore escape taxation in France. France has also a very strange peculiarity regarding the law, which is quite abnormal for a so-called "Democracy". Before prosecuting a potential tax evader, it is necessary to go through the "Lock of Bercy"[105], meaning that any complaint regarding tax evasion must be approved by the Ministry of Finance. This situation is quite shocking for a so-called "democracy". This "lock" was almost removed recently thanks to a proposal voted by the Senate, but the government finally rejected that proposal[106].

On the other hand, other legal arrangements, the "tax niches", allow the richest to pay less taxes, but this represents "only" a loss of 15 billion Euros per year.

These figures can be put in perspective with those of fraud regarding social benefits, which are also difficult to estimate, but which are generally accepted as being about one billion Euros per year. But of course the government always blames the social "cheaters" for the French deficit rather than anything else.

Some people will tell you that "tax havens exist only because taxes are too high in our countries". Maybe. Just try to do better than the Bahamas: 0% income tax, 0% capital tax, 0% inheritance tax[107]. How do you pay for your education system with that? And how do you pay your debt along with its interest? So, in fact, taxes are high in our countries because the wealthiest manage to escape them thanks to Fiscal Paradises.

So, what should we do to solve these problems? The solution of the French president is to reduce the tax on the wealthy further, by limiting taxation only to real estate, and thus allowing holders of large stock market portfolios to completely escape tax. It is a great gift to the wealthy, but this will need to be compensated somehow.

What about reducing housing benefits? The government is already thinking about it.

The general logic that is invoked is that taxing the rich is not a solution because it causes them to run away to foreign countries, such as Gérard Depardieu who is always given as an example in such discussions. But in reality, the main assets of the wealthiest are already abroad in fiscal paradises, as we have just seen. Unless France becomes as fiscally competitive as the Bahamas, Panama or Bermuda, it's inevitable, the richest always go where it's most advantageous for them if you give them the chance. And at the multinational corporation level, relocations have already taken place for everything that was economically profitable.

The fight against tax evasion by our governments is not going to happen tomorrow. As an example, here is a French story. During one night in December of 2015, the Parliament votes and adopts a text to limit tax evasion and tax fraud in general, by asking some transparency in the earnings of big companies. At one o'clock in the morning, the socialist government halts all discussions for 40 minutes (instead of 10 minutes which is normally the legal duration), and imposes a second vote that cancels the first one[108].

To re-establish a balance that would be beneficial to all, debt and its interest should first be rethought. As we have seen, the interest on the debt is an unsustainable burden for the state, which partly explains the disproportionate taxes which it forces on its citizens.

But one of the aspects that is rarely mentioned is the attractiveness of France in terms of dividends.

5.5 Work vs. Dividends

What are dividends?

For each share held on a stock exchange by a shareholder, he receives each year some "dividends", that are taken from the profits of the company corresponding to that share. The general idea is to make the ownership of profitable company shares more advantageous than those of non profitable companies. It's a bit like the annual interest that you can earn when you have a savings account, but it is conditioned by the success of the company in which you have invested. While the idea itself may seem a good one, it also has its disadvantages. One of them is that these dividends are "captured" by investors instead of being reinvested in the company, which may put the company in difficult situations for the future.

France is by far the European Champion of dividend payments to shareholders. While being the gold medal in Europe, it has the silver medal in the world, just behind the United States. This is very good for France, because it means that companies listed on the Paris Stock Exchange are very profitable. But it also means that this is a very juicy market for shareholders, which are certainly not going to run away elsewhere anytime soon, even if you tighten their conditions a little.

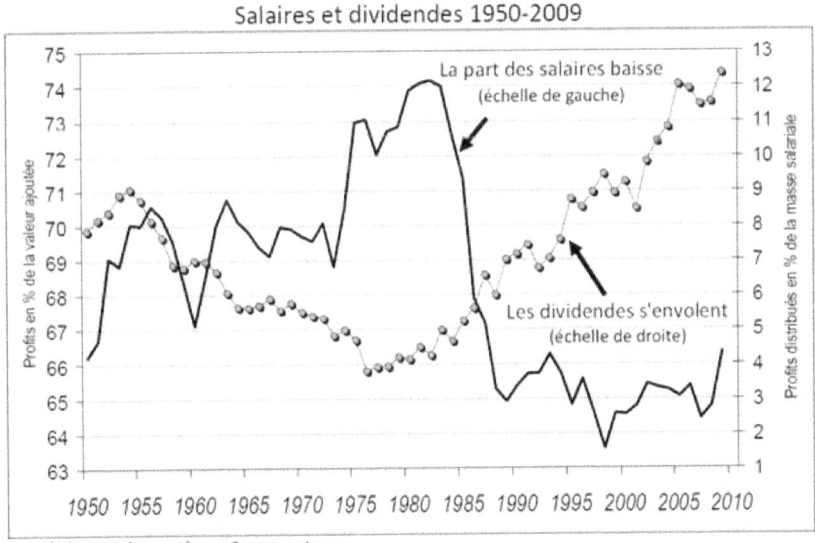

14. *The full curve is the one of salaries, and the dotted one is the one of dividends, between 1950 and 2010. Various sources including a report from the French Senate.[109]*

But while shareholders are boosted with dividends, the employees of these companies constantly see their salaries fall in comparison, as shown by the curves in figure 14.

It shows that the proportion of the share of salaries fell sharply in the 1980s, while the share of dividends has ever increased over the same period. Recall that the pressure on wages is mainly obtained thanks to a high rate of unemployment, which we have seen is linked to the fight against inflation.

5.6 The "Tickle-Down Theory"

This situation is difficult to maintain over the long term because the middle class of a country is the "lungs" of its economy. As the millionaire Nick Hanauer points out in a TED Talk that is out of the ordinary[110], the middle classes buy the products, which constitutes the main part of the economy of a country. Thanks to what they buy, they create a demand that in turn creates jobs. Without any demand, no company can create jobs. Ford understood that a century ago, when he doubled the wages of his employees back in 1914, so that they could buy his cars[111]. Nick Hanauer explains further that a rich man, however rich he may be, does not spend as much as thousands of middle-class people with decent salaries, and therefore does not create enough demand on his own to keep the economy running[112]. And finally, he points out that taxing the rich induces a redistribution in the economy that allows entrepreneurs to do business and keep their businesses alive.

The "Pareto principle", commonly known as the "law of 20-80", explains that a minority always produces the majority of wealth. This principle is often put forward to explain global inequalities between the richest and the poorest on the Earth. But this is a bad justification, because real geniuses rarely become rich. They concentrate much more on their creations that are "useful to society as a whole" than on the accumulation of personal wealth which they generally don't care about at all. On the other hand, the qualities required today to acquire wealth are greed, selfishness and a certain insensitivity to the fate of your fellow humans, as George Soros proved us quite cynically by "breaking" the Bank of

England in 1992.

On the same note, the "tickle-down theory", often put forward by the Liberals, asserts that the enrichment of the rich "drips down" towards the rest of the population and that it is therefore necessary to "water the rich" so that the poor may also benefit from these riches. The IMF itself has been doing research about this dogma, and its conclusions are very clear: the tickle-down theory is not verified in the real world at all[113], as we may have already suspected with a little critical mind. However, it is still important and reassuring to have an official confirmation of our intuition. The IMF also confirms the logical reasoning presented by Nick Hanauer in his TED Talk.

On the other hand, while the diagnosis is well established, the official guidelines of the IMF and other institutions have not changed a bit, and continue to advise budget cuts, more "flexibility" in labor laws, without taxing the rich. The governments themselves apply self-censorship on this subject, as for the financial transaction tax, which is regularly postponed since 2011 in France[114]. And if ever a European state wants to tax dividends, European watchdogs do not fail to put it back where it belongs[115]... We know the diagnosis well and we even openly display it, but the actions are a little slow to follow.

I am far from being a communist. I strongly believe that someone who produces more wealth than his neighbor for the community through his dedication and hard work should be rewarded in a way or another, compared to the one who doesn't come up from his couch all day. But in the last few decades, the uninterrupted accumulation of wealth by a minority becomes unsustainable. Moreover, the mass media regularly remind us that the number of billionaires increases every year[116]. They generally forget to mention that this comes at the expense of others. The richest 1% possess as much wealth as the 99% of the rest of the world's population. By 2015, only 80 people possessed as much wealth as the poorest half of the world's population[117]. This year, this figure has gone down to 8 people[118], which illustrates perfectly the increasingly uncontrolled flight of capital going up the social pyramid. It is humanly impossible to justify such inequalities. Do these 8 people really create as much wealth for humanity as 3.5 billion people combined?

One of the symbols of these inequalities are the dividends, where "money works by itself", and the simple fact of owning more makes it possible to earn more and more. I do not deny the fact that investing on the stock market may be risky, especially when you can not afford a team of financiers to manage your portfolio. But how can we continue to have millions of people dying of hunger while the shares in the stock market of a minority allow them to live in luxury without actually contributing anything to society? And the "generous donations" of these patrons widely advertised in the media are most often motivated by the tax cuts associated with these "gifts", while polishing their image with the general public.

Let's stop bashing the "1%". They use the system as it is, and do whatever they can to consolidate their position. It's a very human-like behavior. But the system ought to be changed in order to avoid such extreme situations and we should require it to have mechanisms to limit their power. From this perspective, it is important to take into account the Pareto principle to build a better world, not to mention human psychology and the quest for power. This brings us to a quick analysis of the world economic situation.

Summary:

Forcing states to borrow from the markets instead of creating their own currency requires them to be "profitable", as if they were corporations, in order to repay interest.

Tax evasion is a plague that also drives countries into debt, and the overall cost in Europe represents at least the equivalent of Spain's GDP (or half of France's GDP). Yet, not taxing the rich is damaging since the "tickle-down theory" doesn't work in practice. There is nothing to lose by controlling tax evasion, since the delocalization of assets and jobs has already been carried out. In the case of France, its large dividends are sufficiently attractive to hold investors.

Moreover, deregulation of the labor market increases inequality and doesn't create jobs.

Chapter 6
Money and the World Economy

The World Economy has been dominated since WWII by the US. This is why we will start looking at the domination of the US Dollar in the last 70 years.

6.1 USD Domination

During the Bretton Woods discussions in 1944, John Maynard Keynes proposed to introduce a kind of world currency, the "Bancor". His proposal also added regulations on the trade balances of all countries worldwide. Any country that would export too much would be forced to pay a "fine" that would encourage it to import from others, and vice-versa. His vision was to encourage all country's trade balances to be even. The British were in favor of his proposal, but the Americans discarded it and imposed the gold standard model, with the US Dollar as a reference for world trade. We saw how this whole scheme ended by the collapse of the gold standard in the 1970s.

> *Just a little note on Keynes' model. In his system, there could be no fiscal paradise, since any fiscal paradise has a very high incoming flow of money, would have been severely punished, and wouldn't have been able to survive...*

At the time, the gold standard is not new, since it was used throughout the nineteenth century and it has already shown its disadvantages: gold reserves are limited, money is therefore restricted and its rarity leads people to keep their money rather than spending it. Inevitably, it leads to the contraction of the economy and therefore to a crisis. Keynes called the gold standard a "barbarous relic"[119].

So with the Bretton Woods agreements, the US Dollar becomes the reference world currency, indexed on gold. From then on, the majority of international trade happens in Dollars, and the price of oil, for example, is expressed in Dollars still even today.

This is not without problems for the United States, whose currency becomes both the national currency of the US and the world currency. In 1960, an American economist, Robert Triffin, showed that such a currency could not satisfy both national and international requirements. He explained that the overproduction of Dollars to fuel world economic flows necessarily led in the long term to a loss of confidence in this hybrid currency. We can draw a parallel with the Euro, which must satisfy the constraints of the economies of very different European countries.

The Dollar is not only worrying the Americans, it is also the symbol of American hegemony in the world, and in 2006 Iran and Venezuela tried to sell their oil in Euros instead of Dollars[120]. While the attempt is a failure, it inspires others and Iran tries it again in 2016[121]. Saddam Hussein in Iraq, then Muammar Gaddafi in Libya both tried to sell their oil for Euros instead of Dollars[122].

We've seen what happened to them.

But little by little, the hegemony of the USD crumbles. China and Russia are already trading in their national currencies since 2014[123], while Russia is one of the largest producers of natural gas. Venezuela seems to wish to get away from the USD as well these days, and use a "basket of currencies" instead[124].

Why is the USD getting less and less popular? Maybe because, while the situation of the European countries in terms of debt is not so great, the position of the United States is even less so. With more than $60,000 worth of debt per person (compared to $37,000 for France), the US national debt stands at $20,000 billion, of which $6,000 billion is due to overseas countries, including $2,000 billion to China (which then holds 10% of the US debt). In total, the US public and private debt, by adding the national debt and the debts of companies and individuals, amounts to 68,000 billion Dollars. This debt is partly due to the dual position of the US Dollar, both a national currency and an international global reserve.

To have a good laugh, there is an excellent site where you can have a look at the debt of any country of the world, just choose your country:

http://www.nationaldebtclocks.org/#countries

Have fun! To have more fun, you can click on "World" at the top of the page and see how much interest have been paid worldwide to the bankers since you came to the site. It's quite entertaining!

6.2 The Special Drawing Rights (SDR)

In the meantime, when the Bretton Woods system collapsed in the 1970s, a global currency is created very discreetly: the Special Drawing Rights, often abbreviated "SDR". It is not "money" strictly speaking because it is a basket of currencies, like the old European ECU, exactly as expressed by the Venezuelan President Maduro.

Its value actually depends on the value of five currencies: the US Dollar, the Euro, the British Pound, the Japanese Yen and since October 1, 2016 the Chinese Yuan (also called Renminbi). This inclusion highlights China's growing power in international trade. The next revaluation of the basket is scheduled for 2021 if everything goes well.

As a quick anecdote, the French Post already uses the SDR to declare the value of packages sent to international destinations. The US Postal Service also uses the SDR to quote the value of goods in a package[125].

In fact, it would be simple enough for the IMF to decide to put in circulation more SDR so that they gradually (or not!) take the place of the USD as an international exchange value. In a 2009 speech, the governor of the People's Bank of China, Zhou Xiaochuan, proposed to revive the Keynesian "Bancor" proposal, using the SDR as an international currency. The inclusion of the Chinese Yuan in the SDR can lead us to think that the proposal may not be taken lightly by the IMF.

Finally, the SDR have probably already came within an inch of officially becoming the new world currency. On February 10, 2011,

Dominique Strauss-Kahn, the head of the IMF at the time, strongly supported the SDR as a new International Monetary System, in a series of publications on the IMF website[126] in which he states "increasing the global stock of SDR could help alleviate global imbalances". On 18 May, 2011, he is forced to resign from the IMF, following his arrest in New York[127].

> *Maybe his position regarding the SDR didn't really suit the Neo... ahem, some people on that side of the Atlantic, but few have made the connection.*

In 1988, "The Economist", a newspaper mostly owned by the Rothschilds, showed on its front page the possibility of creating a real world currency, which they called the "Phoenix", by 2018. The deadline is getting close! Many conspiracy theory websites have pointed to this article, which actually exists. And the current financial situation makes it not so crazy to think that the "prophecy" could realize itself sooner than we may think.

15. January 1988: "The Economist" predicts a new World Currency in 2018. Source for the cover: coverbrowser.com[128]

6.3 Globalization and Free Trade

When it comes to money and the economy, it is important to have some basic knowledge about the principles of globalization and free trade. This has a direct influence on global capital flows and justifies some decisions such as whether to create a global currency or not, like the SDR.

Free trade starts from a simple principle, invented as early as the 18th century. It states that each country should switch its production to domains in which it is most competitive, in order to optimize the global world production. According to the theory, every country on earth, in cooperation with the others, specializes in what it does best. From there, countries exchange freely and without taxes with others, its exports balancing its imports, in a Utopian scenario of "free and undistorted competition". In its ideal version, free trade makes it possible to reduce the prices of all products for all countries, since everyone reaches their top productivity. Finally, to finish painting the ideal scene, one of the arguments in favor of free trade is that it promotes peace in the world, since there is no conflict or restriction in trade between countries.

I'm not sure that wars have completely disappeared yet. Maybe it's because we don't have enough free trade?

Free trade is highly "recommended" by economists and liberals in general. One of the biggest arguments in its favor is that it promotes growth, which is true. But we have seen that "growth" is only a necessary parameter of the money-debt system, so the bankers and economists who advocate growth and therefore free trade are obviously in a massive conflict of interest.

Free trade is the exact opposite of protectionism. Protectionism, in its extreme version, taxes every single product coming from other countries sometimes in such a way that it gets impossible to import certain products. It can also require some transparency on the production chain, or impose health or environmental standards to be observed along with many other restrictions, including totally banning some products. Excessive protectionism is not an ideal solution: in its extreme version, the country is cut off from the rest of the world, and nobody wants to trade with it.

I hate extremes. So, I do agree to condemn obsessive protectionism which is counter-productive anyway. But in that case, don't accuse me of communism if I criticize free trade, especially its extremist version...

If free trade seems like a good idea at first sight, it also has many drawbacks.

6.4 General Criticism of Free-Trade

One of the first and most important theoretical criticisms made against it, which is still current, dates back to the 19th century, and was formulated by one of the original defenders of free trade: Robert Torrens. He found that free trade treaties, which are therefore "contracts" between countries, can encourage blackmail and pressure from the dominant country towards the weaker one. These pressures are much more limited in the case of protectionism. When a weak country protects itself from others, and a strong country tries to force it to pay high prices, it can import from other weak countries. Somehow, protectionism pushes "weaker" countries to communicate with each other and even support each other against bigger ones.

Independently from the theory, it is observed that free trade suffers from many flaws when put into practice.

In many cases, it prevents countries from imposing food and health standards, transparency on the production flows or traceability of imported products. This is particularly troublesome when the different countries do not have the same standards of production or hygiene at all.

Besides, free trade implies direct competition between companies that have potentially completely different constraints in their respective countries, and therefore in conditions that are very far from a "free and undistorted competition". Health standards, environmental and social norms are very different in France and China for instance, not even to mention salaries. Free trade therefore favors a general downgrading of conditions, to the expense of the environment and social advances. This is mostly due to non-discrimination clauses in international treaties. These clauses force countries to abolish any restrictive laws towards their partners, in order "not to be unfair" to them. And other clauses forbid states to create new laws or have policies that would be more restrictive than the current ones.

A very interesting book by Erik Reinert[129] analyzes the reasons for wealth disparities in the world between countries. It shows that not all productions generate the same profits. Typically, the production of raw materials (mainly minerals) and agriculture generate relatively little profit, while high value-added industrial production is very lucrative. Thus, African countries that are confined to low-yielding productions remain logically poor, while other countries such as some Asian countries have managed to switch to profitable productions and thus to get richer, little by little.

Along the same lines, the specialization of each country exposes everyone to the fluctuation of demand for its production by the rest of the world. If the demand suddenly drops, the entire country is hit hard economically. This can be seen, for example, with the fall in oil prices, which seriously affects the countries whose wealth depends on oil, and few have been wise enough to diversify their production.

Another very negative aspect of free trade is its impact on the environment, as it pushes all countries to consume products that are made at the other end of the planet, which has an environmental cost: transportation. Back in 2009, a study published by The Guardian[130] showed that the 15 largest cargo ships created as much pollution as all cars on the planet, especially because of sulfur and nitrogen dioxide. Since then, the situation has improved a little thanks to new standards about the fuels used by those ships. In any case, free trade inevitably implies global transport, which in turn creates pollution, instead of relocating the productions as closely as possible to consumers. As a reminder, world freight transport rejects the equivalent of 10 gigatonnes of CO_2 each year, and the main energy currently available for long distance transport is based on hydrocarbons.

Maybe we should try out nuclear cargo ships? Or maybe not.

Another commonly used argument in favor of free trade is that it brings the best of technical progress to all without any restrictions. In reality, free trade agreements favor the robbery of new technologies, often from the weakest to the strongest.

6.5 Free Trade Treaties in Practice

Free Trade Treaties and Organizations are subjects on their own, addressed in many studies and books[131]. However, our object here is money, so I will keep it short. I will still give you some outlines and examples to give a general idea on the subject.

Free Trade Treaties are "contracts" which specify the rules to be observed when exchanging goods or services between nations. There are hundreds of treaties worldwide. They are generally thousands of pages long, and use very technical vocabulary that can only be understood by legal experts.

Wait a minute. Isn't Free Trade supposed to fit in a single page saying "let's trade everything freely"?

These treaties are always negotiated behind closed doors within organizations such as the World Trade Organization, abbreviated WTO. Powerful countries come with a lot of very specialized negotiators, while poor countries generally send one ambassador, who is even sometimes shared between several countries. Blackmailing is often part of the negotiations. Typically, many countries in the world, especially "poor" countries, have large amounts of debt towards organizations such as the WTO, the IMF, or the World Bank. These debts are an easy way to remind those countries that they can't afford to negotiate much. In fact, the New York Times itself published an article in 1990 titled "A Crowbar for Carla Hills"[132], in reference to the the "negotiating power" of Hills, who was the US's Trade Negotiator at the time.

It is easy to imagine the US negotiator entering the negotiation room with a big crowbar...

Note that a country which has no representative during some negotiations automatically agrees with everything that will be signed there.

This is especially a problem to smaller countries, who generally have only one representative, while several negotiation rounds are often negotiated at the same time in separate places.

One of the most clear evidence of injustice is the very existence of the "Section 301" of the Trade Act of 1974. This section forbids any country in the world to have policies that would "burden or restrict US commerce". If a country does not obey this, the President of the US can "take any appropriate action" to put it back on track[133]. Of course, if any other country tried to do the same, it would cause a diplomatic scandal.

These treaties are not only negotiated by countries. They are also written for and by international corporations, through lobbying within the various institutions worldwide[134]. For instance, treaties within the European Union allow corporations to sue countries whenever they think some laws or policies are not good for them. For example, a European energy giant corporation recently filed a complaint against Germany, claiming "potential losses" after the Germans declared they were abandoning nuclear power. The corporation asks for a total compensation that could amount to 20 billion Euros, all based on no actual loss[135].

The exact same situation happens with international treaties. With the CETA and TAFTA, these complaints could take on a totally new dimension for Europe. These treaties provide for the expanded use of the "International Tribunals for Private Arbitration", of which the judges, lawyers and prosecutors are business lawyers. Thus, any US multinational company who wouldn't be happy about a European state's laws would be able to file a complaint to one of these tribunals. But these tribunals are totally independent of the national laws of the country in question or even European laws. Moreover, their "judges" are business lawyers, who are in clear conflicts of interest with the private corporations they serve. We can guess that such trials wouldn't have "fair" judgments. This seems incredible, but it is real[136]. These courts already exist within the European Union, but by signing the TAFTA and CETA, it is the American and Canadian companies that could come and write the law in Europe through these tribunals. Of course, a State can not file a complaint to these tribunals in the event of a failure by the multinational corporations: the complaints can only be filed by the private sector.

Let's also not forget that these treaties are huge, not always very clear, and sometimes filled with contradictions. This allows the "judges" to cherry-pick whatever they want to advantage whoever they want when they pronounce their judgments. And as these "judges" are business lawyers, they can hardly be seen as "activists for the common good". The accumulation of many treaties also creates confusion and collisions between them. The most famous example is the GATT vs the Lome Accords during the 1990s[137].

Another example of one-sided advantage through these treaties is found in Algeria. Free trade agreements signed with the European zone are very damaging to Algeria's economy, according to Algerian analysts[138]. To summarize, the EU benefits from the Algerian oil at low prices, but the Algerians don't benefit as much from what they get in return.

Another effect is that, in the real world, "free and undistorted competition" doesn't exist. For instance, subsidies (typically allocated to agriculture) create an effect of unfair competition in the absence of taxes between countries. One of the most obvious examples for this can be found with the US subsidies for their corn production. Under the "NAFTA" treaties (North American Free Trade Agreement), where Mexico is forced to import US food without taxes, this poses a serious problem for Mexican farmers. They don't have subsidies, and they obviously cannot match the US prices for corn, unless they produce at a loss. As a result, while Mexico was self-sufficient in food before the NAFTA treaties, now they have to import 40% of their food products. The poor in Mexico were 14 million before these treaties, but now they are 50 million. Moreover, we speak of "free trade" of goods, but rarely of people...

6.6 Who Benefits from Free-Trade?

So, free trade seems to have a lot of negative effects, who really benefits from it?

First, it mostly benefits the big multinational corporations and allows them to increase their profits. Thanks to free trade agreements, they can safely relocate their production in countries where the cost of production is less, while still selling their products at the same price in countries with higher wages. Other beneficiaries of free trade are traders who buy and sell the products on the world market for profit and with fewer restrictions.

People in the richest countries also benefit from free trade because of very low import prices. But they also suffer from it. The first thing that comes to mind is the relocation of the productions, which causes unemployment in their countries. The second thing we tend to forget is all local norms that are abolished by free trade, such as ecology, traceability or things like regulating GMOs.

To summarize, if free trade was to be viable and fair for all, all the countries of the world should be similar and have the same climatic, geographical, geological, social and cultural conditions. It is obviously not the case in real life. Each country is unique, and as such it is normal that it should be able to decide what it considers to be fair, rather than force it to accept everything without saying a word.

Finally, if "Free Trade Treaties" were really what they claim to be, they should contain just one page stating that no restrictions can be applied to the importation of products on both sides. But this is obviously not the case, given the size and complexity of these treaties. Robert Torrens gave us a hint back in the 19th century that explains why they are so big: the stronger can force their will on the weaker inside these treaties. In the end, they result in not being "Free Trade", but rather "Rules of the Strong" to submit the weak, including some democratic states, which become simple puppets when facing a powerful organization such as the WTO, as we will see in the next chapter.

Summary:

The US Dollar is the worldwide reference currency, which is problematic because of the "Triffin dilemma". The Special Drawing Rights, a basket of currencies such as the European ECU before the Euro, could ultimately become the world currency and replace the USD as such.

Free trade in practice is counterproductive, as much as extreme protectionism is. Free trade as it is implemented today leads to strong financial pressures on states, especially the weakest ones, typically through blackmail. On the other hand it truly benefits multinational corporations by limiting the possibilities for States to defend themselves, through "private tribunals" which overrule the laws of the states.

Free trade could only function correctly if all countries were identical and with full transparency, which is obviously not the case. Besides, as different types of productions do not generate the same profits, it creates inequalities all over the world. Finally, free trade is greatly detrimental to the environment because of the transportation it generates.

Chapter 7
The Independence of Nations

7.1 Why We Really Need Regulations

"All this is well and very idealistic, but why do we need so many regulations, anyway? Why should the states be authorized to interfere with the business of private companies in the first place? Aren't the regulations the very things that push companies to relocate their production abroad? Too much bureaucracy is making it so difficult for companies to operate."

How many times have we heard that from very sincere people who really believe in what they are saying?

Let me repeat the fundamental purpose of a private enterprise: to make money. And if it doesn't, others will and that company will not survive. So, for a company, nothing else matters more than money, everything else is just useless idealism.

How do you increase the money you make when you are a company? You have to spend less when manufacturing your products, and earn more from selling them.

To earn more money, companies:

- use child labor without any remorse[139],
- thrive on poverty, don't care about the working conditions[140] even if it means that a whole factory can collapse on its workers[141], or if the area is at war and making the people's lives absolutely horrific[142],

- don't care about pollution, toxic air fumes, toxic leaks, or even simply rejecting toxic liquids in the environment[143],
- use toxic pesticides in food even if their toxicity has been proven[144],
- blatantly lie in their advertisements, as the one featured in figure 16.

The list goes on and on, I don't think I need to make more points here.

So the people who support removing regulations from the states, whether they realize it or not, actually support that:

16. *The reasons why we need regulations. Sources: various images on the Internet.*

Of course, some companies choose a different business model. Either because their owners do care about all these problems, either because they calculate that the people will buy their products thanks to their good behavior, and they can even sell their products at very high prices.

One example of a "good behavior" is a small European company, called "Fairphone", which has taken upon itself to build phones by minimizing its negative impacts in the world[145] while not raising its prices much. But this is an exception.

Others develop "fair" or "ecological" labels which guarantee to their customers that they are limiting their negative impacts. There are some growing suspicions towards these labels, as it has been uncovered that some of them thrive on the label itself to sell very expensive products without necessarily delivering on their promises[146]. This doesn't mean you should stop buying any such product, some initiatives truly have positive effects. Just be cautious and don't rush on the latest labels, which are sometimes only marketing tools.

But again, all these are generally polishing their image towards the general public, in the hopes that people will buy their products at high prices.

It is already very complicated to buy any product these days. Depending on your beliefs, you have to watch out for preservatives, aspartame, non organic products, gluten, and so many other things. And of course, the price. It is already such a mess that you can't ask every person to make a full inquiry on where the product was made, whether child labor was involved, or if the environment was heavily damaged in the process.

The reason for the very existence of a state is exactly that: protecting its citizens against this kind of problems.

It doesn't only have to make sure that domestic products comply with high standards, but it also has to make sure that imported products do as well. And if they don't, it should simply ban them or at least impose very strong taxes on them so that these practices can be abolished worldwide.

Governments do this through their laws.

Can the governments deliver on these promises? Not anymore, "thanks to Free Trade Treaties".

I say "thanks to", because if you see it from a certain

perspective, the one of multinational corporations, it can be a positive thing. It's only about which side you are on.

Now, you may think that this book drifted very far away from its primary subject: money. I am not advocating socialism or any other ideology, I'm simply looking at the hard facts and how things happen in the real world when private companies are allowed to do whatever they want. And I am presenting all this for you to realize how much money's influence can reach very far in our society and our lives.

Money as it is in our financial system allows for wealth to be concentrated by a minority of people. It allows a few to be powerful enough to build empires. It in turn allows them to become multinational giants which take over our states through international treaties and organizations. It has permitted organizations such as the WTO to accumulate much power, to the point that they can dictate their will to governments.

I'm not the only one expressing concerns over this. Many people question the monopolies of the giant multinational corporations. Some even wonder if we should nationalize them (the question is, in which country...)[147].

Finally, deregulations favor all kinds of traffics (drugs, weapons, humans...), which also benefit from crises when they launder their money even more easily[148].

7.2 International Organizations

Free Trade Treaties could not be signed without the help of international organizations such as the World Trade Organization, which has 164 member countries.

This organization combines all main powers together. Treaties are "laws" for the different countries, so it has the legislative power. It also has the role of watching the countries and notifying them if they "misbehave", so it also has the executive power. And finally, it has special courts[149], which can judge countries whenever there is a conflict, so it finally has the judicial power.

> Combining these three powers in one organization is a very strange idea: why do you think we always separate these powers when designing the management of a state?

Besides the treaties, the WTO, the IMF and the World Bank play their own roles at an international level. Their "help" is always conditioned by "austerity measures" on the states: government subsides are cut, public services are reduced and sold to the private sector, and states are forbidden to get loans from their own national bank, you get the drill. Through these actions, the IMF causes more poverty in those countries, and additionally puts them into debt[150]. Even lead economists protested against the IMF, such as Milton Friedman[151]. Because "austerity" is only for the population. The credits that are given to these countries go mostly to the private sector, especially from abroad.

To illustrate how this operates, there is one simple mechanism to put developing countries into debt. The first step is to convince officials of these countries that they need top infrastructures to bring their country to the next level, and show them magnificent projects to achieve this goal. The second step is to make them finance these projects with debt: they make a loan to the IMF or the World Bank. The problem is that these mega projects, while most of the time built by foreign companies, don't deliver the promised advances to the country. And generally, they have other agendas.

For instance, the building of huge dams in Congo that need a lot of maintenance, but in the end which profit mines that are operated by foreign companies[152]. Foreign investors and international organizations knew very well before the construction of such dams that the population wouldn't consume that much electricity. In the meantime, these countries are sunk in debt. In the end, they are put under the administrative supervision of the IMF, by programs that are modestly called "Structural Adjustment", and their infrastructures are privatized "to pay back the debt".

> Does this remind you the recent case of Greece by any chance?

7.3 National Debts

Following the centralization of institutions and free trade treaties which tend to transform the world into a large single market place, you may wonder whether the next step could be the creation of a world currency. It could be simply accepted by governments, or forced upon them. One of the ways to force it would be to put some pressure on the indebted states, offering to cancel their debt in exchange for the adoption of this new currency. But it is difficult to erase a debt that is due to private entities without causing major disruptions in the economy.

Let's reflect on the Quantitative Easing program by the ECB. It is "buying state debt from private hands", with very little effect. In other words, without changing much to the economy, states hold more and more debt toward the ECB and less to private entities. So could the reason for the ECB's quantitative easing programs be that states would be easily blackmailed to accept the SDR or another currency in the future? This is a theory that I put forward, it might be totally far-fetched, time will tell.

One thing is certain, when you have to negotiate a debt that you are not likely to repay anytime soon, you are in a serious position of inferiority, and the consequences are often fatal, as Greece can testify. Not only has it been humiliated as a nation, but it has simply lost its sovereignty. Its government must follow exactly what is imposed by its creditors, including the robbery of its public infrastructures, airports, harbors, energy distribution, highways, railways, everything is auctioned to the vultures[153], such as multinational corporations, banks, billionaires... the scenario resembles Russia in the 1990s when the mafia was battling over the juicy cake of privatizations for crusts of bread, by means of tanks and Kalashnikov.

We could also talk about the scandals related to Greek privatizations, such as the national lottery, the OPAP, which was sold while its stock was at its minimum, enabling the buyers to buy it at a discount[154]. And it gets interesting when you match this information with the resigning of the Greek privatization chief, caught flying on the OPAP buyer's private plane a little while later[155].

I am not saying that Greece did not make any mistakes, especially regarding taxation, their successive governments have their share of obvious responsibility. But before giving any lessons to others, perhaps we should deal with our own tax evasion problems first. And how is Greece supposed to reach financial stability in the future, now that all profitable activities such as the national lottery have been taken away and given to private investors? What kind of long-term logic is this?

Besides, austerity policies that are promoted worldwide to "stabilize" the debts of the states do not address the real causes of the problem: Debt-money, with its associated interest and speculation. Instead, they always declare that "when we have cut enough budget, the economy will restart"[156]. In reality, we have been observing for decades that budget cuts slow down the economy and weaken the states, and cut short all their hopes of becoming competitive in the future. One sure thing: these cuts certainly don't help pay back public debts.

Some others, like Portugal, have bet on the totally opposite model, and have succeeded so far even if the road to full long-term recovery is obviously still long[157].

7.4 Privatizations and National External Debt

Note that public debt doesn't accurately represent a country's debt. For instance, Turkey managed to get rid of its debt to the IMF by privatizing parts of its economy[158]. It is obvious that in a country where everything is privatized, the public debt is much lower than if everything is nationalized.

To be fair, it is then necessary to look at the overall private debt as well as the public debt of a country to get an idea of its overall debt. So yes, Turkey did pay its debt to the IMF, and the Turkish State has managed to cut off most of its public debt. But this doesn't mean that the country is out of debt as a whole. While most liberal economists praise Turkey for its "miracle recovery" from the "disastrous 1990s", and thanks to its "austerity measures and privatizations", the picture is a little different when we look at Turkey's "Total Gross External Debt", as shown in the following graph:

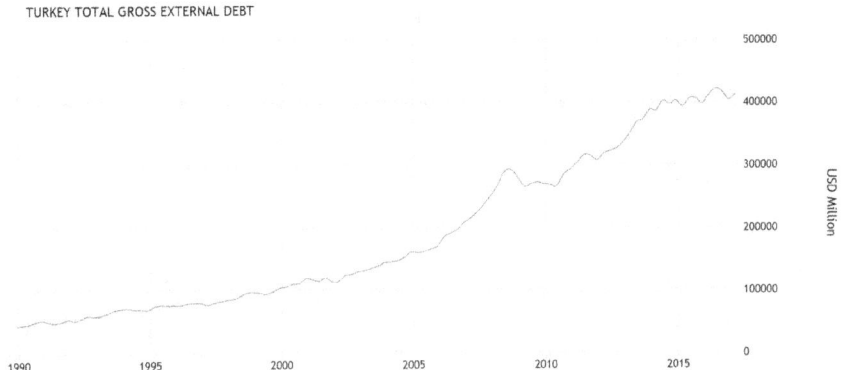

17. *Turkey's Total Gross External Debt. Source: tradingeconomics.com*[159]

As we can see from the curve, Turkey is far from being "debt-free", it has only transferred its public debt to an ever-growing private debt. And most countries in the world have similar curves when it comes to their total external debt. Except... Iceland. Check it out for yourself, it's worth it![160]

We should also note that privatizing entire parts of an economy with the current debt system has very little overall benefit for the population: the interest to the banks is then paid by private companies rather than by the state, it doesn't change a thing, instead of paying with your taxes, you pay higher prices for basic services. However, the big difference for the wealthy is that those companies which can buy such massive infrastructures are all on the stock market, so they also have to distribute dividends to their shareholders. So there is more money going back to the wealthy, instead of being reinvested into the local economy and benefiting the population.

Besides, there is absolutely no reason why those infrastructures would be less competitive when managed by people paid by a well-managed state than when they are paid by private companies. In the end, whenever something is privatized, prices skyrocket: electricity, gas, water, freeways... these profits do need to come from somewhere. In fact, this knowledge is not new at all[161], but is rarely shared on the news.

Of course, many will take some examples where privatization and opening a market to competition has lowered the prices of products or services. But these examples are very rare, and besides, it is a quite common practice for companies operating on the same market to have secret agreements to keep prices high[162]. These are of course illegal, that's why they are secret!

As for the classic example of the USSR to show the dangers of nationalizations, it is a very bad example. If the USSR had been a democracy, it could be a valid example. But it was a deeply corrupted autocratic regime operating on fear. This was the major reason for its demise, regardless of any economic considerations.

7.5 Counter-Powers?

For the lasts decade, new powers have emerged, such as China or Russia, which joined the WTO recently[163]. This caused a halt in many negotiations: it is a little more difficult to blackmail such powerful countries.

Besides, the creation of the BRICS[164] on the international scene, as well as the new "Silk Road" initiated by China, is creating a big shift in world trade and economy, including in developing countries. Now, the Chinese also want their share of the African cake.

For instance, the Chinese copper deal with Congo in 2009 created some panic in the West. Following the deal, the IMF and the World Bank started blackmailing Congo of not wiping off its debt if it proceeded with the deal[165]. In 2015, Russia also defied the West by inviting Greece to join the BRICS[166].

> *Caution: one imperialism can easily be replaced by another one.*

There is also another new institution on the world scene: the "New Development Bank"[167]. It is an alternative to the IMF and the World Bank. Unlike the IMF, it doesn't impose any austerity measures on the countries to which it lends money, which is a real positive novelty for the countries that want to recover economically.

7.6 World Finances and the States

The world financiers also have a growing impact on our states, and it is time to put them into the spotlight for a while.

First of all, they control information. Information is key to get the support of the people, especially in democracies where they are supposed to be "independent, neutral and critical". It is no secret that the mainstream media are now in the hands of the wealthiest, since they are privatized. In France, 10 multimillionaires hold all major media[168]. From there, they can easily give directions to their journalists, and give them the subjects that should be put forward and those to be buried. Evictions of journalists are commonplace as soon as they cross the red line[169]. It is the same scenario all over the world.

Simple question : frankly, if you owned a TV channel, would you let its journalists expose your tax evasion plans? Extra question: would they even dare? (self-censorship...)

Then, financiers clearly invade politics. Donald Trump is originally not a politician. In France, Emmanuel Macron, the current French president is, so to speak, the spokesperson of the financial interests. The first steps taken by his government are the best proof of this: tax gifts to large fortunes through the reorganization of the tax on the wealthiest, tax gifts for companies "to revive the economy"...

Interestingly, Emmanuel Macron's program was heavily criticized by the journalist François Lenglet during an interview before the French Presidential election[170]. Just for the record, this journalist can not be called a socialist since he generally advocates neo-liberalism, he was actually at this summer's Bilderberg meeting[171]. In his interview, he was surprised by the very large tax gifts offered to the wealthiest by Macron's program as well as the very large financial deficit of the program. He estimated that if the program were to be put in place, it would cost the French state more than 100 billion Euros annually, and the candidate's answers were pitiful attempts to try and get away from the real subject, which was the debt he is going to transfer to our future generations. Too bad the French people did not listen to this interview and didn't understand the journalist's very valid points. Anyway, the multiple conflicts of interest (Rothschild Bank, Patrick Drahi, Pierre Bergé, Xavier Niel, Alstom and many others, as well as other conflicts of interest within his own presidency campaign team) should have warned the French about him.

No one can serve two masters. During the French Presidential campaign, 40 economists supported Emmanuel Macron[172], while it was clear that his presidential program was a financial abyss as shown by the journalist Lenglet, we may wonder about their skills or their integrity...

Summary:

National regulations are necessary to protect basic human rights as well as the health of the population and the environment, among other things.

The WTO is an organization that concentrates the 3 powers: legislative, executive, judicial. It is above the laws of the states through the treaties that automatically apply to member states.

The IMF and the World Bank help countries, but also impose austerity measures, especially privatization schemes of public services, that drive poor countries into even more poverty and instability.

The "public debt" of a state is not representative of the debt of a country, you need to check its external debt instead which also includes private debt. When seen from this angle, privatization plans only move the public debt to private debt while generally raising prices of services for the population.

Some new Counter-Powers, such as the BRICS, seem to be a new interesting alternative to the historical institutions: WTO, IMF, World Bank.

The states and their politicians seem to be more and more infiltrated by the financiers.

Chapter 8
A World in Crisis

World finances are constantly object to speculation, and thus to bubbles, these passing trends completely disconnected from reality, made possible by excessive centralization and globalization. All this looks like a paper giant based on nothing concrete: too big to be transparent. The only explanation for maintaining the system is the blind confidence of the people towards their respective rulers and the "economic analysts" despite the huge mistakes they often make.

8.1 The 2008 Subprimes Crisis

To illustrate what happens during a modern crisis, let's analyze shortly the 2008 "subprimes crisis". It seems complicated when explained by most economists, but it is actually very simple.

After the burst of the Dot-Com bubble in 2000, the Fed decided to lower its interest rates to boost the economy, thus encouraging US consumers to buy homes. Rates were very low, banks didn't ask so many guarantees to the borrowers and began to make very risky loans, called "subprimes". These loans will be called later (too late...) "toxic" loans because of their fragility. The banks were very aware of the risks they were taking with these loans, and they began selling them on the financial markets. The way they did this was through a process called "securitization"[173], which is a very bad name for a very risky practice. Basically, they offer to investors "packages" of various speculated values, including truly interesting ones, to "hide" the bad ones. These "packages" are generally praised by venture capitalists and rating agencies, the logic being that "diversified" investments are "safe". So rating agencies didn't see a thing, and these overall toxic financial products started selling like hotcakes, not only to American banks, but to the whole world. This is the main risk about speculation, and especially "derivatives", which is "speculation on speculation", whom Warren Buffet called "Weapons of Mass Destruction" back in 2003, long before the 2008 crisis.

In 2005, the Fed, believing that the economy had recovered, suddenly raised its interest rates. However, as I have already mentioned, most loans in the United States are not at fixed rates: they follow the evolution of rates fixed by the Fed. So, on the one hand, many borrowers of these risky loans found themselves overnight having to pay much higher repayments, which they couldn't afford. The banks seized their homes and tried to sell them to compensate for their losses. On the other hand, with the rising rates, there were fewer borrowers on the market since less people could get loans, as banks also tightened their conditions. Real estate prices fell 30% on average between 2006 and 2009, and the banks found themselves with a bunch of houses they couldn't sell, and 7 million Americans... without a home in just a few months.

Panic spread, the rating agencies, realizing (a little late) their mistake, began to put very negative notes on these toxic products, making the panic even worse. You would think that the Fed would be wise enough and lower their interest rates to calm everyone down. Well, that is not really what they did at first. They believed there was a "liquidity crisis", which means "not enough money in the economy", so they began flooding the economy with money. This of course had no effect, and when they finally lowered their interest rates it was too late.

They did a blood transfer while the patient was actually choking... this is the type of mistakes "top" economists actually make.

Finally, many banks went bankrupt, many of them were nationalized, and Lehman-Brothers won the prize of the biggest bankruptcy, partly bailed out by the Fed. The crisis spread throughout the financial markets to Europe, although it had little impact on the population in France, which was protected by its fixed interest rates.

At the end of 2008, it was discovered that a certain Bernard

Madoff had made elaborate schemes, in the form of a Ponzi chain based on the confidence of his investors, for a total amount of more than 60 billion Dollars, and which were not guaranteed by anything. He was not a bank, so he was sentenced to 150 years in prison. See you in... 2139.

From this lesson of history, it seems of course obvious that subprimes had to be eradicated from the markets in order not to repeat this crisis in the future. But you would be surprised to learn that, on the contrary, these risky loans are used everywhere nowadays, not only for housing, but also for cars, for students... and they are making a strong comeback[174].

Madmen![175]

8.2 Europe and the European Banks

The interest rates fixed by central banks around the world are currently very low. On the other hand, as we have seen, the ECB has flooded the market with fresh money, which could translate into galloping inflation in the event of an economic recovery.

On the other hand, let's look at one of the biggest banks in Europe: Deutsche Bank, the biggest German private bank. It is not in a very good financial health. Its stock value was listed at €150 in 2007, but it fell to €10 in 2016, and is now at €15, which means that investors believe that it is not worth much and it is a risky investment. There are reasons for this, and I will mention only two of them.

First, this bank has accumulated "mistakes" in the last decade, and was accused by the United States of having been a major actor of the subprimes crisis, asking it 14 billion Euros in fines. The bank's leaders have also been repeatedly condemned for market manipulation scandals including its part in the Libor scandal, accused of money laundering or even cooperating with "terrorist" countries, and repeatedly helping with tax fraud.

But it doesn't stop here. Analysts see that it is massively exposed to derivatives, and thus potentially at risk. The amounts of these derivatives vary from 52 to 75 trillion Euros according to analysts. If these derivatives were to default as in the subprimes crisis, no one in Europe could bail out such humongous amounts... as a reminder, Germany's GDP is 4 trillion Euros, and less than 19 trillion for Europe as a whole.

In the meantime, central bank are gradually rising their interest rates and the ECB recently announced that its quantitative easing program is coming to an end[176], as recommended by the President of Ifo in May 2017[177] in a publication titled "Inflation is back", which is the nightmare of the Germans and therefore of the ECB.

As we have seen, the stock markets are subject to "butterfly effects", and the picture which is shown here doesn't look so great.

Last June 2017, the Spanish bank "Banco Popular", the sixth largest Spanish bank[178], was saved at the last moment from bankruptcy and was bought back by another Spanish bank "Santander"[179]. It was choked by "toxic assets", very similar to subprimes mortgages, and all the ECB's attempts to rescue it failed. These toxic assets are now in the hands of another bank, which is supposedly "too big to fail" as well.

Italy is also in the spotlight that same month, since several banks were saved by the Italian government, bail-outs costing a mere 17 billion Euros of tax payers' money[180].

All this really doesn't smell good at all...

8.3 Crisis, Cash and Gold

In spite of all this, and even if a crisis is quite likely in the next few years, we must not give in to the sirens of many "analysts" who have things to sell, and who have for years predicted that "Armageddon comes tomorrow". While some of the things they say are true, they do not know more than you or me when the next crisis is going to happen, and they certainly don't know how big it will be. Fear is their business, they use a good old technique for which IBM paid the price in the 1960s, "FUD", "Fear, Uncertainty and Doubt".

By the end of the 1960s, IBM sellers became aware that the new computers of their competitor Control Data were likely to take their market share seriously. So in order not to lose their customers, they spread false rumors about a supposed new IBM machine that was going to revolutionize the market. But this machine didn't exist at all. IBM lost its trial against its competitor at the time.

On the other hand, it doesn't mean you should bury your head into the sand. Risks exist. The system as a whole is a huge house of cards.

There is some important information to know if you have more than €100,000 in a European bank account (all in one account) or €70,000 in life insurance in France (if you do have a large life insurance plan, check out the limit in your country). It wouldn't be surprising if these amounts are revised downwards in the future[181], so you should monitor this very closely if you have large amounts of money in your bank account. European laws have been passed in recent years to seize accounts that have more than these amounts in the event of a crisis. The plan is, instead of the state bailing out the banks, to first block customers' savings, then take them and give them to the banks[182]. This has already been the case in Cyprus during the 2012-2013 crisis. Moreover, according to the very serious Reuters news agency, the European Union is seriously considering the possibility of blocking all current accounts in the event of a "systemic risk" (including "series of bank bankruptcies")[183]. So even if you don't have much in the bank, they might just close the ATMs overnight for an undetermined amount of time, as they did in Greece or Cyprus. Remember, they absolutely don't have enough cash to cover all deposits, so they cannot afford having everyone knocking at the door to withdraw cash.

At the same time, there is a clear desire from both governments and financial institutions worldwide to get rid of cash. The most frequent reason is fighting terrorism and the black market. But terrorists all have bank accounts. Even Osama Ben Laden had one[184]. Another reason that is often put forward is the cost of producing banknotes and coins. This one is a total joke given the flows of money in the economy[i]. Deutsche Bank boss John Cryan said on January 20, 2016: "Cash I think in ten years time

---

i Estimates of the cost of printing money are some tens of millions of dollars a year, nothing compared to the thousands of billions of debt around the world.

probably won't exist. There is no need for it, it is terribly inefficient and expensive."[185]

See you in 2026...

Denmark has already made this wish several years ago[186]. In the rest of the world, other countries take this project very seriously: Sweden, Norway, Canada, South Korea (total removal of cash by 2020[187]).

In November 2016, the Prime Minister of India, Narendra Modi, announced that the 500- and 1,000-Rupee banknotes were declared "canceled" overnight, causing an unprecedented crisis, which affected the poorest who had some savings under their mattress. The justification was to fight again "terrorism" and the "black market". Banks were stormed by panicked Indians in an attempt to replace some notes by the new versions, after explaining where their money came from. Banks got short of banknotes very quickly, in an incredible confusion[188]. In France, such a decision would undoubtedly cause riots, but electronic payments already represented 55% in France in 2013, compared with 2% in India. Needless to say, the Indian panic has certainly served the businesses of MasterCard and Visa among others…

Ah, Visa… those who offer a $10,000 reward to businesses who refuse to take payments in cash?[189]

Almost a year later, the economy of India has been suffering due to a lack of cash in circulation. Meanwhile, the Central Bank reports that it has got back 99% of all the "canceled" bank notes. So the operation, which was supposed to hurt "corruption" and "terrorist networks", is a huge fail, as reported by the very serious "The Economist" [190].

So, all this chaos, all this suffering of the population, was for nothing. It was like digging the Panama Canal with a teaspoon.

In Venezuela, it is the 100-bolivar bill, the banknote with the highest face value, which is scrapped within 72 hours[191].

Getting rid of cash raises the issue of privacy, coupled with the risk of piracy of this very sensitive data that is the monetary transactions of citizens. Another aspect often ignored by those who support "fully electronic" payment systems is the risk of network hacking: how do you pay for your bread if the network is not operational? As we have seen recently, piracy has very important impacts and some studies show that the Internet as a whole could be brought to its knees by large groups and that some "very large organization" is testing its limits[192].

> Some people with sharp tongues also imply that the removal of "cash" is essential to set negative interest on your savings... it does make sense!

Eliminating cash is also associated with the control of gold. In France, the purchase of gold is regulated as much as the purchase of firearms. Payment in cash for gold is restricted by the law, and any purchase of gold must be recorded in a ledger with the ID of the buyer. The main idea is that the state wants to know who owns gold, and how much of it, to be able to seize it in the event of a major crisis. It becomes even easier if you "purchase" gold from a bank and let them store it for you rather than bringing it back to your home, which is a common practice.

> Of course, in the event of a crisis, it is obvious that you will never ever hold this gold in your hands.

India, following its "coup" on the banknotes, also intends to seriously regulate imports of gold. Gold is nevertheless a taboo subject in this country, where gold jewelry makes most of the wealth of the people.

As for the various countries of the world, Russia[193] and China[194] stand out by creating huge gold stocks in recent years. On the other hand, in what should be a state scandal, a certain French minister of the economy has forced the Bank of France to sell one fifth of its gold stock between 2004 and 2009, just before the value of gold went up. The loss suffered by the French state due to this bad operation is a shocking 10 billion Euros in 2010 compared to the foreign currency portfolios that were bought with the gold[195]. In the meantime, Germany is calling its gold back home[196].

8.4 How Can We Improve the System?

Before going any further, I suggest we take a look at the system with a global view, to measure the challenges we are facing.

A World in Crisis

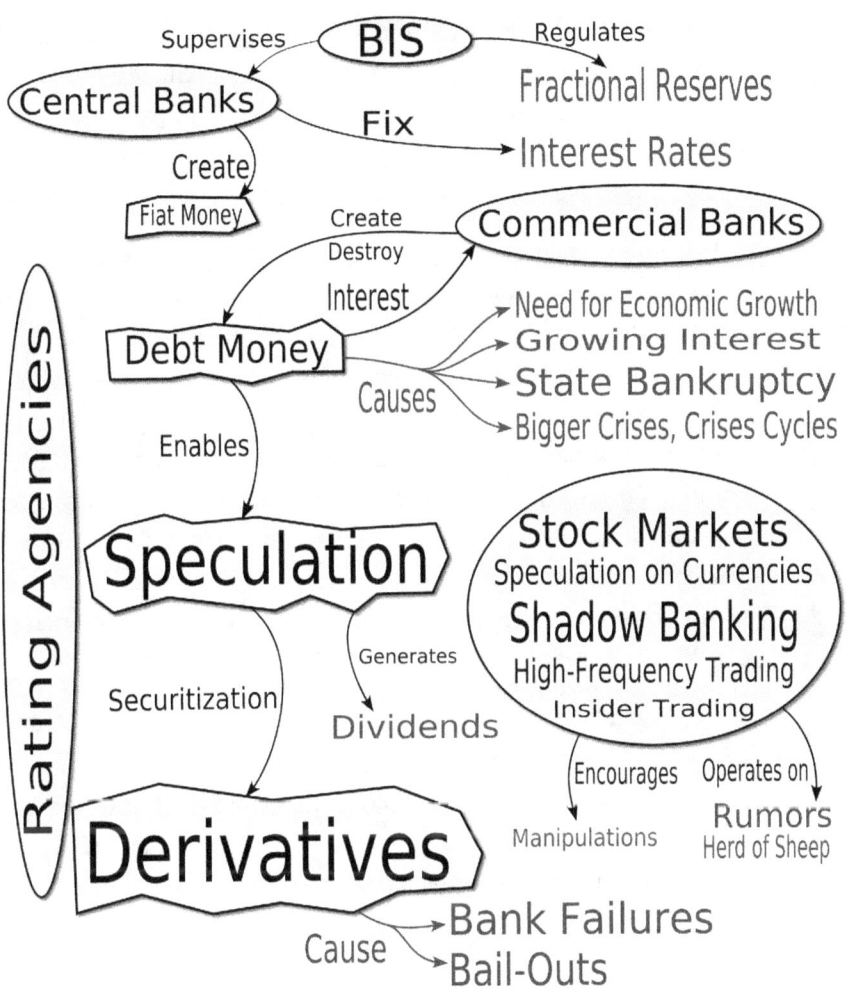

18. Summary of the whole financial system

- The BIS fixes overall regulations such as Fractional Reserves limits. Central Banks fix Interest Rates that Commercial Banks apply when granting loans. Central Banks create Fiat Money, which represents a tiny fraction of the circulation of money.

- Commercial Banks, with adequate Fractional Reserves, create Debt Money through credits at the Interest Rates given by the Central Banks. This money is then destroyed when loans are repaid, but the interest remain in the bank's account. The Debt

Money System, through the underlying growing interest, causes the need for Economic Growth, and causes Bankruptcy of States, which are then forced to dismantle their public infrastructures. As Banks grant loans only when the economy is thriving, they also create crises cycles, and bigger crisis effects.

- Debt Money enables Speculation in the Stock Markets, which generate dividends for the stock holders when companies make profits. Most stock holders are after short term profits, and speculate based on rumors, which creates "sheep" behaviors, causing regular massive downfalls of stocks. High-Frequency Trading by robots totally dehumanize speculation, and accumulate profits on transactions in micro-seconds, which also enhances the "herd of sheep" behavior. Speculation favors Insider Trading and Corruption, which can hardly be regulated in practice. Stock Markets are totally unpredictable and vulnerable to the "butterfly effect", sometimes in very short periods such as a single day.

- Rating Agencies are the "Sheep Dogs" of the Stock Market, and are followed blindly by speculators, even if they have regularly proven that their ratings were not reliable. Rating Agencies are often accused to be in major conflicts of interest, especially as they are paid by the very companies they have to rate.

- Shadow Banking is just like Stock Markets, but without any regulations. It is growing thanks to the current extremely low interest rates, which Central Banks now cannot raise anymore without causing a major financial cataclysm. Besides, speculation on national currencies is not regulated and big players such as hedge funds have fun with them as if they were playing Monopoly.

- Derivatives, which are accumulated layers of speculation, mostly by securitization which enables hiding toxic products inside "good-looking" packages, are the ultimate step of investors totally losing contact with reality. Speculation, especially Derivatives, causes massive Bank Failures, especially those that are "too big to fail", typically when interest rates go up.

- States are forced to bail-out banks when they go bankrupt, with the tax payer's money.

What???

The system described in this way seems totally insane. So how do we come back to our senses? The Gordian Knot cannot be untangled: what is at stake here is the price of raw materials, including those of primary necessity, it is the financing of companies, real projects, and for which the entire world population depends for its survival, for the better and for the worse.

Optimists say that the system regulates itself on its own, and that when it has a hiccup, the impact is limited and everything goes back to normal very quickly.

I'll let you explain that to the millions of Americans who lost their homes back in 2008...

Until now things have still gotten back under control every time. But in the process, many lives are spoiled with every "crisis", and always for the benefit of some minority. In any case, nothing allows to be so optimistic for the future, since economists themselves admit that we are in a situation that has no precedent and that there are no reliable models to predict what could happen[197]. This can largely explain the mistakes they make repeatedly and their inability to predict and therefore prevent crises[198]... I'm not sure we should trust Janet Yellen when she says that "we are likely not to see a new financial crisis in our lifetime"[199].

I'm not sure whether I want to laugh or cry. Up to you!

On the other hand, this system favors to the extreme a minority of actors who direct the international financial institutions. These people have an overall view of the state of the system and the actions that will be implemented in both the short and long term, enabling them to make the right choices at the right time to get richer at the expense of the world's population as a whole, and in a totally non-transparent way.

Their status makes them completely immune to justice and guarantees that nothing can be brought against them. The recent trial of Christine Lagarde, director of the IMF, has shown that she was convicted of "carelessness" when she was the French Minister of Finance, but she was neither condemned nor dismissed, while the IMF "renewed its confidence in her"[200].

It is, however, easier to get rid of a director by other means when it is needed...

With this in mind, it is difficult to make anything happen at the level of these institutions. We could require more transparency, but how can we implement it in practice in the face of the enormous stakes and the powers that we face?

We could also ask that robots be removed from speculative markets. Alas, the recent advances in artificial intelligence especially in "deep learning" can only make us fear that these robots will become more efficient in the near future. Efficient to earn more and more for their masters of course, not to "improve" the condition of humans who depend on the system but do not run it.

For the record, I am not "anti-robots". On the contrary, I find that it is great that technology frees mankind from tasks that are tedious, repetitive and unrewarding. But this technological switch should also come with profound society changes, which I absolutely don't see coming...

We have also seen that, in the course of history, humans have a short memory. They regularly get stuck in a gold standard that causes deflation. Then, realizing the problems of deflation and seeing the economic system falling into crisis, they start a spiral of debts, uncontrolled monetary creation that leads to inflation and then hyperinflation. At the collapse of this "new" system, in reaction, they go back to something "solid", and a new cycle starts with the gold standard or another restrictive monetary creation system. How do we get out of this endless cycle?

Finally, how can we design a system in which money doesn't make more and more wealth for a minority, while we know perfectly well that this doesn't "tickle-down" towards the majority of the population?

What can we do? Give up? Give in to the system? Try to selfishly play your cards right within it while others are starving on the streets?

Summary:

Speculation, which depends directly on rating agencies, raises corruption problems and is generally not based on any economic reality. Stock markets are subject to the "butterfly effect' and are unpredictable. The analysis of the subprimes crisis and the comparison with the state of European finances is staggering. In the meantime, regulators seem totally overwhelmed.

Resist scaremongers.

Cash seems to be an endangered species. Beware if you have more than €100,000 in a European bank.

The whole system looks like a paper giant which cannot be strengthened nor reformed.

Chapter 9
Alternatives in the World

During the past 100 years, alternatives to the system have emerged around the world. When things go well, nobody looks for alternatives. But when everything goes wrong, people turn to other options, invent new systems, and try to solve their problem. So alternatives flourished especially during crises, when the currency of the state and banks was lacking. We will study some of them, as well as their limitations, but it would not be reasonable to list all of them here. We will nevertheless try to make the most exhaustive overview of the different systems.

9.1 Silvio Gesell's "Freiwirtschaft" (Free Economy)

Pierre-Joseph Proudhon, a French politician and often considered as the originator of the anarchist movement, held the opposite theory of Karl Marx in the 19th century. He believed that the only way the workers could free themselves from the capitalists was not by making strikes, but on the contrary by working harder than ever. His theory was that, by multiplying constantly the available resources, they would overflow the capital, which would become unnecessary and obsolete. Following further, he proposed to replace money with goods, and went on to create exchange platforms and cooperatives. It was a big failure which contributed to discredit all his theories.

In the 1910s, the German merchant Silvio Gesell, without knowing Proudhon's theories, had a similar reasoning, but which led him to different conclusions[201]. He discovered that the problem did not arise from the existence of money itself, but from the use of money as a "Store of Value", giving money an unfair advantage over goods. The "gold standard" was the norm at the time and the coins were very attractive simply because they were made of gold. This led him to the conclusion that the solution to the problem of the never ending enrichment of the capitalists could be resolved by the elimination of that unfair advantage, the store of value, compared to the goods. To do so, he devised a currency system in which money would constantly be devaluated, thus preventing anyone from hoarding it. In this system, nobody would prefer to have money rather than a real commodity, since the value of both would be decaying at the same speed.

Silvio Gesell called it "Freigeld" in German, which translates to "Free Money" in English. As "Free Money" doesn't really describe that type of currency, I'll use the term "Melting Currency", which is a nice depiction of such a currency: it "melts in your hands" when you own it. There are two main ways to implement Gesell's Melting Currency. You can apply some devaluation of the banknotes over time by indicating on the banknotes themselves indications of their value at a given time. You can also apply a periodic tax on every banknote. This devaluation process is called "demurrage".

19. A banknote from the 1930s in Wörgl, Austria. Source: Wikipedia.

Gesell's theory is an inspiration for modern local currencies, even if the "devalued coin system" was not entirely new. Indeed, it was already used in the Middle Ages, especially in the Holy Roman Empire between the 10th and the 15th century, with coins called "Bracteates"[202]. These coins were valid for short periods of time, and needed to be regularly exchanged for new coins of slightly lower value. The population was therefore active in creating wealth and exchanging these coins as much as possible, and did not want to keep them, since they were depreciated regularly, exactly on the same principle as the one expressed by Gesell. People then valued much more goods, land, stone buildings, rather than their ever depreciating money. This period is the one of the building of huge cathedrals throughout Europe, which were long-term investments that attracted foreigners and were boosting the local economy. But in 1495, the sovereign Maximilian I, who wished to force a general tax on the whole Empire, imposed the "Common Penny" which replaced these local currencies. For the record, the ones who were creating these local coins were the local sovereigns, which was very clearly favorable to them, at the expense of the population.

Gesell's "Freigeld" is in fact one of the components of an economic system which he called the "Freiwirtschaft", "Free Economy". Along with this currency, he prescribed the abolition of property, replaced by going back to the "commons". So in his system, the state owns the land, you cannot buy it, but you can rent it. He also advocated a generalized free trade. Savings could be realized through investments in bonds or shares.

The Melting Currency principle gave birth to local experiments, especially in Germany and Austria in the early 1930s during the economic crisis. The effect was spectacular and revived the local economy wherever it was experimented. The authoritarian states of the time didn't like it much, and they quickly made these currencies illegal.

The Chancellor may not have been the easiest to negotiate with at the time...

One of the main limitations of this system is monetary creation: in Gesell's vision, it is the duty of the state to create money regularly, "depending on the needs of the economy". We fall back into the trap of leaving a group decide whether the economy "needs" new money or not,

9.2 The Swiss WIR

While Germany experimented with Melting Currencies in the early 1930s, the WIR is created in Switzerland in 1934. At its start and until 1952, it was also based on Gesell's Melting Currency system. Later on, it became a regular currency using loans with interest, but at very low rates compared to "official" banks. Unlike the neighboring dictatorship, the Swiss allowed the experiment to go on, and the WIR still exists today. Originally, the "WIR" was a non-profit association, it has evolved into a bank which is ironically located in Basel at less than 600 meters from The Bank for International Settlements.

Switzerland, which I dearly admire, is really the country of all surprises.

Only private companies can have a WIR account, which is currently a purely electronic currency. It is estimated that one in five Small and Medium Enterprises in Switzerland uses WIR with a turnover of 5.4 billion Swiss francs and 14 million profits in 2016. It has lost some of its attractiveness in recent years due to exceptionally low interest rates in the traditional banking sector, but it remains very much alive thanks to the trust of its regular customers.

You never know... the Swiss are patient and careful people.

The WIR Bank insists that WIRs should not be exchanged for other currencies, in order to keep WIRs for local exchanges only, as a complementary local currency.

The WIR is a very interesting experiment, some economists even suggest that it has probably contributed to the financial stability of Switzerland since its creation. However, it is still held by a bank, with all the drawbacks of a centralized authority and which makes benefits at the expense of others.

9.3 The LETS and Local Complementary Currencies

Local Exchange Trading Systems, abbreviated LETS, are most often local associations, whose goal is generally to stimulate local exchanges in a limited geographical area. There are currently over 600 of them in France.

Some of these associations create for their own needs what are called "Local Complementary Currencies". All exchanges within the group are then made using this local currency rather than the currency of the state. There are about thirty of these local currencies in France, about forty of them in Germany, and 400 LETS in Great Britain with many local currencies. Overall, they find it difficult to gain popularity because most people don't even see why they should bother with a local currency[203]. That's probably because they ignore the problems of the state financial system.

They haven't read this book (yet)...

These currencies ensure for companies and individuals who participate in them that the money is used locally, which stimulates the local exchanges. In practice, we really observe a boost in the local economy. Besides, it keeps the creation of wealth local and stops it from escaping into Euros which then go into speculation. In a way, this gives back to money its primary purpose: that of exchanging goods and services.

Most of them in France are indexed to the Euro, which means that each unit of the local currency is exchangeable directly with the same number of Euros. The same is applied in Germany, and in Great Britain they are indexed to the British Pound. Other currencies exist around the world using the same principle.

One local currency that deserves a special mention is the Chiemgauer. It was launched in 2003 by an economics teacher and his students in a small German village of about ten thousand inhabitants. This project literally took off and reached €2.3 million in cash circulation in 2016. It is a "currency with demurrage" as prescribed by Silvio Gesell and has become a reference in terms of local currencies. It is, however, indexed to the Euro.

20. Chiemgauer banknotes. Source: Wikipedia.

The problem is that these local currencies are totally dependent from their corresponding national currencies since they are indexed to them. This seriously reduces their scope and benefits and makes them vulnerable to variations of their corresponding currencies. Some people are aware of this, for instance there are discussions to make the BerkShares in Massachusetts independent from the USD[204]. Another problem is again how the currency is created, by whom and on which grounds.

Some other currencies that are a little more original are based on time: one unit corresponds to a "working human time". These currencies are obviously mainly used for services, but some also use them to trade goods, by estimating the time needed to manufacture these goods. One of the criticisms that immediately comes to mind is whether one hour of different services is actually equivalent in value... you are free to decide.

Finally, these currencies only have a real impact when there are economic loops within the area where they circulate. If you are an individual who gets his paycheck in Euros or Dollars, and has nothing to sell to anyone with the local currency, the impact is very limited, since you have to constantly exchange your national money with the local one. There isn't much advantage in that case. But this works perfectly well if you own your own small business, for instance, and you exchange only with other local small businesses, then you can even get rid of the national currency altogether, and this is where local currencies reveal their potential. Remember the cycle between the baker, the butcher and the grocer? This is the exact situation where local currencies can efficiently "lubricate" the local economy.

9.4 The Universal Exchange Garden

Daniel Fargeas, a French economist, creates in 1998 an original system, which he calls the "JEU" (which means "game" in French), "Jardin d'Échange Universel", "Universal Exchange Garden" in English.

It is based on a very simple principle and requires no centralized structure: every person has a ledger or account book. This book corresponds to that person's own account, it can in fact be a simple notebook manually transformed into a ledger. All transactions on that account are written by hand in this ledger. For example, if Peter wants to give 5 units to Wendy to pay for a good or a service, they must write this transaction on their respective ledgers, along with their personal information and signatures. This way, it is possible for the future partners who will want to exchange something with Peter to verify that the transactions on the ledger are accurate, by calling Wendy to double-check that the transaction in the ledger really took place, for instance. In the original "JEU" system, one unit is the equivalent of one minute of service.

This system is indeed very simple and doesn't need any centralized authority to organize it or print banknotes, but it does have a major flaw: security and trust. The simplicity of the system comes at a price: it is simple to cheat in such a system, including by having multiple ledgers. This in turn introduces the problem of solvency. In other words, it is possible for your account to be as negative as you want, there is no limit to it. But then, who stops you from buying everything you want, without selling or offering anything in return? And once your account is deep in negative values, who stops you again from starting from scratch with a new ledger?

These are the reasons why this system does not take off, especially among professionals, for whom it would be very tedious to check all past transactions for all their customers to ensure their solvency. Despite this, the system is used in many places in Canada and in France, although the number of participants is very small.

While a paper ledger is very easily forged, a computer tool allowing this kind of transaction register in a secure way is much more interesting.

9.5 The "Community Exchange System" and the "Sardex"

In 2003, an Australian starts the "CES", the "Community Exchange System", which is exactly based on the "JEU", but the ledgers of all are centralized on a website. It gets more difficult to cheat (although it is still possible to open multiple accounts).

In January 2010, 5 Sardinian friends, who are not economists but very resourceful, create a new exchange system, the "Sardex". Their system works exactly the same as the CES, but their users are only Sardinian private companies. These companies must register on the Sardex web site which verifies their validity and existence to prevent any cheating. In exchange for a small annual fee, each company has its own account, and can then trade with other companies within the system. Employees of these companies can also get part of their wages in Sardex. This system literally took off, and even if it still represents 0.7% of Sardinia's GDP, it amounts to 70 million Euros exchanged in 2016.

Italy still requires companies to pay their taxes in Euros, so the system will not be able to grow as much as it would otherwise. The creators advise companies not to do more than 20% of their exchanges in the Sardex system, in order to keep enough Euros to pay their taxes. However, a whole network is building in Italy, and even gets subsidies from the Italian government, it currently looks at expanding internationally.

But whereas the original JEU system was totally decentralized, both the CES and the Sardex run on centralized infrastructures, this is the price for security. There are some other similar initiatives around the world.

Some of these exchange systems also add extra rules to avoid some users to get too rich or too poor. Typically, some taxes can be taken from the richest accounts and distributed to the poorest.

> *Well, in that case, you better be always as negative as possible...*

Again, just like in the JEU, one of the biggest challenges of these systems is that anyone can have their account go into negative values and are counting on the "good faith" of the users to use their accounts in a responsible manner. We can argue that after a certain limit, some people will not want to trade with a person whose account is "too negative", as it already happens in the CES. We can also suggest forbidding users to go beyond a certain negative value. But then the question arises: how should this limit be set? By whom? According to which parameters and which principles? Again we base everything on the "needs of the economy", and other arbitrary decisions which take over the monetary system. And we have seen that such human intervention is very detrimental to the system as a whole.

9.6 In-Game Currencies

Although these are not "Complementary Currencies", they are worth mentioning, since they play their own small role in the world economy.

The creators of games or even some websites, have imagined a system of "in-game tokens". These tokens can be bought by the players or users in general with "real world" money. They can then be used within the game or the website, to purchase items, extensions, special powers and so on. This is useful because players don't need to take out their credit card each time they want to purchase something within the game. They just buy a bunch of tokens once, and they can spend them as they wish later on. You can actually consider them as the tokens used in casinos.

Some of these "tokens" have become quite a phenomenon. The most well-known is probably the "Linden Dollars", the tokens of the virtual world "Second Life" (which is not considered a "game" by its fans). In Second Life, the "player" impersonates a "virtual person" in a "virtual world". In this virtual world, he spends and earns "money" as in real life, and this money is actually "Linden Dollars". It is also possible to buy "Linden Dollars" from "US Dollars" or any other real-world currency through an exchange platform, called the "Lindex Exchange". Because of this, it is possible to calculate how much the Linden Dollars economy is worth in terms of US Dollars, for instance. Wikipedia reports that Second Life's GDP was about $500 million in 2015[205], which is more than some real world countries! And some people really manage to get rich within the virtual world, which in turn makes them earn money in the real world[206].

Another "classic" is "World of Warcraft's Gold". There are many others, like Pokemon Go's "Coins", or "Pokemon Dollars" in the original game.

Most of these currencies can be exchanged for "real-world money", so they do have an interaction with the real world. Of course, all of them are totally dependent on the company that owns the game, and these companies have full authority to do whatever they want with their "internal currency", including creating money, setting arbitrary regulations and so on. They are the Central Banks of their own universe.

9.7 M-Pesa

In developing countries, the problems met with "official money" and especially the lack of it generate very interesting initiatives. In some African countries, people started to exchange their unused phone credits for goods or services. So these phone credits became a means of exchange, some form of "currency".

Some researchers pushed the concept, and soon local mobile phone companies used this to develop a whole financial system for their users, including micro-credits. This system is now used in many third-world countries, and expanding rapidly[207]. The main advantage is that people only need a cellphone to be able to use the system.

This system grew so much that it started irritating some financial institutions, which tried to block it or slow it down, for instance in Kenya. But so far, governments have tolerated it, and still don't consider this system as a "full banking institution". Of course, although it does have some benefit for its users, I have no doubt that the phone companies also act with their own interests at heart. Who doesn't dream to have a captive customer base who make their daily transactions with your systems?

9.8 Get Rid of Money Altogether?

We can also quickly mention the theories which think that we can get rid of money altogether, and operate through "gifting economy", like Jean-François Noubel's project of "collective intelligence". I will not get into much detail, because it would be a subject on its own, and it seems to me that society as a whole would need to make profound changes before implementing such money-less solutions.

One of the main criticisms I have is that these theories often take abundance of resources for granted, while the earth is finite and the world population is increasing. On the other hand, there are many examples of very small groups operating in this way throughout history and even today, but it is strange that no example can be found with larger groups. We can probably find an explanation to this by studying human psychology.

In the meantime, I strongly believe that humanity as it is today needs something in-between, so that mentalities can shift slowly, and society as a whole can take a new direction, before we can truly start seriously and practically thinking about going "money-less".

Summary:

Many local currency initiatives flourish around the world, partly inspired by Silvio Gesell's "Freigeld", which we can also depict as "Melting Currencies". Some of them are really taking off and even have a positive impact on the local economy. They also trigger questions about money in people's minds.

Unfortunately, almost all of them are indexed to the currencies of their respective states, and most are centralized. Their monetary creation is their main weak point.

Other alternatives such as the CES or the Sardex have an interesting approach but they suffer from other problems such as arbitrary limitations on negative accounts.

Chapter 10
Bitcoin and the Blockchain

We can't cover all aspects of Bitcoin and cryptocurrencies here, that subject alone would require a full encyclopedia. But it is important to understand the basics of these new technologies to grasp their advantages and disadvantages. It's sometimes a bit technical, but hang on, it's not that hard to understand, and it's the only way to make your own opinion. The stake here is that these technologies will very probably disrupt society as much as the Internet did. You'd better be ready for them.

10.1 What Is At Stake?

Very few major media speak about Bitcoin. Actually, journalists even mock it and generally don't know anything about it. They believe it is a toy for specialists that has absolutely no impact for the "average Joe".

If you still believe that Bitcoin is a "toy for geeks", you should know that it is referenced at the New-York Stock Exchange since 2015, and that its total market capitalization is more than $70 billion (it was 60 just a month ago[208]).

Yes, $70,000,000,000.

And governments around the world announce that they are developing their own national cryptocurrencies. Sweden, very proud of being the first country to print banknotes in Europe in the 17th century, would really like to be the first to launch its own cryptocurrency[209], the Ekrona. But it may very well be double-crossed by China, which is currently building its own cryptocurrency to replace cash[210], Russia is in the race too[211], the Bundesbank, the German Central Bank, also invests in this technology[212]. Japan is also making steps towards dematerializing cash with a crpytocurrency, the J-Coin[213].

In fact, blockchains are flourishing all over the world, and not only in the world of finance:

- A group of financiers among the most powerful like UBS, HSBC, Barclays, Credit Suisse, or BNY Mellon (if you don't know this one, it "only" manages 30,000 billion USD worth of assets...), are currently testing USC, a blockchain that would enable them to exchange assets, and the launch is planned before the end of 2018[214],

- Another group of European banks asks IBM to build a platform based on a blockchain to fund Small and Medium Size Businesses[215], in fact, the bank Naxitis is already trading oil on a blockchain[216],

- Giants in the food industry also develop blockchains to promote transparency in the food chain[217],

- The Bank of France already uses blockchains as well as the French bank BNP Paribas and Credit Mutuel[218],

- Estonia state services, including the management of the identity of its citizens, have been running on a blockchain for years now and its Stock Exchange, which is run by the Nasdaq, will soon be running on a blockchain[219].

The list goes on and on, in the energy sector[220], cars and mobility services[221], health care, it won't take long until it comes to your country and your industry, wherever you live and work. Blockchains are currently in the same development state and hype than the Internet was in the second half of the 1990s which led to the burst of the Dot-Com bubble in 2000, but today the Internet is deeply rooted in our lives.

What on earth is a blockchain anyway? Given the stakes as we have just seen, maybe it's time for you to wonder and learn a bit more about it! To answer that question, we have to go back to the creation of Bitcoin.

10.2 The Creation of Bitcoin

Where does Bitcoin come from? In 2008, a white paper published under the pseudonym "Satoshi Nakamoto" on an Internet forum describes a secure system to record transactions digitally, based on existing technologies but blending them into one single system. We still don't know today who wrote this article, many suspect that it wasn't written by a single person, but rather by a group of people[222]. In 2009, an implementation of the model described in the article was created by some computer developers: a new currency called "Bitcoin" was born. The implementation is open source, which means that everyone can read the source code of the program and check that what runs on their computer is correct and examine the code for flaws.

21. Common Bitcoin logos

The official financial name for Bitcoin is XBT (the "X" meaning that it is not attached to any nation), but it is most of the times abbreviated as BTC, and represented with the sign ₿ (just like the $ or € signs).

Until 2013, it remained quite confidential, known and exchanged by a handful of "geeks". In 2010, a user bought two pizzas for the modest sum of 10,000 Bitcoins. Then the phenomenon accelerated a little bit, Bitcoins being exchanged with Dollars for $1 per Bitcoin, then $10, then $100, and at the end of 2013, it literally takes off in a giant bubble, exceeding $1,000 per Bitcoin before bursting and even falling to $150 in 2015. It went back up to almost $3,000 recently before coming down again and it now seems like it is heading for $4,000.

10.3 Bitcoin's Peer-To-Peer Network

The Bitcoin network consists of computers spread all over the world, which run the Bitcoin software. In fact, you can simply download and run this software on your computer, it will automatically be part of the Bitcoin network and start communicating with other computers.

The original idea of the founder was to create a decentralized currency "for the people", in order to free themselves from the banks, where everyone could run the software at home and participate in the network.

Each computer in the network communicates with others, and they all exchange information directly from one computer to another through the network, without going through any server: this is called a peer-to-peer network (often abbreviated in "P2P"), where each computer is called a "Node" of the network.

In the Bitcoin P2P network, each node can create a new transaction in order to exchange Bitcoins, and notifies other nodes about this new transaction. If other nodes consider this transaction as a valid one, they accept it, otherwise they discard it. For instance, they can check that this transaction is not spending more money than the source account actually contains. If a transaction is accepted, then it is integrated into the "blockchain", a common ledger shared by all the nodes in which all transactions are recorded.

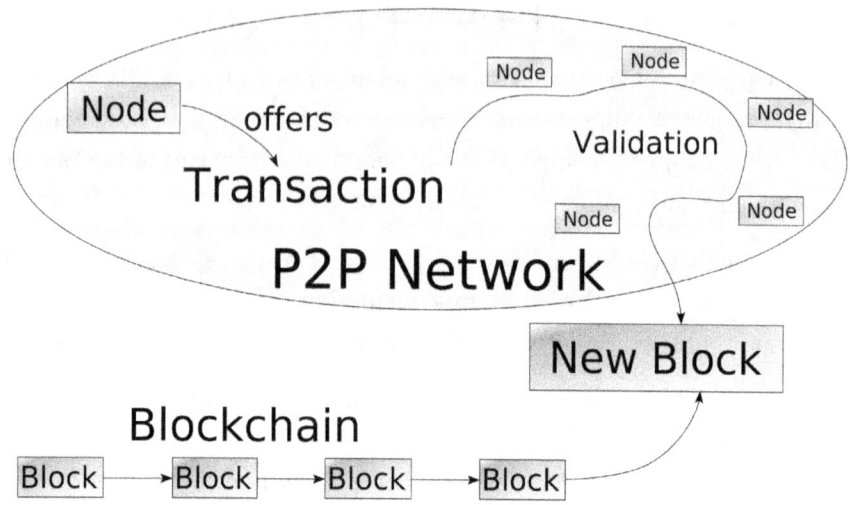

22. Illustration of the Bitcoin P2P Network

10.4 The Blockchain

It is important to understand the basic mechanism of Bitcoin so that it does not remain a "vague idea" in your mind. It is not so difficult to understand it and it is very likely to become part of our daily lives. As we have seen, beyond the currency Bitcoin, the "blockchain" mechanism is a growing trend in a huge bubble, attracting many investors and banks. Some experts even predict that 10% of the world's GDP will be stored on blockchains by 2025[223]. It's as important as that.

The blockchain is in fact a ledger containing transactions, we can make an analogy with a paper ledger. We write transactions on every page. When reaching the end of a page, someone "signs" this page as a valid one with an unforgeable stamp that "freezes" the page as it is so that nobody can change it afterwards. It is exactly as if you were covering the page with a plastic film at the time of stamping with a seal. Once this page is acknowledged by everybody, the page can be turned and everyone goes on to the next page to write new transactions.

23. A quick illustration of the contents of the blockchain

One of the technical challenges that needed to be overcome when Nakamoto wrote his white paper was to find a way for this unforgeable mechanism that stamps each block (or page) to avoid any further modification. In the meantime, some system had to be found to create new blocks, that is to say turn the pages, at relatively regular intervals of time, so that the ledger could move forward at a relatively constant speed. In the remainder of this description, to help you understand, you can replace the expression "create a block" with "turning a page", if you want a more visual representation.

The mechanism invented by Nakamoto to solve this problem is quite simple. Each time a new block is created, it offers a "difficult challenge" to be solved, which is based on cryptographic technologies. And before it can be integrated into the blockchain, the solution to this problem must be found. So when a block has just been released on the blockchain, all nodes on the network start trying to solve the challenge for the next block. This challenge requires many cryptographic calculations to secure the block. It is exactly as if you were asked to throw lots of dice billions of times on average before you can find an acceptable solution.

Besides, the challenge also depends on a "difficulty" which is adjusted according to the current speed of new coming blocks. The more difficult the challenge, the more time will be required for all nodes to solve it. So if too many blocks were recently created compared to the desired speed, the algorithm increases the difficulty for the following blocks, slowing down the rate at which the new blocks are created and vice versa if the rhythm becomes too fast.

To illustrate this mechanism, just imagine that I ask you to throw 10 dice many times, until you find at least 4 dice with a "1" in a single throw. To find a solution to my problem, you will need to throw the dice a bit more than 14 times on average.

If I want to increase the difficulty, I will ask you to find 5 dice with a "1" instead. This time, you will have to throw the dice 65 times on average to find a solution. It will take you more time to find solutions than previously.

And if I want to decrease the difficulty, I will ask only for 3 dice with a "1". This will only require 4 to 5 throws to find a solution.

With this system, I can easily change the speed at which you find solutions. Back to a system based on a blockchain, adjusting the difficulty enables to change the speed at which new blocks are solved, so that they are generated at relatively constant intervals of time. Within Bitcoin, the desired "ideal" interval is fixed to 10 minutes.

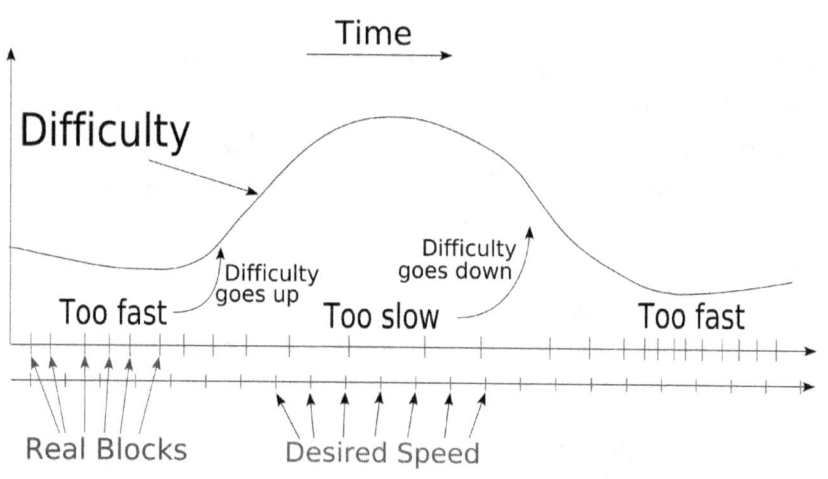

24. Illustration of how the difficulty works

This whole system is ingenious because it ensures that:

- each block is effectively secured, due to the cryptographic challenge associated with each block,
- blocks are created at regular intervals,

- all the actors on the network can participate in securing the blocks.

At the Bitcoin P2P network level, every node communicates with others and at every moment it can receive new transactions that are given by its peers, as well as newly created blocks. From all this information, it then compiles a new block with all new transactions it is aware of, and tries to solve the challenge for that block to validate it.

It should be noted that in such a system, trust is based on a series of transactions signed within blocks stamped by cryptographic techniques, all of which are public. Therefore, anyone can verify at all times the integrity of the whole blockchain. So there is no longer any need to trust any "third party", or "the human being" in general, the trust is provided by well-known cryptographic technologies and a public blockchain. This is why these currencies are called cryptocurrencies.

No one can falsify the blockchain, and when a transaction is written there, it is irreversible. It can be seen both as an advantage and a disadvantage, depending on the point of view. You can always think that, in a public system where everything is visible to all, a transaction that was made in error can always be "canceled" by performing another transaction which returns the funds to its original owner. But then, it is about trusting institutions or other individuals, and has nothing to do with the blockchain anymore.

One advantage of blockchain technology is that it can be applied to many fields. While Bitcoin has confined it to monetary transactions, others have extended it to broader uses, such as electronic voting or generally speaking contracts with free content between two entities. The "Ethereum" blockchain, another cryptocurrency, allows to create "Smart Contracts", which are computer programs, that can be activated directly on the blockchain, to obtain an "Autonomous Decentralized Organization" (DAO). People using this system "sign" and "activate" contracts with others, which are then published on the Ethereum blockchain.

One organization even went so far as to create a system of virtual and digital nations, based on a blockchain. Thus, anyone in the world can register to "Bitnation" and join decentralized nations, which eventually should be able to provide state-of-the-art services, such as identification, legal services, and so on, all running on blockchains. As we have already seen, the country of Estonia has already switched its national services like identity management to a blockchain and offers all European citizens to become an Estonian e-citizen, in order to attract foreign investors.

10.5 Forks, Blockchain and Democracy

If two nodes located at the other end of the planet find a solution to a new block at the same time, the network is for a time in a state called a "fork", and the blockchain branches into two chains. Indeed, if the two blocks are found and valid, then there is no real reason to refuse and accept the other: they are both legitimate blocks. The way the network solves this problem is to always stay on the longest chain and discard shorter chains. So the fastest chain is then chosen over slower chains, if there are any.

Let's say that when mining block number x, a miner A mines a block x_A and at the same time, a miner B mines a block x_B. Until the next block, the network is split in two: one part is trying to find a block $x+1_A$ and the other part is trying to find a block $x+1_B$. If $x+1_A$ is found first, then the chain of x_B is discarded and the whole network goes back to the A branch, and vice-versa if block $x+1_B$ is found first.

This kind of involuntary "fork" happens regularly, and is solved very quickly, as we have just seen. But there are two other cases of "forks", which on the other hand are voluntary.

We have seen that each node on the network can check the blocks presented by the other nodes. But this means that if members of the network want to change one of the software's operations, their modifications must be accepted by the majority of the other nodes in order to become valid. It is this notion of "majority" that must be compared with the notion of "democracy". In the universe of cryptocurrencies, the "people" participating in "democratic" decisions are in fact the set of nodes that calculate blocks, where the weight of each node is often proportional to its computational power.

When a change in the behavior of the software is proposed, it is only adopted when the majority of the computing power of the network approves it. It is a form of "computing power democracy". A problem can arise if a group of nodes that hold more than half the total computing power of the network make an agreement to add a modification that is favorable to them, to the detriment of the rest of the network. It becomes a kind of "dictatorship of the majority", knowing that we are talking here of "majority of computing power", which in the worst case can very well be held by a single person or a single organization. This is often called a "51% attack".

It is then necessary to distinguish two cases: either the modification is compatible with the old blocks of the blockchain, either it introduces modifications in the structure of the new blocks.

In the first case, if the modification obtains the majority of the computing power, it is likely to be automatically adopted. In this scenario, nodes with the modification compute blocks faster than the rest of the network, and will therefore nullify any attempt by other nodes to create their own chains without the modification. This is called a "Soft Fork", because it is only a change of software.

In the second case, the new generated blocks are incompatible with the old software, so they are automatically rejected by the nodes that do not integrate the modification. Just imagine that while you are building a brick wall, they suddenly offer you two different sizes of bricks: you have the choice of keeping the old size or taking the new ones. You have to make a choice, you can't afford to randomly pick bricks of different sizes to finish your wall if you want it to be solid.

In this situation, a "Hard Fork" takes place. In some cases, it is possible that the two chains may live their lives separately, the nodes running the old software continuing their own chain, and the nodes with the new version creating a new chain. This means that from one original blockchain, two blockchains are born, which means that from one original currency, two new currencies exist from the moment of the hard fork. One currency still uses the old brick size, and the other one uses the new brick size.

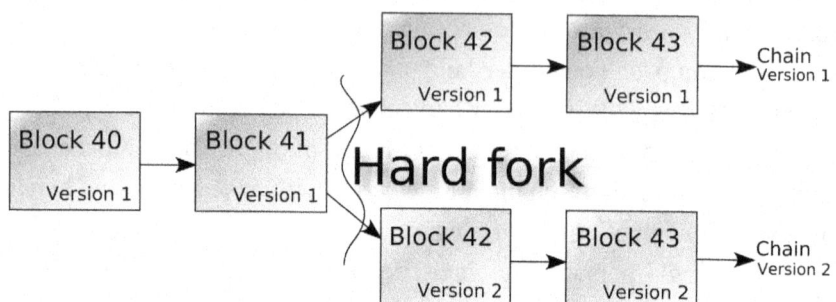

25. Situation of "hard fork" where one single original chain is split into two chains that can "live" separately from one another, creating in effect two separate currencies.

One strange and interesting side-effect is that an account that wasn't empty before the hard fork is therefore not empty on both of the new chains, which also means in both of the two new currencies. So the owner of that account suddenly doubles his number of units of coins, if the community accepts both currencies of course, which is actually quite rare.

10.6 Addresses and Transactions

While the concept of "blockchain" can be used in many areas, Bitcoin and many cryptocurrencies use it for the only purpose of storing monetary transactions.

The Bitcoin ecosystem is based on a set of unique addresses, where each address represents an account, comparable in some way to a bank account number or rather an electronic purse number.

Each address is represented by a long series of characters, and is created in two steps. First, a Bitcoin client creates a "key-chain" using a cryptographic mechanism based on complex mathematics. This "key-chain" contains two keys: a private key that the user must keep secret and a public key that can be safely published to the world because it is impossible with current computers to compute the private key corresponding to a public key.

Here is an example of a private key and public key of the same key-chain (do not use this since the private key is published in this book):

- Public key, to be shared with the world:
1BFLCmWb6za5CLSjYcLbELVYaEN4b8gBnd

- Private key, that needs to be kept secret:
L2V1iV4aFUmE4sSnDTTENeiTAxt5kY5as6oVxxph6aDNxo5FYQ3L

This pair of keys can then be used to encrypt or sign computer messages. If Alice wants to send a secret email to Bob, she only needs to use Bob's public key to encrypt the email. Only Bob can decrypt it using his private key. Similarly, if Bob wants to send a signed email to Alice to make sure that no one has changed his email during the sending process, he only needs to use his private key to sign the email. Upon receiving it, Alice can verify the integrity of the email and its signature using Bob's public key.

From this pair of keys, the second step is to generate a "Bitcoin address" using another very secure cryptographic method. This address corresponds to an "account", or rather a "purse", which can then receive some Bitcoins. If someone who already owns Bitcoins wants to send them to this address, he only needs to create a transaction where one of the destinations is the address in question. To prove that he is really the creator of the transaction, he signs it with his private key. From there, everyone can double-check the authenticity of this transaction by verifying the signature using his public key. Once received, these Bitcoins can then be used in a new transaction to other addresses[i].

Here is one Bitcoin address, which corresponds to the key-chain published earlier (do not use this, anyone who reads this book can empty any coins in this address since everyone has the private key now):

---

i   Beware: a transaction empties all Bitcoins present in the source address. It distributes them to other addresses. Most Bitcoin clients "mask" this to the user, by redistributing the coins to other internal addresses that are generated automatically. This way, the user believes he has only one account, just like a bank account, but in reality there are multiple addresses behind it.

1DyTUhMgCLzB68GEkmr2BRdmeHJEEemcww

These transactions between addresses are not encrypted, and are written as is in the blocks of the blockchain. It is therefore easy to go back to the source of each Bitcoin currently in circulation, following the different successive transactions through which it was transferred.

Finally, to ensure that transactions can be made with the smallest amounts possible, a Bitcoin can be split into 100 millionths of a Bitcoin, the smallest usable unit, also called a "Satoshi", in reference to the creator. It is somehow equivalent to the cent for "regular" currencies, but pushed a little further! One Euro can be split into 100 cents, but one Bitcoin can be split into 100,000,000 Satoshis.

10.7 Bitcoin Mining

As we have seen, the "stamping" of a block requires many calculations using complex cryptographic operations. But in order for the mechanism to be truly secure, sufficient computing power must be involved, otherwise an organization with supercomputers could very easily compute all the future blocks and take full control of the blockchain.

This is why Satoshi needed to encourage network members to use their computers to participate in the stamping calculation as much as possible. So he decided to give a reward to the miner who would discover a block. He did this by giving to the miner's address some brand new Bitcoins. This is why these stamping operations are called the "mining" of Bitcoins. The analogy being the miner at the bottom of the gold mine, digging hard to find a gold nugget. When he finally finds one, he actually gets his reward. Thus, people and machines participating in the "mining" of Bitcoins are called the "miners" of Bitcoin, and have an interest in putting their maximum computer power in order to mine as many blocks as possible and thus winning many Bitcoins as a reward.

Another reward mechanism is also provided: Bitcoin users may indicate "transaction fees" for each of their transactions, which are paid directly to miners when they include this transaction into a new block.

10.8 Advantages of Bitcoin

Bitcoin has many advantages.

The first one is that it is an innovative and unprecedented attempt at freeing people from the control of the banks, and even potentially from any authority. And in practice, anyone can use Bitcoin with a cellphone or a computer from anywhere in the world, no need to "open an account" and "be accepted" by a bank, you just need to have access to the Internet.

Besides, it is not possible to "block" or "freeze" an account within Bitcoin, unlike any centralized system. Banks and other money managing systems have their own policies, and they do whatever they like with peoples' accounts, such as freezing them all in case of a bankruptcy (remember Cyprus in 2013). The same goes with any centralized organization. For instance, Paypal suddenly blocked Wikileaks' account. Whether you like Wikileaks or not, this gives Paypal a totalitarian political authority, which is a slippery slope. Tomorrow, they may target You. On the other hand, no one can block Wikileaks' Bitcoin account. In this regard, Bitcoin is a truly neutral currency. And if anything illegal can happen with Bitcoin, many illegal things currently happen with cash or even financial institutions. Illegal stuff can and should be addressed by justice, not with arbitrary decisions from private corporations.

Bitcoin also provides some kind of anonymity towards your peers. Your neighbor doesn't know what your Bitcoin account is so you can safely make public transactions without worrying if he will manage to find out your little dirty secrets. On the other hand, authorities have the means of tracing illegal transactions, as we will see later, so that shouldn't be a problem regarding terrorism or money laundering. In the meantime, the blockchain is totally public. So if any institution for instance published its own set of Bitcoin addresses, the people as a whole would be able to see the money coming in and out of these addresses, thus promoting transparency.

Bitcoin also offers a very highly secure environment that has been running for several years now, without experiencing any kind of hack on the system. However, you need to have your own full access to your address in order to be protected. Leaving your Bitcoins in the hands of a third party, such as "currency exchange sites", or "web wallets" puts your money at risk of vanishing overnight. Would you entrust your wallet with your credit card in it to the first stranger you met in the street?

As a world currency, it also gets rid of excessive bank fees when doing international transactions. This is currently a little less true since transaction fees are raising, but some technological advances may find solutions for that.

Another advantage is that, for sellers, there is no "charge-back" risk with Bitcoin since no transaction can be "canceled". Additionally, a transaction that has been validated automatically indicates that the funds were available, so there is no default risk.

Despite all these advantages, Bitcoin also suffers from many drawbacks, as we will see in the next chapter.

Summary:

Bitcoin is an unprecedented attempt to free human beings from the power of the banks. It was created by an anonymous in 2008, who called himself "Satoshi Nakamoto".

The blockchain is a promising technology that could disrupt society. It provides a secure environment in which financial transactions can be recorded, as well as potentially any other digital data. States all over the world and big financiers have already started using blockchains and even creating their own cryptocurrencies.

Blockchain technology is decentralized and based on existing cryptographic technologies to create "trust".

Within a blockchain, "democracy" operates through the decisions of the majority regarding the changes to be made on the software that runs that blockchain.

Chapter 11
Cryptocurrencies in Practice

Now that we have seen how Bitcoin works and its main theoretical advantages, it is time to see how this goes when put into practice.

11.1 Bitcoin's Monetary Creation

Bitcoins are created only by the "mining" of blocks, and this creation matches a curve that tends towards 21 million.

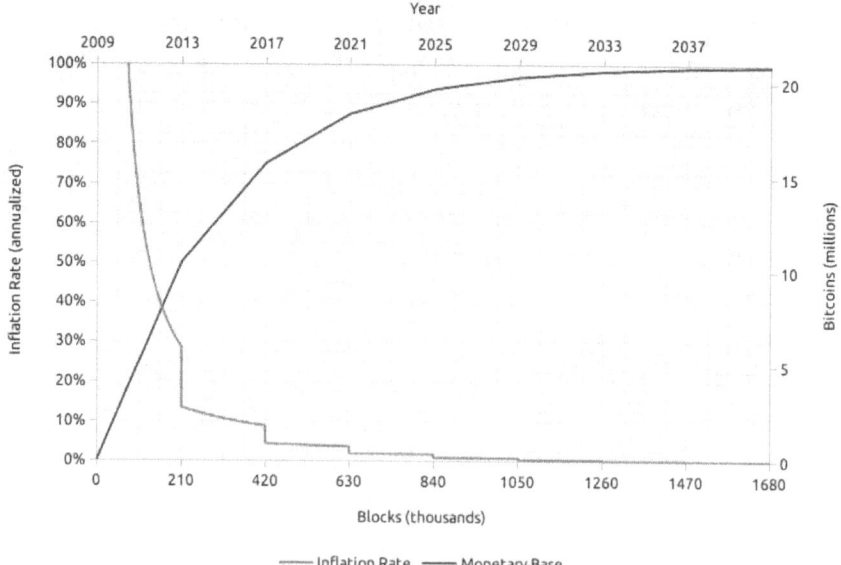

26. Curve of the total number of Bitcoins (in blue) created, it tends towards 21 million, and will reach this value in 2040 (block 1,680,000), and annual "inflation" rate (in red) which tends towards 0. Source: a discussion on the bitcointalk.org forum, the data is directly computed from the Bitcoin code.

In other words, there will be a maximum of 21 million Bitcoins in existence, never more. In practice, there will be even fewer in circulation, because Bitcoins can become inaccessible and therefore be "lost" if a person forgets the private key of one of his addresses, and thus lose access to his Bitcoins. Another reason for losing coins is when someone sends them to a wrong address owned by nobody.

The figure 26 represents the number of Bitcoins generated since its start, and as well as the rate at which the number of Bitcoins grow each year. We notice that:

- in 2040, at block 1,680,000, all the Bitcoins that will ever exist will have been created,
- in 2017, already three thirds of all Bitcoins have been created,
- in 2013, there was a sudden drop in the creation of new Bitcoins, which can partly explain the 2013 "bubble", since Bitcoin was becoming rarer, it is not surprising that it triggered some interest for some,

27. *History of the price of Bitcoin since 2012. The sudden interest in 2013 and 2017, as the monetary creation slows down, are clearly visible. Source: xe.com*

- it is interesting to see that since 2013, Bitcoin's value has stagnated, and it suddenly went up again in 2017, just after the second "drop" in its creation... see you in 2021, although the impact might not be as big and other parameters may play a bigger role until then.

Some people call Bitcoin a Ponzi scheme, since the new buyers of Bitcoins "pay" the previous members. Indeed, the higher the number of Bitcoin users, the higher the price of a Bitcoin in Euro or USD, which "pays" the first Bitcoin owners, although it is not strictly speaking a Ponzi Chain.

Let's examine how it could perform as a currency "for the people". As the number of Bitcoins will eventually reach a maximum and never grow again, it will become increasingly rare as it is adopted by more and more people in the world. So it is an excellent asset to hoard, even much better than gold, and consequently a very bad currency which can only result in contractions of the economy and crises.

Maybe Satoshi skipped his economy classes?[224]

I find interesting that the debate of the built-in deflation of Bitcoin is not subject to more debate within the Bitcoin community. Everyone seems to think this is great. Obviously, it is very great for early investors, who spent very little money and will get filthy rich in return, which may be the very reason why they speak so little of it. But for people who "adopt" (or are forced to adopt) it later, it is more problematic. At some point, they won't even be able to get a cent of a Bitcoin, forget even one full Bitcoin. While others will have paid that Bitcoin less than a Dollar.

The reaction of the community is that "it's normal for people who take high risks to get high returns". Again, I'm not a communist, and I find normal for someone who takes risks or who creates some great value for others to be rewarded. But when inequalities get too big, they automatically create hate between people, growing insecurity, wars and bloody revolutions. We certainly don't want Bitcoin to be the cause of those, do we?

11.2 Who Owns Bitcoins?

Even if it is not always possible to know who owns every Bitcoin, it is possible to trace most existing Bitcoins, and know who owns how many of them.

A 2014 study showed that a majority of Bitcoins was already in the hands of a very little minority.

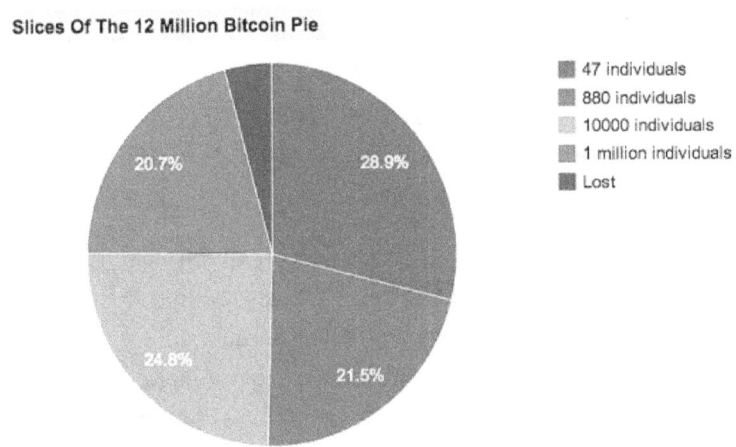

28. Number of Bitcoins owned by a group of individuals. 28.9% owned by 47 people, 21.5% by the next 880, 24.8% by the next 10,000, 20.7% by the next million, and an already quite large part that was lost... Source : this graphic appears in many sites discussing Bitcoin.[225]

This graph shows that 47 individuals alone own nearly 30% of the existing Bitcoins, and half of the Bitcoins are owned by less than 1,000 people. When compared with the current economy, where the richest 1% own half of the world's wealth, there is an even worse difference in inequality in Bitcoin. Indeed, 1% of the world population still represents 70 million people, while by comparison less than 1,000 people own half of the Bitcoins. And when we remember that 75% of the Bitcoins have already been mined, we can understand that it is not Bitcoin that will free the world from poverty.

The inventor of Bitcoin, Satoshi Nakamoto, owns probably about one million Bitcoins, which he has never spent, and which are currently worth more than 3 billion Euros. Our great philanthropist is probably waiting for the right time to donate them to charities...

Let's take a very caricatural but very real example. Suppose that Bitcoin has become the world currency, and that Satoshi hasn't spent any of it. He owns 1 million Bitcoins, and the rest of the world owns 20 million of them. To make sure you understand the implications of this, let's calculate quickly how rich he is. He owns 1 out of 21 of wealth, which means 4.76% of the world's wealth. Also note that this is the "minimum" and "most conservative" estimate. In this scenario, the average amount possessed by an individual would be 0.003 Bitcoins (21 million Bitcoins divided by 7 billion individuals). Anyone owning 3 little Bitcoins is thus potentially 1,000 times richer than the average person.

On the other hand, it is known that the mining of Bitcoins is the work of a minority which has the means to pay for huge "mining farms", whose equipment is now very expensive and often located in China because electricity is cheap there: more than 80% of Bitcoin miners are located in China, but owners of the systems are not necessarily Chinese.

> Why am I saying that? Well, recently, "Chinese" miners, who represent 80% of Bitcoin miners, agreed on a common decision, as we will see later. You'd believe that they would have signed a "Beijing Agreement", or a "Honk-Kong Agreement", right? Nope. They supported a "New York Agreement"[226]. Any other question?

You may say I'm jealous of those who have "been smart enough to invest early in this revolutionary technology". But the day 7 billion people on earth will realize how they've been scammed, the 10,000 top Bitcoin holders better brace themselves...

11.3 Bitcoin and Scalability

One of the current problems of Bitcoin is scalability. When Bitcoin was a small project with few users and transactions, there was no particular problem, but as the number of users grows, the scale problems begin to arise. It is very difficult to estimate the number of users of Bitcoins, but there are probably a few million, perhaps a maximum of one or two tens of millions. Coinbase, a large site that offers Bitcoin services, recently announced that the number of their users has grown by one million in less than a year, which can give some ideas of orders of magnitude.

More users means more transactions per day. And Bitcoin is facing a choice between the size of the blockchain as a whole and the number of transactions that a block can contain. The Bitcoin code is designed to create a block every 10 minutes, and each block has a maximum size of one megabyte. With a small simple calculation, this means that the blockchain potentially grows by 144 megabytes per day, and 52 gigabytes per year if all blocks are filled to the maximum. Until recently, this was not the case, and Bitcoin's complete blockchain currently weights "only" 140 gigabytes.

This already means that it will be more and more difficult to operate a Bitcoin node on a small laptop, for example, and that the power requirements to run a node may concentrate the nodes more and more on a limited number of powerful computers. There are already many services that offer to store the blockchain for their users, and customers only connect to these services to perform the transactions. But in this case we must blindly trust this third party...

Yet there are technical solutions to this problem. One of these is to create "snapshots" of the state of all accounts at regular intervals. With this technique, it would then be possible to store only transactions since the last snapshot rather than storing all transactions since the beginning of time. Of course, some bigger nodes would still retain the full blockchain "for everyone's reference". To become a reality, this solution needs to be accepted by a majority of miners. But for them size is not a problem since they already have very powerful computers to do the mining, and they absolutely don't care about individuals with their small laptops.

I had warned you about the "dictatorship" of the majority of miners. And these miners are a very little minority of the population. Democracy!

On the other hand, because the blocks are limited in size, this implies that they may contain a limited number of transactions. And if the flow of transactions sent over the network exceeds this storage capacity, this poses a big problem: the network is potentially delayed and transactions take more and more time to be integrated into the blockchain. This is what has already been happening for several months now. As a result, it becomes absolutely mandatory to pay transaction fees because any transaction with no fees is systematically rejected by miners. There are currently about 350,000 Bitcoin transactions per day, and the network is clogged.

Despite a declared goal of being a currency for the average people, the transaction fees charged reach 0.001 Bitcoins, currently over 3€. Difficult to pay for your bread under these conditions... People started admitting that Bitcoin as it is today is designed much more for the Stock Market than for the everyday life of an average person[227].

To try to solve this problem, it has been proposed to double the block size, which would allow twice as many transactions to be processed in the same amount of time. But on the one hand this only buys some time until the next congestion, on the other hand it doubles the size of the future blockchain to be stored on each node of the network. It also causes an increase in network traffic. And so the vast majority of miners are opposed to it.

On the other hand, the team in charge of the core of the Bitcoin software proposed another modification, called "Segwit", which is the abbreviation of "Segregated Witness". This proposal makes it possible to relocate part of the transactions in a parallel network to the Bitcoin blockchain, the "Lightning network". This is not really favorable to miners in the sense that it causes them to lose some power because of the delegation of part of the transactions outside the Bitcoin network. On the other hand, it would be a good news for people since it could potentially provide micro-transactions without any fees.

After months of conflicts, this proposal was accepted by a majority of miners on July 22, 2017, it is very likely we will hear about the "Lightning Network" in the near future. In the meantime, some miners really wanted to raise the block size, and this proposal didn't make it to the recent Segwit soft fork. So they created a hard fork of Bitcoin on August 1st, creating a new currency, "Bitcoin Cash". So if you had one Bitcoin before that date, you now have one "Regular Bitcoin", and additionally one "Bitcoin Cash". You kind of have two different Bitcoins now. One Bitcoin Cash is roughly worth one tenth of a Regular Bitcoin so far.

11.4 Other Technical Problems of Bitcoin

One of the problems raised most often about Bitcoin is the energy needed for the mining of new blocks. As we have seen, the system is designed to encourage nodes to deploy the maximum computational power to find as many blocks as possible in order to gain mining rewards. This system is essential to secure the blockchain and to ensure that the power used is sufficient to avoid a hack by a pirate who would be able to mine all blocks.

This already poses a serious problem: the race for power has been ever increasing since the beginning of Bitcoin. While the first miners could actually mine on their laptops, it is totally useless to try that today: you will pay large electricity bills and overheat your laptop, without ever finding any block.

Smart programmers first discovered that they could use graphics cards to speed up the calculation needed to mine blocks compared to conventional computer processors. Next came the programmable logic circuits. And finally, as Bitcoin mining became more and more profitable, specialized Bitcoin mining processors were created, called "ASIC". There is no point in trying to mine Bitcoins today without these specific processors, which are very expensive. The advantage is that the electricity spent by these specific processors is much less than conventional processors in relation to their calculation speed. Nevertheless, the energy spent today for the Bitcoin network is estimated at more than 14 terawatt hours per year. This is the equivalent of the electricity used by one million American homes. Bitcoin therefore consumes the equivalent of a city of an average size, 0.07% of the world's energy, which is quite huge.

Bitcoin's supporters say the banking cartel is also using much resources. This is true, but the majority of financial transactions today are done electronically, and when you compare the cost of a Visa transaction with a Bitcoin transaction, you realize that the Bitcoin transaction consumes 23,000 times more energy than the Visa one!

As mining requires a lot of energy, miners can be found where the electrical energy is the cheapest. Currently it is China that has the lowest price records, which explains why the overwhelming majority of mining facilities are in China at the present time. Some even set up mining farms illegally next to the hydroelectric power stations and steal some of the energy to mine Bitcoins... This situation is not so great, because it means that the miners, who normally are supposed to be scattered around the world, group themselves in a single geographical area. This makes the whole network vulnerable to natural phenomena: massive floods, earthquakes, infrastructure failures, etc. And depending on a single country and therefore the goodwill of its leaders may not be a great thing either.

It would be fun if the Chinese government decided to ban Bitcoin, effective today.

One of the other problems is the calculation of the difficulty. As we have seen, the difficulty of calculating blocks adapts according to the speed with which the preceding blocks have been mined. However, if a large part of the computing power suddenly disappears due to problems on the network, the blockchain may be blocked for a long time because of a difficulty that is too high compared to the remaining computing power. The blockchain would be literally stopped.

Of course, as anything that relies on the Internet and computers, one of Bitcoin's challenges is security. It has been quite resistant to attacks and not breached for the last couple of years. However, it is not totally impossible that some unexpected attack might happen when it is least expected. Bitcoin investors certainly can get filthy rich in the future, but they could also very well lose everything in the event of a massive attack on the cryptocurrency.

And if it was to become a world currency "for everyone" in the future, then you would lose everything too.

Finally, still in terms of security, as Bitcoin is based on cryptographic principles, it implies to closely follow the progress of technology. It is known for example that Quantum Computers will be able in the near future to compute the private key corresponding to a public key such as the ones used in Bitcoin[228]. Fortunately, as far as we know, a public key can not be found from the corresponding Bitcoin address. But you have to know that the public key of an address is revealed only when a transaction uses that address as an input, so it is very important not to reuse Bitcoin addresses if you don't want your funds being stolen in the future.

11.5 Social Problems of Bitcoin

The first social problem related to Bitcoin has to do with privacy. Contrary to the common rumors that Bitcoin allows to make "anonymous" payments, it is easy to trace the origin of transactions since they are all public. Some governments, such as Denmark[229] and the United States[230], publicly announced that they are developing specific Bitcoin tracing tools. Other governments are probably doing the same, without necessarily shouting it from the rooftops.

Do you really believe the Russians and the Chinese don't have tracing tools while they allow Bitcoin in their respective countries?

One mythical example of the use of traced Bitcoins by the authorities is the creator of the website "Silkroad". The guy thought he could make a fortune by selling drugs "anonymously" on the Internet, paid in Bitcoins. The FBI was quick to locate him. More recently, in the current investigation over the MtGox case that is still taking place, the investigators can easily trace the Bitcoins even if getting back to the suspects can be tricky[231].

So while governments tell you that Bitcoin is a vile tool for terrorists, the "geeks" know well enough that there is nothing easier to trace, at least for a government or a somewhat large organization. On the other hand, for the average person, it is very difficult to trace anything. This raises the problem of unilateral transparency: no privacy for individuals with respect to the powers in place, but no transparency for big holders towards the general public.

So some people devised solutions to preserve the anonymity of transactions for all in order balance the problem a little. For instance, there are "Bitcoin mixers" that make the origin of the Bitcoins actually difficult to trace. But at one point in the chain, an IP address appears one day or the other, and anonymity is broken. As we have seen, the problem is not so much that transactions are traceable, but rather that they are traceable by a minority and not by the majority. One must have a blind faith in the governments and the powers in place to not see that as a major problem.

Bitcoin is also very slow and not really designed to be a "currency for all". As we have seen, the Bitcoin Network generates a block every 10 minutes. But for a transaction to be accepted reliably, it is estimated that it takes about 6 blocks, that is, one hour. It is thus difficult in these conditions to use it as "everyday money". You won't wait one hour at the baker's for your payment to be approved.

Bitcoin also suffers from a bad reputation since the MtGox affair, called "piracy" to try and discredit Bitcoin further. But the problem was not "piracy" of Bitcoin as such. In February 2014, MtGox, a trading platform of Bitcoins closed its doors, claiming to have been hacked and unable to continue its operations. While the exchange has indeed been the victim of piracy because of blatant negligence, the director is also accused of running away with the money, with sums that amount to tens of millions of Dollars, in very troubled circumstances... he was arrested and charged in Japan[232]. More recently, the same scenario has repeated with another exchange site, of which the CEO is still on the run, probably somewhere in China[233].

> *The Bitcoin universe sometimes resembles the James Bond universe...*

Another challenge is the legality of using Bitcoins[234]. The main challenge reported by authorities worldwide is the one of "money laundering"[235], which is quite ridiculous since Bitcoin amounts are magnitudes lower than any tax evasion or money laundering scheme in Fiscal Paradises... Anyway, while most "democratic" states let Bitcoin grow so far, it is not always the case in other countries such as China or India, where the Bitcoin exchange platforms have regular problems with the authorities. In France, like in most European countries, the government has not really legislated, but Bitcoin, like all other cryptocurrencies, is not prohibited. In Russia, Bitcoin was strictly banned until the government suddenly announced in November 2016 to everyone's surprise that it was legal.

Maybe they were just waiting until their tracing tools were ready... just saying...

In fact, as I mentioned in the introduction of this chapter, China, Russia, Germany and others are currently looking at creating their own cryptocurrencies. Even if it is not clear yet how these will work in practice, it is a safe bet to assume that the legal authorities will be the only ones allowed to create new money in these systems. So I see this as an attempt to "bring back cryptocurrencies within the institutions". Forget about freeing the people.

It is also legitimate to wonder who is this mysterious inventor and what were his real intentions. His public intentions were to free us from the banks and create a decentralized currency for the people. But we see that the parameters of monetary creation are all to the advantage of the powerful and at the very detriment of the people. Besides, those who defend Bitcoin often possess large amounts of it and therefore have an interest in promoting it so that the value of Bitcoin rises in the future to increase their earnings. Since we do not know the real identity of the original creator, we can ask ourselves whether his true intentions were actually those he displayed.

What about if it was a trick from the banks[236] or the NSA?... given that governments and financial organizations seem to want to scrap cash, and with the catastrophic state of the current monetary and financial system that can go down the drain any day, it seems that Bitcoin is a God-sent. But hey, you create your own luck, and in the case of Bitcoin it comes really at the right time, from "anonymous and providential" hands.

The last problem I will discuss here is the "totally decentralized" aspect. While this is undoubtedly an advantage in some ways, it can also be seen as a disadvantage. In case of a problem with the system, there is no one to complain to, there is no door to knock on, nobody to call, and overall it is not possible to organize an event such as "Occupy Wall Street", there is no possible "Occupy Bitcoin".

Besides, for those who lose Bitcoins or get their Bitcoins stolen, nothing can be done, the game is over. In this system, everyone is responsible for their own security, the security of their account and the computer that hosts them. We have seen with the MtGox story and others that even computer geeks can easily be hacked if they are not extra careful. The ideal being to store large amounts on "paper wallets", which are totally disconnected from the Internet. But it is necessary to acquire a certain level of technicality in order to achieve decent security. It is not impossible, but it is a point to be taken seriously.

11.6 Altcoins

Let me remind you that Bitcoin's source code is "open-source" which means that anyone can read it, you can simply copy it on your computer. From there, you can modify it slightly in order to create a new cryptocurrency, which is quite easy for a programmer. So even you could create a new cryptocurrency to try and address Bitcoin's problems.

When Bitcoin became widely known by the end of 2013, many clone projects emerged, often poor imitations, basically bringing very little added value: a nice name, a nice logo, slightly different monetary creation parameters... Note that the overwhelming majority of these copies follows a monetary creation curve similar to Bitcoin. Sometimes, all coins are even created at the beginning of the project and no more coins are created. Therefore, the overwhelming majority of them is based on rare coins, to attract investors.

> *That's logical. Which shark investor would put money today in something he knows will lose its value in the future?*

Almost a thousand "Alternative Coins" exist[237], often abbreviated in "Altcoins", which I will use since it is shorter. Of course, it would be impossible and boring to speak about all of them here, but I will present a few of them that I believe are interesting.

All these Altcoins can be exchanged for Bitcoins or even with each other on exchange platforms on the Internet. But as we have seen with the MtGox story, it is better not to store too much money on these platforms. They can be hacked and it quickly becomes tempting for administrators of these sites to run with the money...

All these innovations are generating tremendous hype waves and massive speculation, just like Bitcoin does. The sudden interest in a new Altcoin and its promises can sometimes create a huge bubble that bursts as soon as the next "revolutionary" Altcoin comes down the road. The world of Altcoins very much looks like the financial markets in the real world.

I have chosen to spend some time to present some "Altcoins" in order to show how money can be handled in so many different ways and human imagination is boundless. When it comes to money, and in order to solve the challenges of the world, we have to think "out of the box". But overall, if these Altcoins all offer very innovative solutions to sometimes difficult problems, they all fail to address the fairness of creation and distribution of coins to their users.

11.6.1 Litecoin

One of the first Altcoins is "Litecoin", which proposed a faster pace for block creation and would then act as "Silver" compared to the "Bitcoin Gold", which explains the "silver-like" logo. But its major contribution is that it chose a new algorithm to mine blocks, which was supposed to resist "specialized mining processors", and be usable only by normal computer processors. Unfortunately, they had underestimated the ingenuity of gold diggers (or rather, silver ones), and specialized hardware to mine it appeared very quickly. Litecoin was not innovative enough to make a breakthrough, let alone overcome Bitcoin.

11.6.2 Nxt

Another Altcoin, "Nxt", also faster than Bitcoin, and adding some "nice" features such as the ability to send messages or to label addresses, also introduces a new block validation system. In this system, which has the advantage of wasting much less energy, the difficulty to validate a block decreases according to the amount of currency possessed by the address associated with the node. Thus, the more they own, the more they mine new blocks, which means the more they have power. "The more you have, the more you get".

Some find this solution "brilliant", but I think that there is nothing new under the sun compared to the current financial system...

11.6.3 Nem

To try and address this problem of the rich getting richer, another cryptocurrency appeared: "Nem". It invented the concept of "proof of importance", which is based on the "activity" of an account, along with its current balance. So in this system, it is not enough to be sitting on a massive amount of coins to be able to create new blocks, the user also has to actively contribute to the Nem economy. It is an interesting and innovative concept, but those with more money still get more importance, provided they exchange funds with others. And finally, almost all Nems have been created at the launch of the project, which substantially favors the initiators of the project to the expense of others.

11.6.4 Ripple

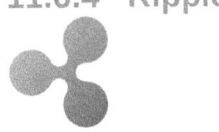

"Ripple" is openly created by and for centralized organizations. In this system, each account or address is "validated", "authenticated", "certified" by a central authority. The purpose is to ensure that the address you are transacting with is not a rogue address. Of course, as it operates on a blockchain, everything is also perfectly traceable, and it is also much faster than Bitcoin. Needless to say, this system is not seen in a very positive way by the general public. But this "confidence security" seems to attract investors, since it is currently the third cryptocurrency by market capitalization. Personally, I do not see any advantage compared to a conventional bank, else that "it's cool" to be on the blockchain.

11.6.5 Dash

Really bothered by relative transparency intrinsic to Bitcoin, a group creates "Darkcoin", which integrates in the core of its system the guarantee that transactions are anonymous. This Altcoin is now called "Dash". It also incorporates another interesting feature: the ability to vote for changes within the community.

The problem I see with this system is that, in order to vote, you must own a "Master Node". The acquisition of a Master Node is done only by putting 1,000 Dash on the table, and 1 Dash is currently valued at almost $200. This system is in fact an ultra elitist tax-based voting system, it then becomes difficult to speak about "Democracy", which is the word used by its advocates. If you think about it, this system finally doesn't bring much advantages compared to the existing "democracy" where the majority of the richest miners decide the future of any cryptocurrency.

11.6.6 Monero

Another Altcoin, "Monero" addresses anonymity problems as well as the specialization of mining by a few. To achieve this, they also changed the mining algorithm, and so far nobody has built specialized hardware, so a simple laptop can mine it, as was originally thought by Nakamoto. This still doesn't solve the race for power and therefore the energy waste. Its monetary creation is interesting since it will never stop, at some point Moneros will be created at a constant rate of 0.3 Monero per minute, to try and continuously attract miners. But its model is still very imperfect as we will see later in this book.

11.6.7 Ethereum

Let us pause for a moment on "Ethereum", the work of a young Russian, Vitalik Buterin, who introduced the principle of "Smart Contracts". The principle is to use the blockchain to secure and register contracts between users, in the form of computer programs, activated by "Ethers", which is the internal currency of Ethereum.

This solution has the advantage that it potentially allows to do everything on the blockchain, we enter a new dimension compared to simple monetary transactions. This is how the concept of "Decentralized Autonomous Organization" came into being, the acronym of which is "DAO". It is a technology that inspires a lot of people.

Unfortunately, it was hacked in the summer of 2016, the pirate managed to steal 3,6 million Ethers, the equivalent of $50 million. The flaw was corrected immediately, but there was a debate about whether to change the source code in a "hard fork" to take back the stolen Ethers from the pirate or not. The problem here is that for many people in the cryptocurrency community, "the source code of the software is the law".

Because of that, many people idealistically believe that the code should be changed as little as possible, except when it brings substantial benefits for the future. Thus, there was no consensus on this subject, because the pirate had only used the existing code, "the law". Following this, the Ethereum blockchain was split into two blockchains and therefore two distinct currencies: "Ethereum" in which the stolen funds were taken back from the pirate, and "Ethereum Classic" in which the pirate kept his bounty. Ironically, he donated part of the stolen funds to the supporters of "Ethereum Classic" soon after the fork.

Another more recent Altcoin, which is exactly based on the same principle than Ethereum but with other technological choices, is called Tezos. It has been one of the biggest ICOs with more than 200 million dollars raised[238].

11.6.8 Iota

Another Altcoin that looks technologically very promising is "Iota", whose name refers to the Greek "iota" which has taken the meaning in English and French of "negligible quantity". This currency is specially dedicated to the "Internet Of Things" which is often abbreviated "IOT".

This currency does not work on a blockchain. Instead, it introduces the notion of the "Tangle", a transaction-oriented graph, in which each new transaction "validates" two previous transactions. The inventors point out that this system does not suffer from the major drawbacks of Bitcoin, since the effectiveness of the "Tangle" increases with the number of nodes that support it, rather than in terms of the overall computing power. It is also possible to do micro-transactions at no cost, and the system is resistant to attacks by quantum computers. By the way, this currency is backed by no less than Microsoft.

The only problem I see lies in the monetary creation: all the Iotas were created and "reserved" by the initial investors of the project. Others must now buy them at a high price, and over the long term it is an economic model which, as we have seen, leads to crises.

11.6.9 AuroraCoin

Iceland definitely likes to do things differently. In 2014, an "Altcoin", "AuroraCoin" is created by an anonymous (this is definitely the norm in cryptocurrencies) to fight against the effects of restrictions imposed by the Icelandic government on the Icelandic Krona. One of the interesting fact about this cryptocurrency is that a large part of AuroraCoins was distributed only to Icelanders, and in fact to more than 10% of the population, after verifying their identity. Let's see what the Icelanders will do with this original initiative in the future!

11.6.10 Siacoin

To conclude, a few words on a too little known Altcoin: Siacoin. This currency offers the possibility of making backups of your data in a totally decentralized and encrypted way. You can offer your own disk storage space to others for them to store their backups, from which you earn Siacoins. These Siacoins can then be spent to "rent" the disk space of others to store your own data. Clever.

Summary:

Bitcoin and most Altcoins seem to have been totally monopolized by the "less than 1%". It is especially possible because of a monetary creation leading to deflation, which would eventually lead to even greater inequalities than the current financial system if they were accepted as "currencies for the people".

Despite its scandalous reputation, its inherent transparency raises questions about the privacy of individuals, while allowing a certain confidentiality for a minority.

Finally, the massive waste of energy, scalability and anonymity, although all technically challenging, seem to have many answers and solutions that develop with constant innovation in many Altcoins.

Overview: The Flaws of Existing Systems

It is time to stop and reflect on what we have seen so far, to get the essence of it, the core problems, so that we can find solutions and build a better monetary architecture.

We have studied the history of money, the current banking system and its alternatives, both with local currencies and with decentralized cryptocurrencies. All of them suffer from flaws that expose their users to injustice. Typically, a small minority of people can always grab most of the wealth for themselves.

Let's examine quickly the flaws we have shown until now.

The current monetary system has multiple problems.

First, the centralization of the creators of money, whose declared role is to act on monetary creation to "regulate" the economy as a whole. It gives them an huge advantage compared to other players in the economy. This is especially true as they have no requirement for transparency on their actions. We see that this does not work, since they have been unable to prevent crises until today, and on the contrary they provoke them. This centralization favors in a totally unfair way the actors of monetary creation.

To make an analogy, let us place ourselves in a village with only one spring of water, on a piece of land owned by a family. Imagine that this family would make everyone else in the village pay for every drop of water that comes out of their spring. This family, which is in a monopoly situation, could safely raise its prices and become filthy rich. If we go further, we can also predict that the other families that are geographically closest to the spring could then sell the water at even higher prices to the more distant families, creating a spatial inequality: those closest to the spring having a strong advantage compared to the more remote ones. The same is true of money, the centralization of its creation introduces spatial inequalities. Needless to say, in a small village where everyone knows one another, this situation would very certainly end very badly. But as you find this situation with money on a much larger scale, the people in general are not even aware of the monopoly itself and its consequence on their lives.

In this perspective, the current European financial system is a perfect caricature of this example. We have central bankers who create and destroy money at will, and let a minority enjoy it. This minority, mostly commercial bankers from Northern Europe, grabs this monetary creation for themselves without letting the rest of the population benefit from it, since the growth of the monetary mass does not flow into the whole economy.

Bitcoin is another extreme example, but this time temporal one instead of a spatial one. The initial creators have stuffed themselves with Bitcoins at no cost, and as time passes, the next ones are having more and more difficulties getting some little pieces of this asset that gets more and more precious.

Then there is debt-money with the problem of the interest that mechanically creates a spiral of general debt, which leads to the race for economic growth, which in turn leads to ecological devastation. Debt-money is also a source of acceleration and amplification of crises, simply because banks lend less during crises and more the rest of the time. This creates temporal inequalities.

Finally, speculation that allows an elite to "play" with the real economy, to "break a bank" or even a currency, to cause crises on raw materials and hence famines, while being totally disconnected from the real world. As we have seen, speculators have reached an enormous proportion in the economy, even more important than the debt based currency. By themselves, through the rating agencies, they run the show, when it is not computer algorithms that strongly disrupt the system.

This financial architecture favors the acquisition by a few of the majority of the resources. This encourages the centralization of organizations and monopolies, with ever-growing multinational corporations and political institutions, which take control over smaller ones, either by simply buying them or by intimidating them. Thanks to "Free Trade Treaties", a very misleading name, they can now bend or even dictate the laws they want to democracies all over the world.

There are also alternatives. While local currencies help strengthen the local economy, they are nevertheless linked to currencies of central banks and are not really independent, which strongly limits their impacts.

Initiatives such as those based on Gesell's "Freigeld", or "Melting Currencies" have an interesting approach which stimulates the economy, but again the question of the centralized creation of money is problematic.

The same centralization problems apply to so-called "decentralized" currencies, such as cryptocurrencies. Their money creation systems favor the initial creators as well as rich miners, and the "others" are left with nothing but the clothes on their back. Bitcoin is typically a currency that leads to deflation. It has the exact superiority that Gesell spoke about when comparing currencies and goods, and history has shown repeatedly how this kind of story ended: people spend as little as possible and store the precious asset, thus choking the economy in a deadly spiral that is feared by economists.

We also have to be very careful about any system that would favor inequalities in general. The human being has jealousy at its core. It is much easier to put up with hunger if you are surrounded by other fellow hungry humans than when others are stuffing themselves with cakes around you. People constantly compare their life conditions with each other. And when it becomes obvious that some riches are not exactly "deserved", this grows from jealousy to hate and to bloodshed. Let us search for a system that at least limits inequalities, while still rewarding fairly and reasonably the most active people.

I also especially insist on decentralization, not only regarding monetary creation, but also in the management and organization of the monetary system. Indeed, the more an organization is centralized, the more it favors corruption. In a small country village, everyone knows the mayor well, but we already know him much less when living in a big city. The prefect of a region is a total stranger to most people and the President of the country is simply inaccessible. Familiarity with a person of power promotes transparency, while distance encourages manipulation, lobbying and corruption in general. It is becoming increasingly visible within the European Institutions[239].

Human beings lust naturally after power and large bank accounts. The more an organization concentrates the power or the resources of a large number of people, the greater the temptations are for its administrators, because the power and / or monetary sums involved are big enough to make anyone's head spin. Current systems, whatever they may be, have insufficient control mechanisms over their administrators and "elected representatives", and centralization is obviously a big challenge to the people.

An acceptable solution for our monetary system must therefore be decentralized, both regarding its monetary creation and in its organization.

A "good" system should also prevent money to be the source for obtaining power or more money and at least not favor extreme inequalities.

Chapter 12
The Relative Theory of Money

We have reviewed many monetary systems, and it is time to go back to the fundamental concepts, the constraints and necessities underlying the use of money. This will allow you to better understand the core reasons for the weaknesses of existing systems, and find a better solution.

In 2010, Stéphane Laborde, a mathematician and engineer, published "The Relative Theory of Money", which will be abbreviated to "RTM". In his book, he lays the necessary foundations for creating a monetary system that is fair to all. I believe each of these foundations are revolutions in the way we approach money. I will present the main lines of his book, with my own explanations and remarks.

12.1 What is "Value"?

In 1916, Silvio Gesell, in "The Natural Economic Order", writes:

The expression "Common Value Measure", which is sometimes applied to money in antiquated economic writings, is misleading. No actual property of a canary, a battery or an apple can be measured with a coin.[240]

He rightly points out that money cannot be used to "measure" the values of objects (and if you believe it can, you belong to a museum!). On the other hand, he does not go far enough in his logic, for he continues to believe that objects have an intrinsic "value" when he speaks of the "qualities" of these goods. Thus he writes:

It very commonly happens that two persons selling the same product obtain unequal income from their labor. The reason for this is that though equal as workers, they are unequal as dealers. Some are better at selling their product at a good price, and when buying goods, some excel at sorting the wheat from the chaff. (originally in German: "die Spreu von den Körnern zu sondern")[241]

While it is true that every person has different abilities, he intuitively associates an intrinsic value with each object, even if he is just using an expression. The farmer or gardener using permaculture value straw much more than wheat. In general, the "qualities" of an object can be advantages in the eyes of one person, and disadvantages in the eyes of another.

Thus, the RTM refutes any "absolute value", in time and space. Indeed, like Gesell, we always tend to think in "absolute" terms, saying for example that "this necklace is valuable". But an object has "value" only in relation to other objects, and every different person, whether in France or China, in the Middle Ages or today, has his own scale of values at a given moment, which even varies with time in the course of his life.

The "value" between two objects is then fixed only at a given moment by two people who perform a transaction: "I exchange my tomato for your apple". At this time and in this place, we mutually declare that me giving up my tomato and getting your apple in return is a transaction that is not unfair to me. At the same time, giving up your apple to get my tomato instead seems to you "a honest proposal". So, the apple and the tomato can be exchanged at that moment. This does not mean in absolute terms that "the apple and the tomato have the same value". Tomorrow, maybe I will not want apples anymore. My tomato-craving partner of today may get tomatoes from someone else tomorrow that he will find more juicy, and even regret having made that exchange with me.

Some love lemons, others hate them. Some prefer ripe fruit, others prefer green ones. You may not have loved contemporary art during a part of our life, then discover a passion for cubic painting. One Bitcoin traded on average for $10 in 2010, $800 in 2016 and $2,500 mid 2017.

All civilizations have sought a "standard", a "common measure" of objects. When you realize the full scope of the relativity of value, you realize that they have all been chasing a rainbow. This negation of "absolute value" and the vision of "relative value" is what I call the "Revolution Zero" introduced by the RTM because it is the foundation, the essential basis on which the RTM and its subsequent "Free Money" are built.

12.2 Value and Cognitive Biases

I allow myself to drift away from the RTM a little to speak about the cognitive biases associated with the notion of value. The subject is so broad that it is impossible to speak about it in detail here, but I will give you some hints to show just how subjective the notion of value is. On the subject, Daniel Kahneman's books are good references, in which he shows the effects of cognitive biases on our behavior, as well as on the stock markets.

What is a cognitive bias? It is a distortion of reality by our brain. Most of the time, it leads us to make mistakes because it twists our judgment. Of course, advertisements and marketing in general use them as much as they can and without us being aware. All these biases are very well documented, they should be learned at school because they make us take bad decisions every day.

12.2.1 Loss Aversion – Endowment Effect – Mere Ownership Effect

We all hate "losing" something, even if we receive something else in exchange. It has been shown that the effect of losing $5 is much more powerful in our brains than finding $5 in the street[242]. Moreover, the effect of thinking "it is mine" makes us give more value to an object we own compared to the exact same object that does not belong to us. This bias can lead to very strange and erratic behaviors, such as people refusing to sell something that belongs to them at prices at which they would never buy it in the first place. Even a $10 banknote in my hand is worth more in my eyes than the same $10 banknote in my neighbor's hand. This effect is the one leading humans to unconsciously wish for their money to "gain value over time", rather than a currency that loses its value over time.

12.2.2 Sunk Cost

You spent $200 to rent a cottage in the mountains for the weekend, and it is non-refundable. The day before your departure, you are very tired and the weather forecast for the weekend looks very bad. A friend offers you to spend the weekend together with some friends doing some activities you like at home. What do you do? Oddly enough, the majority's reaction in this kind of situation is to go to the mountain in order to "benefit" from these $200, even though they are already gone, and it is obvious that you will benefit and enjoy the weekend with your friends much more. It is somehow related to the Endowment effect.

12.2.3 Mere Exposure Effect

The more often we see something, the more we love it, and therefore the more we give it value compared to other products. Advertisers use this effect a lot, as they fill the public space with their products' images. Politicians have understood this as well, and they know that in order to win an election, you have to "be on TV", "generate buzz", have the biggest media exposure possible, even if it sometimes gives negative information on the candidate. Of course, this technique has its limitations, but it is widely used.

12.2.4 Anchoring

This is the effect that "fixes" in our brain the first impression on something. For instance, if you buy a second hand product and the seller has already set a price, this price serves as the basis for the negotiation. It becomes very difficult to aim at substantially lower prices, even if the first price is much higher than the product is worth.

12.2.5 Halo Effect

The halo effect is the one that makes us give more value to products of prestigious brands than to similar products but of lesser known brands. It is also the one that makes us buy the most attractive packaging, regardless of its content. It is again the same effect that makes us elect presidents who are taller than average and also the one that makes us attribute a better personality to people who are physically more attractive[243].

12.2.6 Monetary Illusion

The monetary illusion makes us prefer to earn large sums of money, even if they are offset by a high inflation and it would be more profitable to gain less but with less inflation. This is how we believe we are "earning" something when our savings account has a 1% interest, even if in reality we lose our purchasing power because of a 2% inflation.

12.2.7 Conformity

It is an effect that is also studied a lot. Humans, even the most anti-conformist ones, always do everything so as not to be rejected by their peers, and thus constantly imitate them. It is the one that encourages us to use without question the same currency as our neighbors, friends, colleagues, family...

12.2.8 Bubble Effect

Even if we deviate here from the pure cognitive biases, the economic bubbles all function in the same way: a sudden obsession for a product, often within a minority of people, raises its price. The majority notices this and believes that there is a lot of profit to be made with this growing trend. The herd of sheep suddenly rush on this wonderful and valuable asset. The rise eventually stops, usually at totally crazy heights, and ends up crashing suddenly into a panic where everyone suddenly realized they have been mindless sheep.

The first documented bubble in history and which has gained popularity recently is the one of tulip bulbs in 17th century Europe. Suddenly, the European "high society" becomes fascinated by tulips, so much so that one single tulip bulb can be worth as much as two houses, before the bubble literally bursts and prices get back to normal. The crisis even reached Turkey at the beginning of the 18th century!

The list of bubbles is long, the Dot-Com bubble is the most famous one. But we can also mention the 1987 bubble, when the Dow Jones, one of the most important American stock indexes, loses 22% in one day. The culprit was most likely computer algorithms, which sold everything at the time "in panic mode" because of a transaction that was a little bigger than average. Some even accuse the algorithms of having participated in the formation of the bubble itself.

Men have a short memory...

At the end of year 2013, the Bitcoin bubble is most likely due to computer robots within the MtGox exchange speculating on the Bitcoin stock value, and dragging all human speculators with them[244].

12.3 The Importance of the Frame of Reference

Let's return to the Relative Theory of Money after this little psychological parenthesis. The RTM strongly insists on the importance of the frame of reference chosen to express the "value" of things. In particular, a currency itself is only worth the value humans are ready to give it in relation to other currencies or goods. I would say that this is a matter of trust and I would add that, most of the time, it is the governments that crystallize this confidence in their currency.

Even if we don't notice much, the value of a currency always changes over time. With sometimes significant "hiccups". For instance, the Russian Ruble is subject to a 84% hyperinflation in 1998. It then stabilizes in the 2000s. More recently, it is again experimenting a bumpy ride:

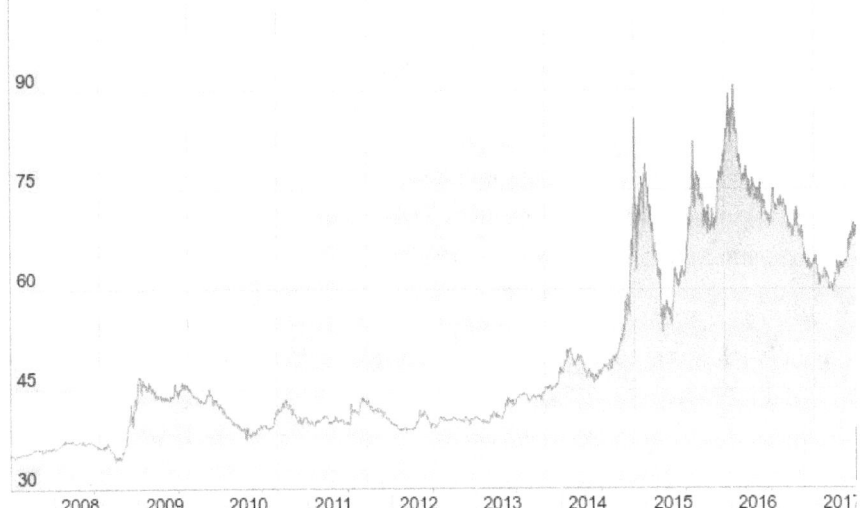

29. *Euro - Ruble exchange rate from 2008 to 2017: the vertical axis shows how many Rubles you need to get one Euro. Source: xe.com*

As you can see, at the end of 2014, you need 50 Rubles to get one Euro, but a month later, you need 90! It then goes back down to 55 Rubles a few of months later. But when we say this, we consider the Euro as a "stable" currency, we take it as a reference frame. However, the Euro is also subject to significant variations compared to the US Dollar during the same period:

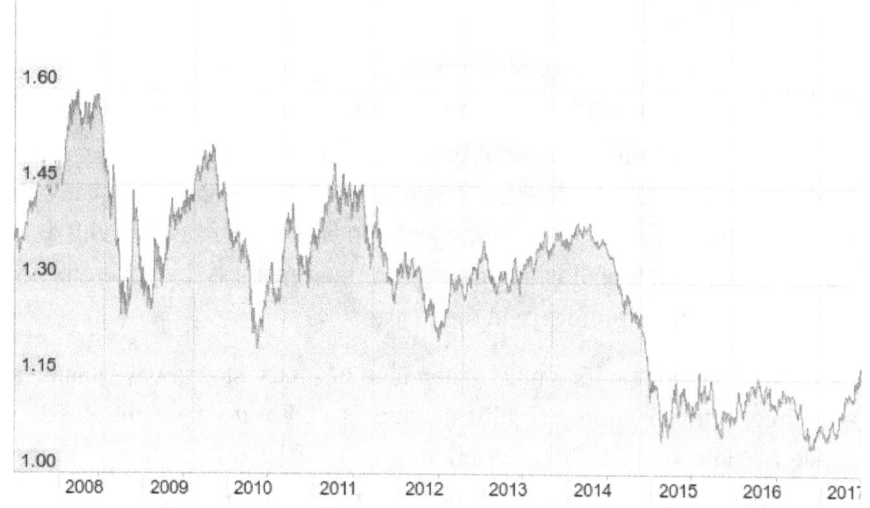

30. Euro – USD exchange rate between 2008 and 2017: the vertical axis is the number of US Dollars you can get with one Euro. Source: xe.com

This chart shows the ups and downs of the Euro – Dollar exchange rate, with variations up to 30% in a few months!

So, as you can see, saying that one currency has gone down, in absolute terms, is totally wrong: it is always the value of one currency that gets lower compared to the value of another.

With this in mind, we understand better that the frame of reference, typically the currency used as a reference, is important and can be misleading if we don't take into account that this reference frame also changes compared to other currencies and other frames of reference.

On the other hand, it is clear from these graphs that money is not a "store of value" in absolute terms. Between the end of 2008 and the end of 2016, in just 8 years, the Euro, this currency that we generally consider "strong", lost more than a third of its value against the US Dollar.

Let us take another example: an ounce of gold. Again, it is a value that we tend to consider as "stable"!

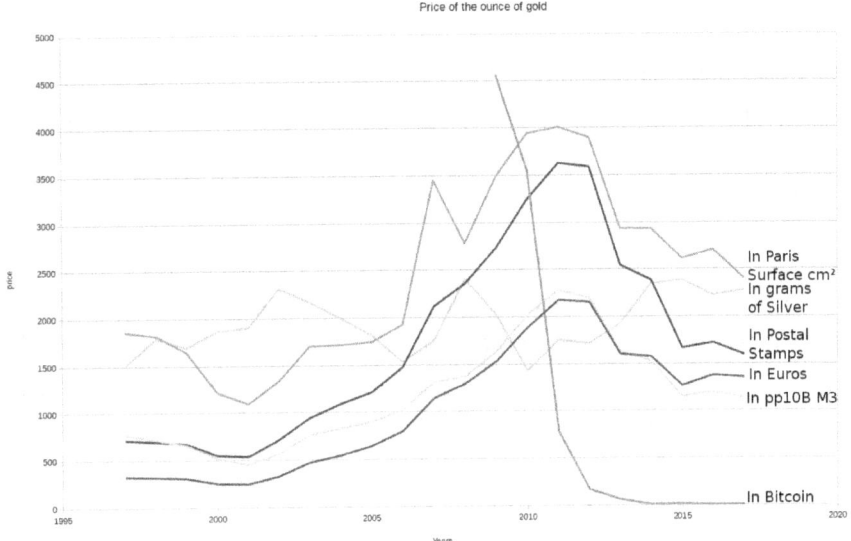

31. *The price of an ounce of gold between 1997 and 2017 if you wanted to buy it in the following values (from top to bottom in 2017) : in square meter of a Parisian flat, in grams of silver, in post stamps, in Euros, in Euro monetary mass M3, in Bitcoin. Source : taken from the Galileo module by Éloïs[245] to which I added some extra data.*

The above graph shows the price of one ounce of gold as a function of a number of other "values". Even with respect to silver, there is a variation of almost 60% between 2010 and 2015. We can easily explain the shape of most curves with the rise and fall of gold between 2008 and 2015 without being a "specialist" or an "economist". After the 2008 crisis, investors started losing their trust in their currency and bought gold, a "stable asset", as well as silver. But by doing this (remember, the "herd of sheep" behavior), their created... a bubble, which burst in the next few years. With that in mind, it's hard to talk about a "store of value" for anything!

As for the "relative stability" of gold compared to silver over time, how can we be so sure that tomorrow a new technology will not be invented, for example new powerful "silver" computers requiring a considerable amount of silver[246], and that the relative values of the two precious metals will suddenly be separated by an abyss? Moreover, it is not impossible either that tomorrow, perhaps, an enormous gold deposit will be discovered, and will cause the price of gold to fall compared to its silver alter ego.

Depending on the frame of reference and of time, there are very substantial variations.

> Question: is it the price of gold that went down or the price of Bitcoin that went up?

A last note to meditate on: all the big investors say that you should never put all your eggs in the same basket... people speak of "portfolio of stocks", that is to say a wide range of shares of different types. If gold, for example, was as safe as it is often assumed, then investors would make gold stocks, and forget about everything else.

12.4 "Value", "Pay" and "Work"

The RTM asserts that the economy exists only thanks to and for the human being. We can remove whatever we want from the economy, wood, iron, even gold, there will always be an economy. On the other hand, if humans are taken away, there is no economy left. Thus, the human being is, and must be, at the center of the economy. From this observation which seems quite simple at first sight, the RTM gives a very different point of view than all other theories. Gesell, for instance, considered money not in relation to humans, but in relation to commodities circulating in the economy, and he deduced that money had a privilege over commodities, which brought him to invent Melting Currencies that get depreciated over time. But we will see that by starting from the primary postulate that man is the basis of the economy, we come to very different conclusions.

The very existence of a human being is a potential for creation of value. And this potential is very difficult to measure. Many geniuses are not recognized as such before their death. Vermeer, Mozart, Van Gogh, Tesla, to name just a few, all had a major influence on our civilization, and all died in poverty without being recognized as exceptional beings in their lifetime. Today, we rely on banks and "investors" to choose which human, which technology, which invention, which artist, has a probable value for them in the future. It is a very big mistake because it is potentially stopping geniuses from expressing their creativity.

"Value creation" is also often confused with "work". It is very common to hear that only those who "work hard", implying "paid jobs", create value. To quote President Macron, you have to "work" to buy yourself a "suit". And yet, nothing can be more wrong.

Value creation is not always rewarded with money. The creators of free software do not ask for a single cent for their creation of value. And yet, such amounts of value get created! The whole infrastructure on which the Internet is based runs on free software. Think a few moments about the Internet's impact on the creation of values all over the world. All the volunteers of associations, and there are many of them all over the world, who are often more efficient during emergency times than official structures, are also part of this category.

On the other hand, money can be "distributed" without any corresponding "labor". Of course, the unemployed who live with unemployment benefits fall into this category. But shareholders at the stock exchange who receive dividends are also included in the same category since they do not "work" but get "money". The same goes with banks which get interest from creating money out of nothing.

Let us also remember that the same creation of value may or may not be rewarded by a monetary transfer. If I mow my own lawn myself, I create value: my neighbors will be glad to no longer see this jungle in front of my house! But no one will pay me for this creation of value. On the other hand, if I ask someone else to come and mow my lawn, I will pay them for it. And yet, it is indeed the exact same creation of value.

We all create value, constantly. This can also be "sentimental" value. The French Post recently uncovered a program where people pay €19,90 for the postman to talk for 5 minutes with Granny in her own village (and that's a special offer, it will get more expensive in the future). If you think about it, the postman already did that before, for free. But now on, it has been decided that "it is a service, a creation of value, that has to be paid for".

And even if you stuff yourself with chips while watching a football game, there is still a potential for value creation: this may trigger a lively discussion the next day at lunch which will put all of your colleagues in a good mood...

And we must beware of our judgment of values created by others. Our descendants will certainly have a very different look from ours on today's creations. Someone perhaps paints pictures, all his friends find that he has a bad taste, that his paintings are too flashy and almost obscene. His name might be Vincent[i].

12.5 The Four Economic Freedoms

In the same way than Richard Stallman stated the four freedoms which led to free software, the RTM is based on the following four economic freedoms:

- **Freedom 0: the individual is free to choose his own monetary system.** It is an inalienable basic right without which other freedoms are meaningless, but it is sometimes considered "obvious" for some freedom advocates, hence the number "0".

- **Freedom 1: the individual is free to use the resources, in a non-nuisance perspective.** In other words, no individual, whether of his own or through the structure of society, should be able to monopolize resources to such an extent that they become inaccessible to others, both in quality and in quantity. All the resources are included in the statement of this freedom, water, raw materials in general, land...

- **Freedom 2: the individual is free to produce and estimate any value.** It is the very principle of the relativity of values that has already been explained.

---

i   Van Gogh of course.

- **Freedom 3 : the individual is free to trade and count in the currency he has chosen.** This is simply the practical usage of the monetary system he has chosen.

In the RTM, Stéphane Laborde mathematically demonstrates that the only currencies that satisfy these four economic freedoms are Free Currencies based on a Universal Dividend, whose value must follow a formula which is calculated in the RTM. To summarize it, the value of the Universal Dividend must be a proportion of the total money supply. This proportion depends on the average lifespan of the humans who are using this Free Currency. On the other hand, any currency which is not based on this Universal Dividend violates at least one of the four economic freedoms.

This is what I consider to be the First Revolution of the RTM. It is a totally unprecedented process to start from fundamental freedoms and to demonstrate the necessary and sufficient properties of the type of currency that satisfies these freedoms. The best way to understand the demonstration and its final formula is simply to read the RTM[247]. I propose in the following chapter additional analogies to help understand it, especially for people who, like me, are more "practical" than "theoretical", and prefer to deduce generalities from examples rather than to demonstrate generalities and then provide examples. This adds nothing to the demonstration, but may help some understand the principles of RTM through examples and analogies.

Summary:

The RTM refutes any "absolute value": all value is relative. This is what I call the "Revolution 0", the basis on which all the RTM is built.

The RTM lays down the four fundamental freedoms:

- the individual is free to choose his own monetary system,

- the individual is free to use the resources, in a non-nuisance perspective,

- the individual is free to produce and estimate any value,

- the individual is free to trade and count in the currency he has chosen.

The RTM demonstrates that only a Free Currency based on a Universal Dividend can satisfy these four fundamental freedoms: this is what I call the First Revolution of the RTM.

Chapter 13
Free Currencies

13.1 The Human as a Frame of Reference

One of the most powerful metaphors used in the RTM is to consider mankind as a pool with a water jet. I suggest to go even further in this metaphor.

32. A fountain, which illustrates the flow of humans with time.

The water in the basin represents humanity. Let us take a "picture" of the basin with its jet of water, which represents a snapshot of humanity at a moment in history. The jet of water is made at this particular instant of a large but finite number of drops, each of them representing a human being alive at that moment. The drops that have just emerged from the jet of water represent the humans that have just been born. Those that are at the top of the jet represent humans in the middle of their life. And the drops that are ready to fall back into the basin represent the humans on the verge of death.

Let's take a new picture a moment later. Each drop went forward a little, new drops have appeared, these are the newborns, others have fallen back into the basin, those are the recent deaths.

Let us now take a film of this fountain: using this metaphor, we see humanity evolving, human-drops continuously appearing, following the others in the jet of water and inevitably falling back into the basin, but the jet of water itself seems stable as a whole, it is always the same. With this same metaphor, we can also consider money as the jet of water: it must evolve in a constant flux like the flow of the jet of water, at the same rate as the humans it serves.

This system therefore ensures that monetary creation follows the flow of human beings, and therefore privileges no one, neither in space since each human corresponds to a monetary creation, nor in time since the new humans that are born also benefit from monetary creation during their life.

13.2 The Universal Dividend

Let's go back a bit to present this idea of a Universal Dividend not by demonstrating it as in the RTM, but by simple iterations, empirically. I again invite you to read the RTM for a precise mathematical demonstration.

The first basic idea is that monetary creation must not depend on the goodwill of a group of individuals who take over monetary creation not only in space at a given moment, but also in time, and in relation to future generations. It must not depend on arbitrary factors such as "the needs of the economy" or "such and such invention needs financing by the creation of money", which are always subjective.

Monetary creation must correspond to the flow of human beings and each human must therefore correspond to a monetary creation. This is what I would call the Second Revolution brought by the RTM. It is a revolution because in history we have never seen a monetary creation by a state or a sovereign in these terms. Except perhaps by chance and partially among the Egyptians with their wheat money that was continuously co-produced by all the farmers of the kingdom. All civilizations have considered monetary creation "according to the needs of the economy", which in practice is completely Utopian since no one has ever been able to objectively measure these needs. This also causes corruption by the very fact of human intervention in monetary creation.

The monetary creation indexed to the human being is a code, a universal and timeless law, in which no human can intervene to his own advantage.

This really deserves to be called a "Revolution"!

Some LETS also apply a monetary creation per human, assigning a fixed amount of money to every newcomer. Thus, everyone in the economy has on average the same amount, it is an interesting system. But what happens on the long term? Suppose, for example, that each newcomer receives 100 units and that there are 1,000 people who participate in that currency in their village. We can simply calculate that there is a total of 100,000 units in circulation. Time passes. Users die. But the units remain in circulation in the economy: they can not be removed since they are potentially scattered throughout the economic zone at the time of each death.

When a lifetime has passed, there is still an average of 1,000 users since newborns have replaced the dead. But this implies that the total money supply is now 200,000 units: 100,000 that is still around from the very first users, and an additional 100,000 from their children, who are the current users. This poses a serious problem. After 10 generations, the monetary mass reaches one million units. But each newcomer still receives 100 units, while the existing currency per user on average is now 1,000 units. Therefore, as time passes, the new generations are more and more at a disadvantage compared to the very first users.

To solve this problem, we have to adjust the amount that is distributed to the newcomers. Instead of a fixed and absolute sum, we have to give them the equivalent of the average possessed by each user at the time they enter the system. So, if there are one million units in circulation and 1,000 users, the newcomer must receive 1,000 units, corresponding to the current average.

We have solved the inequality between the initial members and new members coming to the system later. But the following problem still remains: is it fair that a human of this system who survives up to a hundred years would be given the same sum as a newborn who died the day after his birth? Let us remember that monetary creation must "follow" the flow of humans, like the drops in the fountain, in order to correspond to the potential value creation of this human being during his lifetime. But in the system we have just described, this is not the case: a "human drop" has fallen back immediately into the basin after coming out from the jet, while the drop of the corresponding money goes all the way to the top of the jet of water, as if the human being was alive the same way than any other human in the group. It's not fair for those who live longer.

To solve this problem, it seems obvious that we shouldn't give the whole amount when the user enters the system. Instead, we can give every year or even every day a proportion of the money supply to every human still alive in the system.

We have reinvented, by empirical iterations, the Universal Dividend system.

We can also say that the Universal Dividend "crystallizes" the value creation potential of every human being at every moment of his life.

On the other hand, our little empirical adventure does not tell us the amount of the Universal Dividend, nor the growth of the money supply to be taken into account according to the average duration of the users of the currency. The RTM demonstrates these values mathematically.

This system is in fact equivalent to an unconditional basic income financed by monetary creation, but it also fixes the amount, proportional to the money supply and adjusted to the life expectancy. This is what I see as the Third Revolution brought by the RTM: never in history has this possibility been thought of this way.

13.3 Absolute Money Supply Growth

A Free Currency is therefore a currency in which a Universal Dividend is distributed at regular intervals to every person using that currency. This implies that the money supply in circulation is constantly increasing, when you consider the monetary units. The RTM calculates that, for a population with a life expectancy of about 80 years, the "optimal" monetary growth for a Free Currency is about 10% per year. This means that the money supply grows by 10% per year, and doubles approximately in 8 years. At a human's half-life (40 years), the money supply is then multiplied by more than 37, and in a lifetime, by more than 1,700.

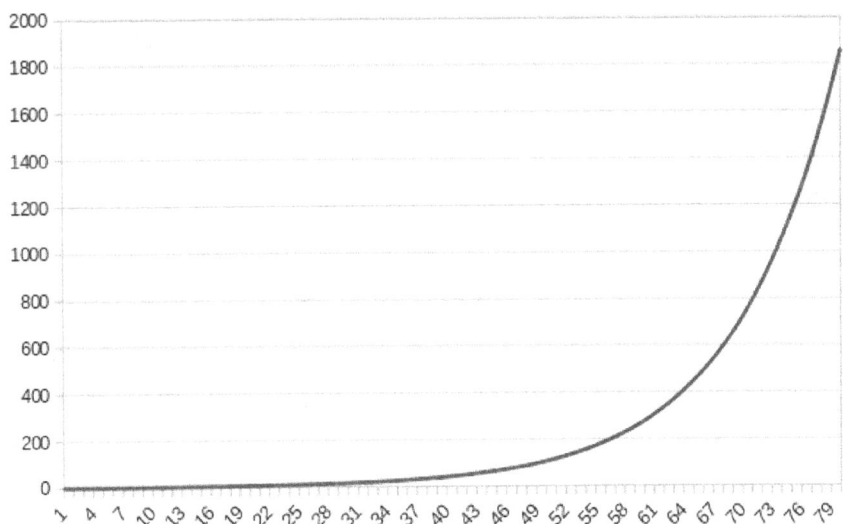

33. *Monetary Growth of a Free Currency during a lifetime, when counting absolute Monetary Units.*

This means that the individual units issued today by each member of the group using the currency "lose value", get "depreciated" over time, since they are "diluted" in an ever growing total mass of more and more units. Back to the analogy of the drops of water in the fountain, when the "drop of money" corresponding to an individual falls back into the basin at the time of his death, it gets gradually "diluted" into the basin.

Since absolute monetary units lose value over time by diluting them in an ever-increasing monetary mass, it becomes tempting to classify Free Currencies as a form of "Melting Currency". We will see that this is not the case.

You can also immediately think that this system can become very impractical: if I pay my loaf of bread one unit of the currency today, by the end of my life I may have to pay more than 1,000 units for the same loaf. And some may even imagine their descendants coming with suitcases filled with banknotes to pay millions of units for their loaf.

When a currency has this type of problem, the most frequent solution is to divide by a certain factor the value of that currency. For example, in the 1950s, the French Franc had suffered such inflation after the war that it was decided to create in 1960 the "New Franc", which was worth one hundred "Old Francs". So, in the case of a Free Currency system, we could decide to divide by 2 the value of the currency every 8 years, and thus remain on the long term at "reasonable" prices. But this type of solution brings a lot of confusion in everyday life. In the 1990s, French people who were born before the Second World War were still using "Old Francs", whereas the division by 100 had occurred more than 30 years before. This solution is socially very confusing.

13.4 Monetary Mass Stability in the Relative Scale

This is where the Fourth Revolution of the RTM steps in: so far, we have only counted the "monetary units" as it has always been the case with coins and notes. But the RTM introduces another frame of reference, the relative scale, based on the Universal Dividend, and therefore indirectly on the money supply.

To understand the relative scale, you can simply imagine the Universal

Dividend, the UD, created every day, as the equivalent of a day of "average value created by an individual". Maybe he mowed his lawn. Maybe he mowed someone else's lawn. He probably did other things that day. In this context, the UD represents a "working time", in a sense. So here we have a new reference frame for our measurements: rather than using monetary units, we can use the "day-work", the UD, as a unit. And this unit remains stable over time.

Of course, it is possible that tomorrow's bionic man may be 1,000 times more productive than today's shabby biological man, we will see!

So from now on we have a new frame of reference for the value of things. Instead of paying a loaf of bread one unit today and two suitcases in two centuries, we pay for instance 0.01 UD today, which corresponds to one hundredth of human-day-work, and exactly the same 0.01 UD in two centuries[i].

Well, of course, provided that bread still exists, that transgenic wheat has not taken over the planet, that the bionic man still needs bread to feed himself...

In the relative scale, we can see that the monetary mass doesn't have any impact on prices, and that it never grows nor diminishes when the number of users remains constant.

Let's use another analogy. In Ancient Egypt, they used grains of wheat

---

i This is only an example. Free Currencies are not indexed on time in the way "value" is evaluated by the actors of the economy when they exchange goods or services for money. The payment for 24 hours of a given service is **not** one UD. This is a fundamental difference with "time-currencies", where one hour is always equal to the same amount of units of that currency, regardless of the service. UDs are **created** in regard to the existence of a human being during a certain amount of time, which is totally different. Users are then free to decide the amount of UDs they are willing to give for a certain good or service. Besides, the RTM doesn't forbid any community from choosing to define "24 hours of service" as equal to "1 UD". But this doesn't seem like a good idea to me for the reasons I have already mentioned. If you believe that one hour of mowing the lawn is equivalent in value to one hour of placing a pacemaker in a patient's heart for him to survive, it is your absolute right. Just be aware that others may not agree with you (especially the patient!).

as money. Every single grain taken on its own was rotting over time, and its value was also getting lower because of storage costs. The grain of wheat is the absolute monetary unit.

On the other hand, you could pay a chair, for example, with a bag of wheat. The unit "a bag of wheat" does not "perish", it is an abstract unit, relative to the average mass of bags of wheat in circulation. This average mass remained relatively stable even during harvests thanks to the large storage of old bags. The "bag of wheat" unit is the relative unit, and the price of a chair in this unit probably varied very little over 2,000 years, except perhaps during famines.

So, in the relative scale of a Free Currency, there is no inflation nor deflation, prices remain "stable". Of course, they obviously vary according to the scales of values of every human, the means of production and the availability of resources, but they do not depend on monetary creation. Free Currencies are therefore not "Melting Currencies" for the members of the groups that use them.

Another way to understand it is by remembering that while the units created yesterday "are worth" perhaps a little less today, this is compensated by the new UD which is created by each member every day.

> We can see here the fundamental difference between Free Money, the result of a demonstration based on economic freedoms, and Gesell's Melting Currency, based on an empirical reflection of the "superiority of money" compared to raw goods.

13.5 Attraction Towards the Average

Another property of Free Currencies is that, assuming that everyone buys as much as they sell, the accounts of each member tend towards the average in the UD relative scale. Whether "rich" or "poor", everyone see their accounts irresistibly attracted towards the average of all accounts.

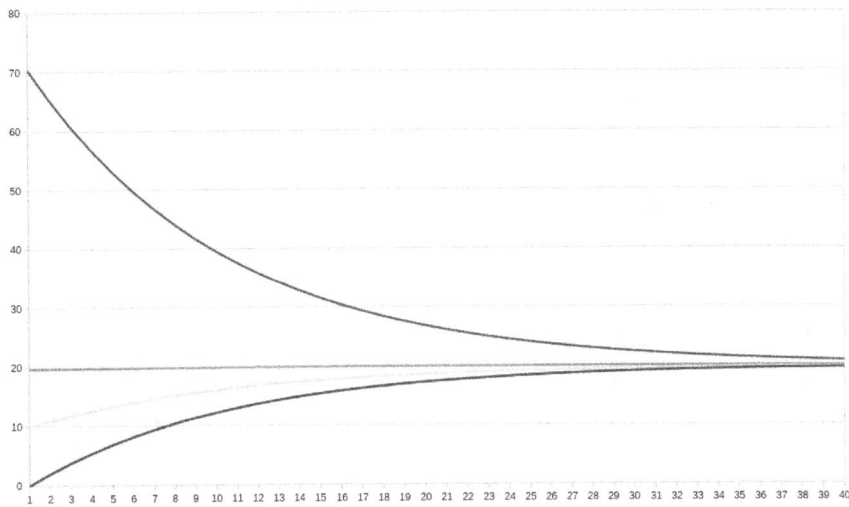

34. Percentage of money held by 5 users during a half life.

In the graph 34 above, we can see the evolution of the amounts of money held by 5 individuals over time with a Universal Dividend system. In year 1, only one individual owns 70% of the total amount of money, another owns 20%, the third owns 10%, and the last two have only a very small part of it. We can see that in 40 years, assuming that all these individuals trade without buying more or less than they sell, all accounts tend to the average of the money supply: 20%, since there is a total of 5 individuals.

The Universal Dividend system can be seen as equivalent to a "tax on the rich", the very big difference is that it is much easier and practical to implement. With a tax system, the "rich" always find a way to be tax evaders. And as we have seen, the loss aversion cognitive bias makes people unhappy if they "lose" something, while "winning" makes them happy with their fate.

13.6 A "Communist" Currency?

You might start thinking that this is a "Communist" currency. But it is not the case at all.

Of course, studying Karl Marx's theories relative to the RTM is far beyond the scope of this book. I will just give some hints here.

"Communism"'s philosophy is to put everything "in common", goods and wages. But no money (or anything else) is "shared with others" in a Free Currency. Someone can sell more than others and actually earn more than the average thanks to the transactions he makes. Those who buy everything and do not sell anything can potentially end up with an empty account one day.

For example, let's imagine a group which, as a whole, does not produce enough to support the whole community. In this group, each member who does not sell anything has a strong incentive to produce something and sell it, otherwise it becomes difficult for him to survive.

Conversely, if a proportion of individuals produces enough for the whole group, those who want to "do nothing" can afford to buy enough from others to survive. We can place the safe bet that those "idle individuals" can then follow their passions "which produce nothing vital", such as artistic activities, and in fact bring value to the group without any external pressure. We all create value.

Silvio Gesell's "Freigeld" was associated with a series of social recommendations: using the "commons" for the land, using of bonds for those who wanted to store value, free trade. He was, moreover, fiercely anti-communist. Typically, he was regularly saying that when you offer to share all wages equally among a group of communist people, everyone becomes silent and starts calculating if it would be advantageous for them or not.

The RTM does not give any of these recommendations. It only describes the monetary creation of a Free Currency system. Individuals and social groups who use such a currency are then free to make their own rules, which might be very different depending on the society, place and time.

It is possible, and I bet on it, that adopting a Free Currency will generate different behaviors in society than the ones we are used to. But these are only "side-effects", they don't come from the theory itself.

While the Universal Declaration of Human Rights stipulates that we are all "equal in rights", we must debunk the misconception that we are all "equal". We do not have the same height, and as we have seen, this seemingly insignificant fact creates distortions within society itself[i]. Women and men are not equal: they are different with their own qualities.

Pareto's theories and many others show that, within a society, a minority always produces much more than the rest of the population. It is now an indisputable fact as it has been systematically verified in practice. In the same way, a minority always tends to grab the majority of resources if we are not careful.

Taking this parameter into account, rather than burying our head into the sand, is very important. Obviously, it has been seriously neglected so far! And we can see the result today. The consequence is that, as most of the wealth is in the hands of a few, the majority adopts "competition" behaviors to try and get their share of the rare money that is left for them.

Instead, by taking this parameter into account explicitly in the second economic freedom, Free Currencies greatly limit the excessive accumulation of wealth by a few while maintaining a strong incentive to produce value when it is necessary. Besides, the individual of a group where everyone co-produce their money feels solidarity with his peers and the group. Thus it seems logical that a society where money is abundant for all naturally turns to "cooperative" behaviors.

13.7 Free Currencies and Universal Basic Income

The Universal Dividend can be seen as a Universal and Unconditional Basic Income funded by monetary creation, but the RTM also sets the amount of that basic income. Thus, distributing a Basic Income to all by creating money seems a good idea, if its amount corresponds to a well-chosen proportion of the current money supply. Having a fixed amount for this Basic Income is of course out of the question! But in France as

---
i   We have shown in chapter 12.2.5 that Presidents are taller on average than the rest of the population, due to the cognitive bias called the Halo Effect.

elsewhere in the world, it would first be necessary to convince the ECB and Central Banks to distribute fresh banknotes to the population every day.

Good luck! Let's make an "Occupy BIS"?

As for the Basic Income that is generally sold to us by the politicians, which is funded by social security contributions, it is a very bad idea for the people.

Let's take the example of Finland. For the past few years, they have been experimenting the Universal Basic Income with 2,000 unemployed people: all social help, unemployment benefit, housing benefit, family allowances or any other social allowance or benefit, are replaced by an unconditional basic income amounting to €560, which is paid systematically to all even if that person finds a paid job. However, this amount is totally insufficient to live in Finland, where prices are among the highest in Europe, whereas this amount corresponds to the amount of the Minimum Welfare Allowance (RSA) in France...

So it seems that, on the population's side, this solution is a very bad idea. But there's more! On the government's side, this idea is also very bad, because if it was to be extended to the population as a whole, it is a financial abyss[248]. The mistake is to fund basic income through social security contributions[249] (through taxes). I am afraid that any effort in this direction will end with the schematic situation described in figure 35.

As I see it, the UBI funded by social contributions seems like a trick to hide more inequalities. On the side of people who have a minimum benefit (such as in France with the RSA) or people who already are in a difficult position such as people with physical disabilities, the UBI would reduce their overall income because it would replace all existing allowances. For the unemployed and the retired, the loss of income is even greater. As for the working classes and the middle class, they could benefit a little from the UBI for a while, but the drastic increases in social contributions needed to finance the UBI at the state level would clearly offset the small additional income provided by the UBI. All this would also mean more debt for the state, which can only end with more interest paid to international bankers and financiers, the only winners in this scheme.

Well, I didn't have enough space for the wealthiest in the histogram, I had to cut it...

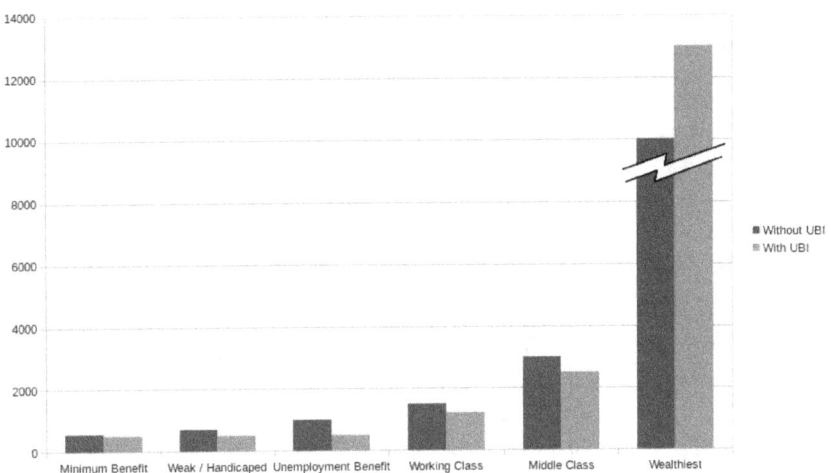

35. *Without the Universal Basic Income in blue (today) and with an UBI funded by social contributions in orange. These are not real values but correspond to a schematic situation.*

One interesting fact to be noted is that one of the leading figures of the UBI, Guy Standing, was invited to the meeting of the very influential Bilderberg Club in the summer of 2016[250].

I would like to say a few words about the "Subsistence Wage". Some people sometimes mistake the Universal Basic Income with a strange notion, the one of "an income to ensure that one can live a decent life". Let's take 10 people on an island, spending their days at the beach, laying on the sand and swimming. No "wage" will provide them with food or shelter. The subsistence of a group is only due to the work of this group as a whole. This notion of a "subsistence wage" has been imagined in a society in which the distribution of wealth was such that the poorest only got the crumbs. Such a system tends to adjust these "crumbs" so that the workers are only able to survive. But within a Free Currency, this notion doesn't even make sense.

However, with the Basic Income financed by social security

contributions, this notion makes perfect sense: we simply make sure that the population as a whole can "survive", but without addressing the real problem, which is the constant capital flight towards the top of the social pyramid.

This really looks like giving morphine to a dying patient.

> Summary:
>
> The RTM bases monetary creation on the very existence of each human being who periodically creates a Universal Dividend within a Free Currency. This is what I call the Second Revolution of the RTM.
>
> The RTM determines the value of that Universal Dividend from the existing money mass rather than from an absolute or arbitrary value. This is what I call the Third Revolution of the RTM.
>
> Finally, I define as the Fourth Revolution of the RTM the introduction of the relative scale based on the Universal Dividend to count monetary exchanges, rather than using the absolute scale based on monetary units. In this framework, the money supply remains constant and there is no inflation, additionally the balances of all accounts tend naturally towards the average of the accounts over time when the exchanges are balanced.
>
> The Universal Dividend is similar to a Universal Basic Income funded by monetary creation. We have also seen that the Universal Basic Income funded by social contributions is a dangerous idea for the people since it could lead to even greater inequalities.

Chapter 14
An Implementation for Free Currencies

14.1 Duniter / Ğ1

Since the publication of the RTM in 2010, some developers have taken upon themselves to code a software to implement a Free Currency System, so that the theory can become a reality. The software is based on known architectures, such as the blockchain, peer-to-peer networks, and cryptography. Test networks are put in place. Bugs are fixed. The final software is called Duniter. It allows anyone to create Free Currencies with the desired parameters.

On March 8th 2017, a real "production currency" is launched in France and becomes usable to do exchanges in real life. It is called the Ğ1[251], which is pronounced "June", \ʒyn\ in the phonetic alphabet.

The parameters of this currency are chosen so that it is a free currency: the annual growth is about 10%. The daily UD is 10 Ğ1 at the launch of the currency, and is re-evaluated every 6 months at the equinoxes to adjust to the money supply.

Apart from the core of the project that handles the blockchain and its security, different client software are developed: "Cesium" works on any web browser, and "Sakia" is a software to be installed on your own machine. "Silkaj" is also a command line tool for the most advanced users. And two marketplaces already exist, where everyone can exchange objects or services in Ğ1[252].

But to be able to come to life, the project needed an additional innovation. So far, transaction management, money creation, security, all already have answers with Bitcoin type architectures. But a major problem was left to be solved: the identification of unique individuals. Indeed, the Universal Dividend is created by each individual in the group, but to do so, it is necessary to ensure that an "account" in the system corresponds to a unique individual. That is, it must be very difficult or risky for an individual to open more than one account in a Free Currency, otherwise there is a risk of multiple accounts, where he could collect many Universal Dividends.

For this, developers based their work on an existing project, OpenPGP, and created their own architecture from it, truly unique, which they called the "Web Of Trust", sometimes abbreviated "WOT".

14.2 The Web Of Trust

It would be tedious to study the Web Of Trust in detail here, especially as we move away from our main subject: money. But I will sketch the basic principles to give an idea of how the Web Of Trust works.

The Web Of Trust is a group of individuals within the currency, they are called "members". To be able to create a daily Universal Dividend in Ğ1, you must have the "member" status within the network, which makes you a part of the Web Of Trust. When a currency is launched, only the initial members of the group who trust themselves because they know each other well enough start at block 0 of the blockchain and initiate the Web Of Trust.

From there, if you want to become a member, you need to get 5 certifications from existing members, who are already registered in the blockchain. One of the most common attacks with this type of structure is called a "Sybil attack". The main principle is that a small group of people manages to create many accounts among themselves. From these original accounts, they grow their own sub-network of accounts, and take over the whole web. To avoid fraud and especially this kind of attack, the parameters of the Web Of Trust were carefully studied and adjusted by the developers: various delays, maximum number of certifications that can be issued by each member, expiration of certifications after 2 years, notion of "referent member" and the distance rule are as many safeguards put in place to make cheating extremely difficult. And let us remember an instinct that is deeply rooted in the human being: the fear of being excluded by his peers. Any cheater caught with multiple accounts exposes himself to the risk of never being certified ever again by the members, and it is already a very effective discouraging mechanism. Besides, the goal is not to have a perfect system, but rather a system where cheaters are such a minority that it becomes negligible at the scale of the whole Web Of Trust.

The advantage of this system is that it is totally decentralized. Of course, you can have as many non-member accounts as you want, not only for individuals, but also for organizations what would like to trade using Ğ1s. Logically, companies cannot be members: only human beings can be members.

The Ğ1 Web Of Trust has been sized to reach a maximum of a few million members, for the basic reason that most thriving economies have such sizes on average. Below that number, there isn't enough diversity, and larger organizations are not homogeneous enough to use a single currency efficiently.

14.3 Why Ğ1 and Bitcoin are very Different

The main criticism I have made of Bitcoin in this book is about its monetary creation, which tends to make each Bitcoin more and more rare over time and thus favors the first owners. Free Currencies work exactly the opposite way. In addition, Bitcoin creates money when a miner mines a block, while Duniter creates no money when a block is calculated but creates currency every day for each member. Therefore, in the Duniter universe, a block is not "mined", it is "calculated".

The second most important criticism is the electric waste generated by the "mining" of the blocks, due to the race for power. But Duniter solves this problem in a very clever way, thanks to the Web Of Trust. In Duniter, only members can participate in the calculation of the blocks, by having one or more nodes on the peer-to-peer network. The big difference with Bitcoin is that every node is identified by the member's signature. As soon as one of the member's nodes finds a block, the difficulty for all the nodes of the member in question skyrockets for a few blocks before gradually falling back to normal values. So, as soon as a member's node has found a block, all his nodes "temporarily give way" to others. Thanks to this mechanism, members naturally take shifts in calculating blocks. The effect is that there is no race to power, a node can work very well and find blocks on a "raspberry pi", a mini-computer that consumes 5 W of power, less than a lamp bulb, and that costs very little money...

To reward members who have computing nodes, an additional service has been created, but it is not part of the core of Duniter. It is funded by voluntary donations and distributes the funds depending on how many blocks each member has calculated.

The only things that Ğ1 and Bitcoin have in common: they are cryptocurrencies based on a blockchain and a peer-to-peer network, so they depend on electricity and the Internet.

> Well, the day we have no electricity and no Internet, I guess we'll have other things to think about in our grotto than free currencies...

One important note at this point: as Bitcoin, Duniter is a Peer-to-Peer system, and is totally decentralized. This means that, in exactly the same way than with Bitcoin, every user is responsible for his own security, there is no "crying at the bank to get your money back" if you lose your coins or if you get robbed. It is therefore highly advised to know what you are doing when you open a Ğ1 account. One minimal recommendation, apart from reading the license, is to read the post from the Duniter forum on your security within the system[253].

14.4 One Fear: Savings

One of the biggest question around Free Currencies, that scares many people, is the one of savings. We are used to have our money yield more money thanks to interest. In reality, the interest you can get is generally not higher than the current inflation, and without realizing it, you are actually losing money. You are just falling into the trap of "Monetary Illusion" we have discussed above. Remember, getting some money doesn't necessarily means you are actually getting richer. Besides, this fear also has its root in the cognitive bias of "loss aversion" that we have mentioned in chapter 12.2.1. When you know where this fear comes from and how irrational it is, you can get rid of it more easily.

All good speculators know that they can only hope to create a "reserve of value" for themselves by spreading their assets in varied resources. The idea that one single currency could guarantee anything in the future is an illusion due to having placed too much trust in a system, often without knowing its actual details.

We have already shown the examples of the Ruble and Indian notes, but the examples of sudden depreciation of currencies are common: Argentina in the early 2000s, Turkey in the 1990s, Venezuela still today, Zimbabwe in the 2000s... This illusion that money can be hoarded over the long term is dangerous. We have also seen that a currency that favors saving it has a very negative impact on the economy over the long term.

We can then wonder how, in a world using a Free Currency, we could buy a house, since it would be particularly difficult to save money on the long term. But no one saves money for over 20 years to buy a home these days, why would it be different in a society using a Free Currency? Community lending mechanisms could very well emerge, or other solutions without involving savings.

Special needs such as health care and insurance could still be provided by mutual organizations, as well as pensions.

And it is still possible to save in the short term with a Free Currency. Someone who saves for two years one third of his UD everyday ends up with the equivalent of 214 UD on his account which is very far from being "nothing".

Some readers, I am sure, may still be perceiving Free Currencies as "inflationary". We are all afraid of inflation, because it is unconsciously associated with all the stories we hear during crises. Prices skyrocket, people's savings under their mattress becomes worthless overnight, the wages do not necessarily follow the inflation... This is hyperinflation, created by crises that are created by... the bankers and their manipulations and mistakes. But if each of us produces some money every day, and it is this monetary creation that creates the rise in prices when counting in absolute terms, we have no reason to be afraid of it. The only serious impact is on those who have hoarded great amounts, in other words "the filthy rich", and who see their reserves disappearing into thin air... we have nothing to fear from this type of "inflation". And we have shown above all that there is no inflation for the one who is part of the system and when counting in the relative scale. This scale will be used for every day transactions, like the bag of wheat in Ancient Egypt.

14.5 What about Multinational Corporations?

In this model, it seems that multinational corporations may not be able to survive. Because those corporations thrive on huge capital, it would certainly not be possible for them to exist within a society in which masses of money cannot be put together on the long term. That seems scary. Aren't these multinational companies the ones that innovate and bring us a better world?

As I have experienced it first hand, you may be surprised if I tell you that, most of the time, they don't innovate much themselves. Why am I saying that? Aren't huge teams that collaborate bringing much more innovations than small teams in small companies?

Well, let you meet with the "Ringelmann Effect", by the name of Maximilien Ringelmann, a French agricultural engineer. He showed in the early 20th century that the bigger a team gets, the less productive it becomes[254]. This is generally explained by the fact that people in large teams tend to believe that their own efforts are not so important compared to the overall effort of the group. This affects very negatively the motivation of all the members of the group, and causes the whole team to be much less productive. Besides, coordinating a small team is easy, communication is simple. But when the team grows, the coordination of its members becomes a real challenge, which can seriously reduce the overall performance of the team. Another key is that it is easier to hide your low performance in a big team than in a small one, this is called "Social loafing"[255].

So, am I just teasing with you now? Don't these huge companies create so many innovations? Of course, they do innovate a little[256]. But most of their biggest achievements come from... buying off other smaller companies, typically highly innovative startups, sometimes abroad[257].

Here is how the process works. They are constantly watching the market and checking the new innovations around that could be useful to them. They look for prey. When they spot one, and if it is ripe enough, they compete to buy it off before their other multinational competitors do. So they get the innovation, and not necessarily keep the people who created them in the first place.

So, besides capital, their survive mostly thanks to innovation that happens outside of them, but their capital is the one that enables them to acquire these new technologies or inventions for themselves.

They also survive because their largest customers, often other multinational corporations, trust their size, which is "too big to fail". Does it remind you of something?

Besides, this system also has a very bad side-effect. If you had spent millions in buying a new critical innovation before others did, would you share it with the world after that? Of course not! So these multinational companies also thrive on secrecy. They keep everything to themselves in order to make more profits[258].

Does all this serve humanity as a whole? Wouldn't we be better off if we openly shared these innovations with others, and let those "others" bring further enhancements? This is typical of what I was referring to when I spoke about "cooperation" behaviors rather than "competition" ones.

14.6 Discrimination

One of the rather absurd criticisms of Duniter and the Ğ1 is that it would be "discriminatory towards non-members". While it is a valid criticism in the case of the "miners" of Bitcoin compared to "non-miners", it is totally grotesque in the case of the Ğ1. Anyone, provided he is a real person, by his simple existence, can become a member and thus create his own share of money. This is not the case at all for the vast majority of monetary systems and in this regard Free Currencies are among the fairest systems.

Along the same lines, some also say that the Web Of Trust as it exists promotes discrimination. It is true that currently, someone living in Quebec or in the Reunion Island is "at a disadvantage" to obtain certifications compared to someone living in certain regions of mainland France. But on the one hand nothing prevents the creation of a ĞQuebec currency or ĞReunion by sufficiently motivated groups, and on the other hand, these problems will diminish with the growth of the Ğ1 WOT, which already has among its members some Belgians and Swiss citizens. As for "discrimination" as it is generally understood, that is, based on race or sexual preferences, there is none in the Web Of Trust. If a member doesn't want to certify someone due to a bias of any kind, it is always possible to find other members who will not have this bias. And the current WOT is already diverse enough for anyone to become a member, apart from geographical limitations, which can always be overcome given the right motivation.

As for "discrimination" because of the quite unfair "democracy" we have exposed with cryptocurrencies, the Ğ1 is in a very different place. We have seen that, to be able to participate in the Bitcoin network, you must buy very expensive hardware (at least $1,000 if you want to earn something). Along with that, if you don't pay for very cheap electricity in the region where you live, you will lose a lot of money since a "small and simple" domestic miner consumes generally more than 1,000 Watts. This obviously creates very strong discrimination as only the richest can afford to mine Bitcoins in some particular regions of the world, and thus to participate in the "democratic" decisions for the future of the currency. On the other hand, as I have already pointed out, the hardware needed to effectively calculate blocks on the Ğ1 blockchain can be as cheap as $35, and consumes 5 Watts. So in the Ğ1 blockchain, any member can afford to participate in the decisions, making it one of the most democratic system we have ever seen.

14.7 Other Criticisms

One clear limitation of Duniter and electronic currencies is that it depends totally on the availability of electricity and the Internet. If you can't live with that, then you should think about creating a Free Currency with physical materials. It is quite challenging, and maybe this is why in the whole history of the world, Free Currencies have appeared only recently, thanks to current technology.

Beyond the electronic aspect of the Ğ1, some criticisms arise on Free Currencies in general or the Ğ1 in particular.

One of them is the "frozen" aspect of the parameters of the currency. But the Ğ1, like any cryptocurrency, can evolve over time, if the community agrees on the modification of certain parameters. And besides, it is always possible for a separate community to create a new currency with other parameters. Of course, in this case, that community would have to technically maintain their own currency.

Another objection about Free Currencies is that the UD is based on the life expectancy of the population using a Free Currency. This criticism must be put into perspective because the RTM shows that the acceptable values for the UD are not fixed, but must be within a certain range that depends on the life expectancy[259]. So the same value for the UD could be valid for lifespans from 60 to 100 years. Of course, there could really be a problem if tomorrow's bionic man lived a thousand years[260]: the optimum monetary growth should then be less than 1% per year. But this is of course an extreme case, and at the worst our descendants would have time to change the parameters of the currency, or even to create a new one, to adapt to the new conditions.

Finally, most criticisms that can be made about the Ğ1 as it exists today are mostly due to the "youth" of the project. The WOT still has only a few hundred members, which limits the possible exchanges for the moment. As the project is still in the initial stages, monetary growth is more than 1% per day, making it difficult to set fixed prices. In general, the currency is still in a phase of instability that can be compared to Bitcoin in its first year. All this should not stop us: everything has to start some day, and it is only thanks to its adoption by greater numbers of people that we will come to a certain stability. Besides, it has been tested again and again by several test networks, so the technical aspects are stabilized.

A last but important aspect remains: exchanges with the outside world. Indeed, if exchanges between members can be counted in UDs, this may be different in terms of exchanges with non-members. They do not benefit from a daily UD, and if they get some Ğ1s in exchange for goods or services, those Ğ1s begin to "melt" in their hands with time. This does not mean that no one will want to trade with Free Currencies, but this means that any outside person has a strong incentive to spend his Ğ1s as quickly as possible. This is actually good news for Free Currencies: this greatly limits the risk of attacks on such currencies by malicious people outside their Web Of Trust. However, it is still possible for others to make exchanges as long as they actively reuse the Ğ1s they receive. And of course, remember that the deprecation of the money for external users is not "hyperinflation", it is only 10% per year.

Generally speaking, when discovering free money, reactions are very diverse and vary over time for the same individual, moving from enthusiasm to incredulity, from doubt to hope. It is a concept that upsets our prejudices, shakes up our vision of the world and inevitably brings up lots of questions. Those have often been asked by others during their own journey, and there are many online resources that provide answers to most doubts and fears.

14.8 What Next?

The Ğ1 WOT is open to anyone who wants to be part of it, it is the

Zero Economic Freedom. On the other hand, you must meet the current members to obtain 5 certifications. Besides, a certification implies knowing the person "well enough" to be able to detect multiple accounts, as described in the Ğ1 license[261]. This implies some strong motivation and, as has already been mentioned, some see it as a certain "elitism" or even a "segregation" by the existing members. But freedom does not come by itself on a silver plate, it is acquired through commitment, sometimes even by daily efforts. And all the current members are diverse enough to allow anyone who wants to join the web of trust by approaching the members of his region, who are now over 300 in France, Switzerland and Belgium.

One of the best ways to discover Free Currencies is to participate in one of the Ğeconomicus games held regularly everywhere in France. This game makes it possible to discover the differences between debt money and free money through experience rather than theory, by living your own life in each of the systems, and observe their effects. This also most often allows us to meet existing members, and thus openly discuss, and create "social interactions".

Still, much needs to be done about Free Currencies, although real exchanges have already begun: restaurants, market places, food, lodging, etc. The exchange platforms are still rudimentary but usable. Many challenges remain, such as the anonymity of transactions. Scalability will have to be addressed, solutions exist, it is only a matter of time and work by the developers. Fast transaction mechanism such as Lightning Networks will also need to be developed, the Duniter software already implements Segwit-like possibilities. All this will come in time, as the network of members expands and more developers join in.

Nothing stops communities using free currencies from creating, for example, common "funds" for certain specific cases. For example, in the case of the disabled, society might choose to help them more than the basic DU to bear the expenses incurred by their disability. But it is a matter of society, not at all a matter of monetary creation. We can already imagine that in a society operating with free money, disabled people would already be in a better position than in the current system of monetary creation.

And in the longer term, individual changes in behavior can lead to important social changes. As can be seen in practice during Ğeconomicus games, ruthless and stressful behaviors in Debt-Money give way to much more altruistic and relaxed behaviors in the Free Currency. Within the current network of members, people also financially reward services that are not usually paid for in our current society.

Again, the impact on society of the use of Free Currencies is difficult to predict. Perhaps the users of Free Currencies will go back to the recommendations of Gesell with his "Freiwirtschaft", which for instance lease the land rather than own it, and somehow switch back to the "commons". Probably, debt-money will never be allowed within Free Currency communities, it would actually not even make much sense anyway. But it is the communities using Free Currencies that will be judges and implementors of such measures. Let's hope these communities will remember and take into account the many situations portrayed in this book, in order to avoid repeating the mistakes of the past.

It is up to all of us to make the changes we want to see for our own future and our descendants. Who would have bet in the 1950s that the United States would have a black president 50 years later? Who could have conceived not so long ago that society as a whole would begin to think about the animal condition and start banishing animals in circuses, for example? Who could have imagined in the early 1990s the enormous disruption of the Internet in our everyday life, and all this operating on Free Software? Nobody knows what the future holds for us. We build it with our own choices, today, whoever we are. We write history.

Some useful links:

- The wiki and main Duniter site: https://duniter.org/en/
- The main technical forum: https://forum.duniter.org/
- The github project: https://github.com/duniter

Summary:

It is already possible today to use a Free Currency, with the Duniter software, based on a blockchain.

This system is very different from Bitcoin, and doesn't have its main drawbacks. It is based on a "Web Of Trust". To be part of this Web Of Trust and become a member, you need to approach existing members to get 5 certifications, after having read and understood the Ğ1 license, which fits in one page.

Nothing stops resourceful computer geeks from creating other Free Currencies all over the world, if they maintain them.

You don't need to wait until tomorrow to start using a fair money system, you can begin today!

Addendum:
Note on Conflicts of Interest

I hate conflicts of interest. This question is especially important since I am using a pseudonym to publish this book. I may be anyone, including working for a bank, or a secret agency, anyone. I have several reasons for not using my own name. There is a marketing one. Most of all, money is a very sensitive subject, generally totally misunderstood, triggering passions and with very high stakes. I don't want to put myself forward. I wish to remain an anonymous private individual. Although you have to take my word for it, I am not a member of any political party: these groups offer fixed menus (a set of ideas) and I prefer to pick my ideas *à la carte*.

Let's examine what possible conflicts of interest an individual could have with the ideas that are put forward in this book.

I do not criticize the current monetary and financial system for no reason. I bring documented facts and figures to support these criticisms, and you can accept or reject them, by doing your own research, and by forging your own opinion. I am a simple citizen who simply asks questions and seeks to understand how things work. As such, I wrote this book only to shake up the reader's head a little, tickle your critical mind, bring you information that you can then verify yourself.

I am obviously taking a strong stance against Bitcoin. What does it bring me? Nothing, but I try to wake up the people who do not own any about the fact that it is not good for them. If Bitcoin were to become an unavoidable currency tomorrow, most of the population would be cheated by the very small minority who captured most of it for themselves. Whether I personally own some or not does not come into play here. On the other hand, if I defended this currency, the fact that I own some or not would definitely need to be taken into account. You can reason in the same way for most of the other currencies or LETS reviewed in this book.

I obviously advocate Free Currencies. Let's be conservative and reasonably assume that I am probably part of the Ğ1 Web Of Trust, and that I therefore potentially have strong conflicts of interest. But the definition of a conflict of interest is that it implies a "personal gain to the detriment of others". If others are not scammed, then there is no conflict of interest.

What personal gain may I obtain by writing this book? Of course, maybe some royalties, but it is not a "conflict of interest" in relation to Free Currencies, it is a possible "monetary reward" for a "work", as if I had written a book about cauliflowers or cosmology. I have nothing else to sell but my book.

My goal here is to attract people's attention and raise awareness about the problems of the current economic system and explain its alternatives. It so happens that, by logical thinking, I came to the conclusion that Free Currencies are the best solution to date.

You might say that I will greatly "profit" if the concept becomes popular and that, like Bitcoin, the exchange rate of the Ğ1 soars. As we have seen, Bitcoin's "inventor" is potentially a multi-billionaire today, and it is reasonable to say that he would be in a big conflict of interest if he was part of a pro-Bitcoin lobby. But for the one who understood the difference between the monetary creation within Bitcoin and Ğ1, it is obvious that these two currencies are not similar at all. In the case of Bitcoin, money is voluntarily "rare", while in Free Currencies it is "abundant". One Bitcoin created in 2009 will become more and more rare as time passes. Conversely, the Ğ1s I have already created will be "diluted" over time in the mass of all the Ğ1s co-created by all members. As for the value of one single Ğ1, the more members there will be, the more my own Ğ1 will become negligible into an even larger monetary mass.

As a reminder, the fundamentals of Free Currencies are to make sure that nobody has an advantage compared to others, whether here or there, today or tomorrow. It is quite clear that I am not going to become a billionaire with the few UDs I have created for the last few months, since, as we have seen, Free Money is not a "store of value", and that past savings "melt" with time. Every account converges towards the average in all cases, which is the exact opposite of Bitcoin.

Actually, this is even a "problem" for Free Currencies in general. No "money venture capitalist" will actually want to invest a dime in this system, and on the contrary they are very likely to diabolize it. I've heard people shout "scam!" about the cryptocurrency Monero when they heard about an ever growing monetary mass[262]. What would they say with Free Currencies? But remember that what is a "scam" for them is a system where they cannot get filthy rich at the expense of others, so it is a "fair" system for the average person. So while no financier will want to "lose his money" in this type of currency, it is us, the people, who should invest our lives and our energy in it, in the way that Proudhon viewed masses of workers peacefully overwhelm capitalists by making their "capital" worthless. The fact that Linux remained free didn't stop it from being the backbone of the Internet. It didn't take over the software industry, but now anyone who wants a free Operating System can have one. It's a choice. You already know that when you buy something, you make a choice, and you "vote" for a system as a whole. Buying from your local farmer is an act in which you vote for your local economy rather than for globalization. It is the same with currencies. The choice of your currency is a "vote" towards a system or another.

Thus, the only "profit" I can make would be if the Ğ1 community grows. That way, my descendants, my peers and myself, can evolve in a world where Free Currencies make it possible to live very probably much better than in the current monetary and financial system. But in this case, I am not the only one who benefits from the system: all those who are part of it benefit equally, today and tomorrow. And everyone is totally free to be part of it or not, you don't need to spend any cent of non-free money or anything else to integrate the network of free money, it is enough to simply be yourself and be certified by five peers.

With this knowledge, it is up to you to judge if I may have any conflict of interest in writing this book.

Glossary

See online: http://money.denislaplume.com/glossary

Scan this QR Code with your phone!

Basic Income: There are many other names, which indicate so many different systems with sometimes significant differences. "Unconditional Basic Income", "Universal Income", "Unconditional Lifelong Salary", all refer to the idea of "an amount paid to each individual of a population, irrespective of his or her age, and regardless of his job situation".

Basket of Currencies: A currency created from a weighted sum of several currencies. The value of such a basket depends on the values of each of the currencies that compose it.

BIS: Bank for International Settlements, located in Basel. It is the "Central Bank of Central Banks".

Blockchain: "chain of blocks" in cryptocurrencies, containing transaction history for the currency, or even potentially any digital data that needs to be recorded.

Bond: a financial asset which describes a debt to be paid to the owner of the bond. When a state or a body issues a "bond", it promises to reimburse it to the "holder" (the creditor). The bonds specify the repayment terms (interest rate, reimbursement schedule, etc.), just like a loan contract.

Bretton Woods: global agreements signed in 1944, making the US dollar the currency used worldwide for international exchanges, and the only currency exchangeable directly with gold. The system collapsed in the 1970s.

Bubble: occurs when the prices of a product, stock market securities of a company or whatever else, become totally disproportionate. It can take a long time to build up, but it ends with the bursting of the bubble and a sudden drop in the prices of this product.

Central Bank: the bank of a state or a union or federation of states, in charge of managing monetary creation and setting interest rates.

Complementary, Local Currency: a currency often used by a LETS, intended to be used in a limited geographical area, in addition to the local currency of the state.

Conflict of Interest: occurs when a person or group of persons have responsibilities that can potentially allow them to obtain personal gains at the expense of others.

Creditor: the one gives "credits", who grants a monetary loan, to whom one has to repay.

Cryptocurrency: electronic money based on cryptographic mechanisms for its security.

Dark Pool: see "OTC market".

Debt-Money: money created temporarily by the granting of a loan by a bank. This money is destroyed when the loan is repaid, while the interest from the loan is kept by the bank.

Debtor: the one who has obtained a loan, who is indebted and who has to repay a loan.

Deflation: lasting and general decline in prices. Deflation is often caused by a growing lack of money circulating in the economy, generating a "deflation spiral".

Devaluation: the decline in the price of a currency in relation to other currencies.

Dividends: share of a company's profits distributed (we could say "divided into shares") to its shareholders based on their shares.

Duniter: a software that implements the basics of Free Currencies.

ECB: European Central Bank, headquartered in Frankfurt am Main, Germany.

Fed: Federal Reserve System, the central bank of the United States.

Fiat Money: all coins and notes, constituting the "physical" money in circulation.

Glossary

Fiscal Avoidance: the fact of not paying the taxes that one has to pay, illegally, often through lobbying or blackmail.

Fiscal Paradise: countries where taxes and duties are incredibly low. These countries help companies and the wealthiest to escape the taxes of the countries where these companies and individuals are actually located.

Fractional Reserves: system requiring banks to have a "fraction" in their reserves of the money they lend.

Free Currency: a currency that respects the 4 economic freedoms defined in the Relative Theory of Money. In a Free Currency, monetary creation is achieved by the production at regular intervals of a "Universal Dividend" on the accounts of each of its members.

Freigeld, Free Economy: a system invented in 1916 by Silvio Gesell called "Freiwirtschaft", composed of a melting currency and social recommendations such as the adoption of the "commons" rather than land ownership.

GDP: Gross Domestic Product. This is basically an indicator of a country's wealth production during a year. It is, moreover, very contested, but used massively by economists.

Gold standard: a financial system in which every monetary unit is backed by physical gold: the value of money thus depends directly on the value of gold.

High Frequency Trading: transactions carried out very quickly (currently in microseconds) by robots on stock exchange platforms.

Hyperinflation: rampant inflation during a crisis, in which the population typically prefers to use another "stable" currency or other values than the country's currency due to its instability.

ICO: Initial Coin Offering, which is a fund-raising to start a new cryptocurrency. This is the equivalent of IPOs (Initial Public Offers) in the world of cryptocurrencies. In other words, investors put money on the table for the creation of a new currency, generally in Bitcoins or other cryptocurrencies.

IMF: International Monetary Fund, an international institution created in 1945 dedicated to the economic cooperation of the countries of the world, whose headquarters are located in in Washington DC in the United States.

Inflation: a general and sustained increase in prices. Inflation is often caused by an uncontrolled large monetary creation by the institutions.

Insider Trading: someone who trades on the stock exchange while having confidential information about the future of the stocks they handle.

Investor: see "shareholder".

LETS: Local Exchange Trading System, an organization whose aim is to boost exchanges in a given geographical area (city, department, region).

Lobbying: pressure on the states to obtain laws and regulations favorable to the lobbying group. Methods vary widely, from the simple publication of a study influencing the politicians' points of view, to corruption by bribes and other "little arrangements among friends".

Melting Currency: a currency that uses demurrage, the depreciation of monetary units over time.

Monetary Mass: the sum of all monetary units in circulation for a given currency.

OECD: Organization for Economic Co-operation and Development. It is an international organization of economic studies, with its headquarters in Paris.

OTC (Over The Counter) Markets, Dark Pools: places where investors buy and sell products directly to each other without going through a stock exchange, usually guaranteeing their anonymity. These markets are not regulated.

Quantitative Easing: A technique used by a central bank to inject money into the economy by buying off debt from creditors and paying them directly with money instead of them having to wait to get their money back from their debtors.

Rating Agency: A company or institution responsible for giving "ratings" on companies, states, securities or anything else.

Relative Theory of Money: theory introduced by Stéphane Laborde, which refutes any absolute value. This theory also sets forth 4 fundamental economic freedoms from which Free Currencies are based.

SDR: Special Drawing Rights, an international basket of currencies including the Euro, the British Pound, the US Dollar, the Japanese Yen and the Chinese Yuan.

Securitization: "package" of speculative securities that can be speculated on. Often used to hide "risky" or even "toxic" speculative assets, such as subprimes.

Share: on the stock exchange, one share represents a part of the total capital of an enterprise. When an investor chooses to buy the shares of a company, he becomes a "shareholder" of the company, which enables him to intervene in the management of the company and to collect dividends.

Shareholder, Investor: I mostly use both terms interchangeably even if they do not mean exactly the same thing. An investor "invests", "makes his money available" to support a project. A shareholder is an investor who invests in the stock market through shares.

Stock market: A place where investors can announce offers to buy and sell financial assets, which may be, for example, shares in companies. These markets are regulated and subject to laws to restrict abuse.

Subprimes Crisis: "subprimes" loans are risky loans that can be sold on the financial markets, at the heart of the 2008 crisis in the United States, causing 7 million Americans to lose their homes.

Subsides: financial assistance given by the state to certain sectors of the economy that are in difficulty.

Tax Evasion: A process by which companies and large fortunes manage to hide their profits and capital, in order to avoid paying taxes in their country of origin. They do so with the blessing of governments and institutions, in a totally legal way.

Think Tank: a non-governmental organization whose purpose is to reflect on issues and then communicate on its findings. They are funded by entrepreneurs, other organizations, or even governments. They have a special status, are exempt from taxes in the United States and Canada, for example. These are usually very powerful lobbies.

Universal Dividend: within a free currency, it is the share of money that is co-created at regular intervals by all members of that currency, and proportional to the money supply.

WTO: World Trade Organization, an international organization that deals with the rules governing international trade between countries, and established in 1995. Its headquarters are located in Geneva, Switzerland.

Peace Mantra

ॐ
सर्वेषां स्वस्ति भवतु / सर्वेषां शान्तिर्भवतु
सर्वेषां पूर्णं भवतु / सर्वेषां मङ्गलं भवतु
सर्वे भवन्तु सुखिनः / सर्वे सन्तु निरामयाः
सर्वे भद्राणि पश्यन्तु / मा कश्चित् दुःख भाग्भवेत्
ॐ शान्तिः शान्तिः शान्तिः

AUM
sarveshaam svastir bhavatu, sarveshaam shaantir bhavatu
sarveshaam poornam bhavatu, sarveshaam mangalam bhavatu
sarve bhavantu sukhinah, sarve santu niraamayaah
sarve bhadraani pashyantu, maa kashchidh dukh bhaag-bhavet.
AUM Shanti, shanti, shanti.

Let it be so ordained (−bhavatu), that all the people (−sarveshaam), experience well-being (−svastir) ;
Let all the people experience peace or tranquility (−shaantir).
Let all the people experience wholeness and completeness (−poornam) ;
Let them experience prosperity and auspiciousness (−mangalam).
May it so happen (−bhavantu) that everyone (−sarve) receives happiness (−sukhinah) ;
Let them all be like saints (−santu) and be in good health (−niraamayaah).
Let them see with their own eyes (−pashyantu) the goodness of life (−bhadaraani) ; And let them not (maa) contemplate in their conscious mind (−kashchidh) any sorrow inducing thoughts (dukh) while they remain beneficiaries (−bhavet) of good fortune (−bhaag).
AUM Peace (shanti).

May good befall all, May there be peace for all,
May all be fit for perfection, and May all experience abundance.
May all be happy. May all be healthy.
May all experience what is good and let no one suffer.
Peace.

References

References can also be found at:

http://money.denislaplume.com/references

Scan this QR Code with your phone!

References

1. It is not always true, adversity sometimes brings the best in us. This wasn't publicized by any English news, but this is the story of people who gather together to help their neighbors fight against evictions by bankers. Here is the news in French: https://reporterre.net/En-Espagne-les-citoyens-font-plier-les-banques-parce-qu-ils-agissent-ensemble
2. Janet Yellen and Lawrence Summers in the spotlight: http://www.nytimes.com/2013/08/14/business/economy/careers-of-2-fed-contenders-reveal-little-on-regulatory-approach.html There is an actual recording of the session in which you can hear her statement with her own voice (at 26'50): http://fcic-static.law.stanford.edu/cdn_media/fcic-audio/2010-11-15%20FCIC%20staff%20audiotape%20of%20interview%20with%20Janet%20Yellen,%20Federal%20Reserve%20Board.mp3
3. An excellent read about money and debt, even if it's politically oriented, is David Graeber's book: "Debt, The First 5000 years"
4. Gold and Silver in Ancient Egypt: http://www.touregypt.net/featurestories/silver.htm
5. A good summary of these practices can be found here: http://www.nbbmuseum.be/en/2012/05/nederlands-geldgebruik-in-het-oude-egypte.htm
6. Bernard Lietaer: "New Money for a New World". Besides, there are many references which can be found on the Internet to wheat, barley and other goods used as payment systems in Ancient Egypt. A transcript of a very interesting and rich interview with him can be found here: http://www.transaction.net/press/interviews/lietaer0497.html
7. Another good read about debt, money, precious metals, and current economy is from the Chartalist Larry Randall Wray, "Understanding Modern Money".
8. See for instance how the decreasing value of gold put Spain into default in the 16th century several times: https://en.wikipedia.org/wiki/Sovereign_default#Examples_of_sovereign_default
9. Notgeld on Wikipedia: https://en.wikipedia.org/wiki/Notgeld
10. Of course, many examples are found in David Graeber's book "Debt, The First 5000 years", but even the very mainstream "The Telegraph" picked on the subject: http://www.telegraph.co.uk/finance/economics/11383374/The-biggest-debt-write-offs-in-the-history-of-the-world.html
11. The first banknotes in China: https://en.wikipedia.org/wiki/Banknote#Early_Chinese_paper_money
12. Playing cards as money: https://en.wikipedia.org/wiki/Card_money_in_New_France
13. Operation Bernhard: https://en.wikipedia.org/wiki/Operation_Bernhard
14. This is mentioned for instance in the Venetian economy, check for instance the chapter starting at page 255: https://www.academia.edu/4536629/The_Venetian_economy_1400-1797
15. This is again shown in David Graeber's book "Debt, The First 5000 years"
16. On this topic, Michael Veseth's book "Mountains of Debt, Crisis and Change in Renaissance Florence, Victorian Britain and Postwar America" shows how

public debt associated to war brought Florence to a decline in the Renaissance.
17 An excellent read on this (unfortunately only in French) is the book by E. Beau de Loménie, « Les Responsabilités des Dynasties Bourgeoises, de Bonaparte à Mac-Mahon ».
18 Deflation is bad: http://www.economist.com/news/finance-and-economics/21644196-low-or-negative-inflation-spreading-around-world-more-worry
19 The collapse of the Bretton Woods system: https://en.wikipedia.org/wiki/Nixon_shock
20 The collapse of Bretton Woods' impact on the first Oil Crisis: https://en.wikipedia.org/wiki/1973_oil_crisis#End_of_the_Bretton_Woods_currency_accord
21 Roosevelt ends the Gold Standard in 1933: https://www.history.com/this-day-in-history/fdr-takes-united-states-off-gold-standard
22 Even if there is some part of speculation in the book, there are also a lot of verifiable facts that are appalling. His Wikipedia entry presents him as an infamous anti-Semite Nazi, but on the one hand none of the very well documented facts presented in his book is refuted, and on the other hand there is not once the word "Jew" in this book. So, he might have been anti-Zionist, but this book is far from being an "anti-Jewish" cabal, and most of the facts he puts forward are based on sources as serious as the New York Times, Forbes, Newsweek... It is easy to try and discredit someone on emotional bases and discard his whole works.
23 The Federal Reserve System: https://en.wikipedia.org/wiki/Federal_Reserve_System
24 A very interesting comparison is held on this page between the structures of the Fed and the ECB: https://www.uni-ulm.de/fileadmin/website_uni_ulm/mawi.inst.150/lehre/ss11/isp/ECB_and_Fed_-_A_Comparison_2011.pdf
25 Article 130 of the Lisbon treaty is very clear. In fact, they even repeated the same thing twice to make sure you got it: http://www.lisbon-treaty.org/wcm/the-lisbon-treaty/treaty-on-the-functioning-of-the-european-union-and-comments/part-3-union-policies-and-internal-actions/title-viii-economic-and-monetary-policy/chapter-2-monetary-policy/398-article-130.html
26 Mario Draghi, the president of the ECB: https://en.wikipedia.org/wiki/Mario_Draghi#Criticism his son is also a trader which does raise other criticism.
27 Isn't it interesting that the first thing that the rebels did, without even have seized power yet, was to create a central bank along with an oil company: https://www.cnbc.com/id/42308613
28 A very good book about the BIS is "Tower of Basel: The Shadowy History of the Secret Bank that Runs the World", by Adam LeBor. The title sounds very "conspiratorial", but it only refers to the actual confidentiality of this institution, whose very existence is generally unknown from the general

public, despite its great power. The book is based on facts and is well documented.

29 Sweden cuts maximum mortgage duration to... 105 years, the previous average in Sweden being 140 years: http://www.telegraph.co.uk/personal-banking/mortgages/sweden-cuts-maximum-mortgage-term-to-105-years-the-average-is-14/

30 Basel III : https://en.wikipedia.org/wiki/Basel_III

31 A little story based on the shipwreck survivors: http://www.michaeljournal.org/articles/social-credit/item/the-money-myth-exploded

32 Interest rates can be found on the website of the ECB, and "main refinancing operations" are short term operations: https://www.ecb.europa.eu/stats/policy_and_exchange_rates/key_ecb_interest_rates/html/index.en.html

33 You can make the simulation yourself on any Internet web site such as: http://www.bankrate.com/calculators/mortgages/loan-calculator.aspx?loanAmount=100000&years=20.000&terms=240&interestRate=1.5

34 Banks await Fed OK to deliver dividends: http://money.cnn.com/2017/06/28/news/economy/fed-stress-test-wall-street-dividend/index.html

35 Banks gamble with your money: https://www.theguardian.com/business/2010/mar/21/bank-bosses-money-larry-kotlikoff

36 Debt crisis in Renaissance Florence: http://www.historytoday.com/blog/2013/03/debt-crisis-renaissance-style

37 Check out online loans that are granted based on an individual's "potential": https://www.washingtonpost.com/business/on-small-business/backers-invest-in-people-not-businesses-through-upstart/2012/11/16/12219c2c-2e8d-11e2-9ac2-1c61452669c3_story.html?utm_term=.45b64416bbb0

38 This article estimates that HFT is now around 80%: http://www.ozy.com/fast-forward/how-high-frequency-trading-is-conquering-emerging-markets/71947
JP Morgan's take on "regular stock picking" vs algorithms: https://www.cnbc.com/2017/06/13/death-of-the-human-investor-just-10-percent-of-trading-is-regular-stock-picking-jpmorgan-estimates.html

39 Rating agencies and conflicts of interest: https://www.nytimes.com/2014/08/22/business/regulators-struggle-with-conflicts-in-credit-ratings-and-audits.html

40 "Flash Crash" of the British Pound in Asia : http://money.cnn.com/2016/10/06/investing/pound-flash-crash-currency-brexit/index.html

41 Emerging currencies crash in 2014: http://www.telegraph.co.uk/finance/economics/11762231/Emerging-market-currencies-crash-on-Fed-fears-and-China-slump.html

42 The crash of the Chinese stock market: http://money.cnn.com/2015/07/09/investing/china-crash-in-two-minutes/index.html

43 Here is one example among so many others: https://www.theguardian.com/business/2010/jul/19/speculators-commodities-food-price-rises
44 The Forex scandal: https://en.wikipedia.org/wiki/Forex_scandal
45 The Libor scandal: https://en.wikipedia.org/wiki/Libor_scandal
46 Hedge Funds speculate on the falling of the Euro: https://www.theguardian.com/business/2010/feb/19/currency-speculating-euro-investor-risk
47 Hedge Funds speculate on the downfall of the Euro... and help it a little: http://www.smh.com.au/breaking-news-world/hedge-funds-pile-up-bearish-bets-on-euro-report-20100227-p9h7.html and then Soros spreads fear: https://moneymorning.com/2010/02/24/george-soros-2/
48 "Dark Pools": https://en.wikipedia.org/wiki/Dark_pool
49 Reuter's analysis on the growing importance of dark pools: http://www.reuters.com/article/us-markets-darkpools-analysis-idUSBREA3605M20140407
50 Reuters on Dark Pools vs HFT: https://www.reuters.com/article/us-markets-darkpools-analysis/dark-markets-may-be-more-harmful-than-high-frequency-trading-idUSBREA3605M20140407
51 Shadow Banking: https://en.wikipedia.org/wiki/Shadow_banking_system
52 BlackRock: https://en.wikipedia.org/wiki/BlackRock
53 A Bloomberg study on shadow banking: https://www.bloomberg.com/news/articles/2017-08-02/how-europe-s-mifid-ii-lets-dark-trading-stay-dark-quicktake-q-a
54 In the book « La finance de l'ombre a pris le contrôle » (in French), Dominique Morisot and Myret Zaki give a deeper analysis of this phenomenon.
55 Mario Draghi is worried and wants to regulate shadow banking: http://www.reuters.com/article/us-ecb-policy-draghi-idUSKCN11S1KO
56 These were from Luxembourg, so unfortunately it's in French: https://www.lesechos.fr/21/07/2014/LesEchos/21732-104-ECH_mif-ii---les-cinq-clefs-d-une-reforme-qui-inquiete-les-marches-financiers.htm
57 New Regulations by the EU Commission attempt to limit trading volumes on dark pools: https://www.esma.europa.eu/policy-rules/mifid-ii-and-mifir
58 The new EU regulation, a "headache" for dark pools: https://www.worldfinance.com/wealth-management/why-mifid-ii-is-europes-latest-regulatory-headache
59 Concerns of large transactions going back to regular markets: https://www.itg.com/thinking-article/mifid-2-impact-dark-caps-algorithmic-trading-strategies/
60 Leverage: https://en.wikipedia.org/wiki/Leverage_(finance)
61 Any Monkey Can Beat The Market: https://www.forbes.com/forbes/welcome/?toURL=https://www.forbes.com/sites/rickferri/2012/12/20/any-monkey-can-beat-the-market/
62 Bitcoin value plummets following Chinese ICO ban:

https://www.cnbc.com/2017/09/04/bitcoin-digital-currency-price-falls-on-china-ico-ban.html
63 A very well designed site, whose data is from 2015 but which still reflects the current situation, graphically represents the different types of money in circulation: http://money.visualcapitalist.com/all-of-the-worlds-money-and-markets-in-one-visualization
64 An estimate of derivatives: http://www.globalresearch.ca/global-derivatives-1-5-quadrillion-time-bomb/5464666
65 The mission of the ECB: http://www.ecb.europa.eu/ecb/html/index.en.html
66 Phillips Curve online: https://www.economicshelp.org/blog/1364/economics/phillips-curve-explained/ For more detailed information, Wikipedia is still around: https://en.wikipedia.org/wiki/Phillips_curve
67 Source (in German): https://www.querschuesse.de/eurozone-monetary-developments-november-2015/
68 Quantitative Easing simple explanation: http://www.investopedia.com/terms/q/quantitative-easing.asp
69 Some think that the current QE program is beyond the ECB's role: https://www.armstrongeconomics.com/international-news/rule-of-law/the-legal-challenge-to-quantitative-easing/
70 France managed to borrow at negative interest rates: https://www.economist.com/news/leaders/21697844-germany-should-stop-whining-about-negative-rates-and-start-borrowing-going-negative
71 Reuters reports the diminishing influence of central bankers: http://www.reuters.com/article/us-global-centralbanks/from-heroes-to-bystanders-central-banks-growth-challenge-idUSKCN0RV3G020151001
72 It is difficult to understand how difficult it can be to just do a "-x" on one side and a "+x" on the other. Banks are making loads of money from fees on international transfers: https://www.theguardian.com/money/2017/apr/08/leaked-santander-international-money-transfers-transferwise
73 Obama accuses China of playing with their currency: http://www.telegraph.co.uk/news/worldnews/asia/china/8812596/Barack-Obama-accuses-China-of-gaming-with-low-currency.html
74 Milk Farmers protest and get subsidies: http://www.bbc.com/news/business-34171946
75 Milk quotas have been finally abolished in 2015: https://en.wikipedia.org/wiki/Common_Agricultural_Policy#The_CAP_today But we see that the problem with milk production is still not resolved.
76 Five countries sit on 90 percent of cash injected by the ECB: http://www.reuters.com/article/us-ecb-banks-cash-idUSKBN17Y1B7?il=0
77 The President of the Ifo recommends to the German State that it should put some pressure on the ECB about the Target System balances (in German) : https://www.wallstreet-online.de/nachricht/9159259-target-salden-bedrohliche-entwicklung-ueberziehungskredite-bundesbank-allzeit-hoch
78 The 2016 IMF study :

http://www.imf.org/external/np/pp/eng/2016/072716.pdf
79 Minimum wages in Europe: http://ec.europa.eu/eurostat/statistics-explained/index.php/File:Minimum_wages,_January_2008_and_2017_YB17_I.png
80 You may read some articles about how "eager" the German elderly are to "work past retirement time". The reality is quite different: they know very well that their pension will not be enough to survive, as many of them get just 600 Euros per month: http://www.dw.com/en/german-retirement-system-leads-to-pensioner-poverty/a-18889839 and http://www.dailymail.co.uk/news/article-2253922/Germany-accused-deporting-elderly-Rising-numbers-moved-Asia-Eastern-Europe-sky-high-care-costs.html
81 The CFA Franc (although this is a very "European" presentation of the subject): https://en.wikipedia.org/wiki/CFA_franc
82 The brutal devaluation of the CFA Franc in 1994: http://www.nytimes.com/1994/02/23/world/french-devaluation-of-african-currency-brings-wide-unrest.html
83 The French newspaper is reporting how everything went well with the devaluation (in French): https://www.lesechos.fr/29/06/1994/LesEchos/16676-002-ECH_devaluation-du-cfa--un-bilan-encourageant.htm
84 Macron blames "civilization" for Africa's problems: https://www.washingtonpost.com/news/global-opinions/wp/2017/07/14/macron-blames-civilization-for-africas-problems-france-should-acknowledge-its-own-responsibility/?utm_term=.3b8c997bf2a9
85 "Good" African countries blame "bad" ones that bring the CFAF down (in French): http://www.rewmi.com/devaluation-programmee-franc-cfa-1-euro-1300-f-cfa-lon-redoutait-desormais-table-de-macron.html
86 Analysis of French inflation (in French) and why having no inflation is not necessarily a good thing: http://tempsreel.nouvelobs.com/economie/20160114.OBS2793/inflation-zero-en-france-pourquoi-il-ne-faut-pas-se-rejouir-trop-vite.html
87 Energy importations in France (in French): https://www.connaissancedesenergies.org/quel-est-le-montant-de-la-facture-energetique-francaise-120328
88 Trade Balance (« Balance Commerciale ») of France since the 1950s (in French): http://economie-bourse.blogspot.com/2013/02/dette-publique-deficit-public-balance.html
89 Many analysts correlate the end of the Bretton Woods system with the cycles of crises that seem to happen since then. Here is one: https://www.creditwritedowns.com/2014/02/economic-crisis-post-bretton-woods-age.html
90 The IMF report for 2013, saying that "fiscal plans to ... move away from indiscriminate spending cuts are broadly appropriate": https://www.imf.org/~/media/Websites/IMF/imported-flagship-issues/external/pubs/ft/fm/2014/01/pdf/_fm1401pdf.ashx

91 There is a big debate about this in France, where the government wants to break all labor laws to allow for more "flexibility". Meanwhile, it gives Germany as a model, but as Le Monde shows, it is the wrong model to point to (in French): http://www.lemonde.fr/les-decodeurs/article/2016/03/16/code-du-travail-le-modele-allemand-pas-aussi-flexible-que-l-on-pense_4884054_4355770.html

92 List of bankers condemned in Iceland: https://en.wikipedia.org/wiki/2008%E2%80%932011_Icelandic_financial_crisis#Judgments

93 Check the OECD website for Iceland, and navigate to the "Unemployment" link on the right. Iceland is currently the country with the lowest unemployment in the whole list. And you can have a look at the history by playing with the time frame at the bottom, just move the rectangles in the "latest data available" section just under the graph: https://data.oecd.org/iceland.htm

94 The debt of France analyzed by Thierry Curty (in French): http://thierrycurty.fr/brisons-mythe-loi-73-pas-origine-dette/

95 Rating agencies downgrade Greece: https://www.theguardian.com/business/2010/apr/28/greece-debt-crisis-standard-poor-credit-agencies

96 Rating agencies make it worse for Greece as help was coming from the IMF and the EU: https://www.theguardian.com/business/blog/2010/apr/28/greece-financial-crisis

97 Süddeutsche Zeitung exposes the gains by Germans from the Greek crisis (in German): http://www.sueddeutsche.de/wirtschaft/griechenland-deutschland-macht-mit-hilfen-fuer-griechenland-milliardengewinn-1.3582710

98 Goldman Sachs helped the Greeks enter the Eurozone by masking its true debt: http://www.spiegel.de/international/europe/greek-debt-crisis-how-goldman-sachs-helped-greece-to-mask-its-true-debt-a-676634.html

99 The Cahuzac affair, for instance: https://en.wikipedia.org/wiki/Cahuzac_affair

100 French tax evasion costs 80 billion Euro a year: http://www.nytimes.com/2013/10/25/business/international/french-fault-banks-over-tax-evasion.html

101 Tax evasion costs Europe 1,000 billion a year: http://www.express.co.uk/news/world/401801/Tax-evasion-costs-European-Union-one-trillion-Euros-a-year

102 Jean-Claude Juncker accused by The Guardian: https://www.theguardian.com/business/2017/jan/01/jean-claude-juncker-blocked-eu-curbs-on-tax-avoidance-cables-show

103 Stéphanie Gibaud: https://en.wikipedia.org/wiki/St%C3%A9phanie_Gibaud

104 One small association called "En toute franchise" has vowed to fight against these groups, David vs Goliath personified! From their information, the French groups would owe to public organizations up to 418 billion Euro for the single South-East region of France called "PACA".

105 The "Lock of Bercy" (in French): https://fr.wikipedia.org/wiki/Verrou_de_Bercy

106 The "Lock of Bercy" will stay (in French): http://www.europe1.fr/politique/fraude-fiscale-les-deputes-retablissent-a-une-voix-pres-le-verrou-de-bercy-3393092
107 Taxes in the Bahamas and other Fiscal Paradises: https://www.expatify.com/advice/10-caribbean-island-tax-havens-worth-moving-to.html
108 The attempt to limit tax evasion in France (in French) : http://www.huffingtonpost.fr/denis-dupre/comment-97-des-deputes-ont-fait-capoter-la-loi-pour-lutter-contre-levasion-fiscale_b_8911440.html The debate itself (in French) is quite amazing if you still believe in "democracy": https://www.youtube.com/watch?v=5SSxEbtXeM8
109 Report on the salaries compared to dividends (in French): http://www.senat.fr/rap/r10-227/r10-227_mono.html
110 Nick Hanauer : Rich people don't create jobs: https://www.youtube.com/watch?v=VLQ3ia6vRTA
111 Ford doubled the wages of his employees, and cut shifts from 9 hours to 8 hours. Then in 1916 he ended special dividends for shareholders to invest in his company instead: https://en.wikipedia.org/wiki/History_of_Ford_Motor_Company#Early_developments_and_assembly_line
112 Some billionaires such as Warren Buffet even advocate frugality, they don't spend as much as you would expect, and certainly not as much as the total expenditure of hundreds of thousands of middle-class families: https://www.gobankingrates.com/personal-finance/7-ways-personal-finance-expert-warren-buffett-lives-frugally/
113 The IMF's report on the "tickle-down theory": http://www.imf.org/en/Publications/Staff-Discussion-Notes/Issues/2016/12/31/Causes-and-Consequences-of-Income-Inequality-A-Global-Perspective-42986
114 The tax on financial transaction postponed one more time (in French): http://www.liberation.fr/direct/element/oxfam-fulmine-contre-macron-et-le-maire_64362/
115 European justice invalidates the French tax on dividends: http://www.reuters.com/article/us-france-dividend-idUSKCN18D1IM
116 More billionaires than ever before in 2017: http://www.telegraph.co.uk/news/2017/05/06/britain-has-billionaires-ever-2017-rich-list-reveals/ , 2016: http://www.businessinsider.com/more-billionaires-than-ever-before-2016-8 2015: http://www.telegraph.co.uk/news/uknews/11563981/Rich-List-2015-Super-richs-wealth-soars-as-new-money-floods-in-from-abroad.html
117 Oxfam reports 80 people own as much as half of the world's population in 2015: https://www.oxfam.org/sites/www.oxfam.org/files/file_attachments/ib-wealth-having-all-wanting-more-190115-en.pdf
118 In 2017, Oxfam reports that 8 people have as much as half of the world's population: https://www.oxfam.org/en/pressroom/pressreleases/2017-01-16/just-8-men-own-same-wealth-half-world

119 In 1923, Keynes challenges the gold standard in his book "A Tract on Monetary Reform", which contains the quote "In truth, the gold standard is already a barbarous relic."
120 Iran and Venezuela attempt to trade oil for Euros:
http://www.wnd.com/2006/02/34742/
121 Iran tries again to get Euros for oil instead of USD:
http://www.reuters.com/article/us-oil-iran-exclusive-idUSKCN0VE21S
122 Trying to sell oil for Euros has some consequences:
https://ellenbrown.com/2011/04/16/libya-all-about-oil-or-all-about-banking/.
The Guardian:
https://www.theguardian.com/commentisfree/cifamerica/2011/apr/21/libya-muammar-gaddafi Besides, Gadhafi's dream of reuniting Africa and giving it a common currency (the Gold Dinar) may have not helped as well:
http://www.nytimes.com/2009/02/03/world/africa/03africa.html Not saying he was a Saint, just pointing some simple facts.
123 Russia and China are trading in Ruble and Yuan since 2014:
http://www.reuters.com/article/us-china-russia-idUSKBN0H40X020140909
124 The president Maduro expressed his wish to get away from the USD and use "a basket of currencies" instead... interesting, isn't it? Wait until you read the next sub-chapter on the SDR... https://www.reuters.com/article/us-venezuela-forex/venezuelas-maduro-says-will-shun-u-s-dollar-in-favor-of-yuan-others-idUSKCN1BJ06O
125 The USPS uses the SDR to quote the value of goods in a package:
https://ribbs.usps.gov/intcustomsforms/documents/tech_guides/Customs%20Technical%20Guide.doc
126 Press Release about Dominique Strauss-Kahn supporting the use of the SDR:
http://www.imf.org/en/News/Articles/2015/09/14/01/49/pr1136
127 Dominique Strauss-Kahn resigns from the IMF:
http://www.imf.org/en/News/Articles/2015/09/14/01/49/pr11187
128 For the reader who wants to double-check:
http://www.coverbrowser.com/image/economist/1678-7.jpg and found on page http://www.coverbrowser.com/covers/economist/34
129 Erik's Reinert's "How Rich Countries Got Rich... and Why Poor Countries Stay Poor" is quite technical about how globalization puts pressure on poor countries, it is a very valuable read.
130 Pollution of the 15 biggest cargo ships:
https://www.theguardian.com/environment/2009/apr/09/shipping-pollution
131 I would advise a book which is now a little old (2003) but still very relevant: "Whose Trade Organization?: The Comprehensive Guide to the WTO", by Lori Wallach and other authors.
132 "A Crowbar for Carla Hills":
http://www.nytimes.com/1990/06/10/magazine/a-crowbar-for-carla-hills.html
133 Section 301:
https://en.wikipedia.org/wiki/Section_301_of_the_Trade_Act_of_1974
134 Lobbying is intensifying in the last decade, especially from new giant players in the market: https://www.theguardian.com/technology/2017/jul/30/google-

silicon-valley-corporate-lobbying-washington-dc-politics
135 Company sues Germany:
http://www.spiegel.de/international/business/germany-s-nuclear-phaseout-irate-power-companies-to-sue-berlin-for-damages-a-768201.html
136 The very serious newspaper "Le Monde" wrote an article on this:
http://www.lemonde.fr/les-decodeurs/article/2016/11/02/inside-ceta-episode-1-are-arbitration-tribunals-a-threat-to-democracy_5024320_4355770.html
Note that they are presenting the brighter side of it, of course.
137 The "banana wars" between the GATT and Lome conventions:
https://www.theguardian.com/world/1999/mar/05/eu.wto3
138 Algeria and Free Trade agreements with the EU (in French):
https://www.algerparis.fr/economie/la-zone-de-libre-echange-euro-mediterraneenne-est-elle-viable-pour-l-algerie-_a-160-5056.html
139 There are too many scandals to list them all here. For some random examples, check out the following links:
 - http://www.dailymail.co.uk/news/article-3256249/Blood-diamonds-dug-African-mines-children-young-11-gold-taken-25m-underwater-kids-aged-9-slave-labour-scandal-jewellery-hanging-neck.html
 - https://www.theguardian.com/uk/2000/nov/19/jasonburke.theobserver
 - https://www.theguardian.com/technology/2013/jan/25/apple-child-labour-supply
 - http://ethicalshopping.com/clothing-accessories/clothes/gap-caught-child-labor-scandal.html
 - https://www.commondreams.org/headlines01/1020-01.htm
140 One among too many to list:
http://www.huffingtonpost.com/2012/03/07/apple-foxconn-scandal_n_1325930.html
141 Bangladesh factory collapses:
https://en.wikipedia.org/wiki/2013_Savar_building_collapse
142 For instance: http://news.trust.org//item/20140818173015-uw8y2
143 There are so many of those, if you haven't heard about any, you must be deaf and blind. Here is one for the record:
https://www.theguardian.com/sustainable-business/2015/dec/30/vw-exxon-lobbying-brazil-mining-tragedy-toshiba-corporate-scandals-greenwashing-climate-change and another recent one (don't click if you are sensitive...):
http://www.hindustantimes.com/mumbai-news/industrial-waste-in-navi-mumbai-s-kasadi-river-is-turning-dogs-blue/story-FcG0fUpioHGWUY1zv98HuN.html
144 Here is just one recent event, but again, there are so many of those:
https://www.cnbc.com/2017/08/11/two-arrested-in-connection-with-europes-toxic-eggs-scandal-eu-commissioner-calls-for-summit.html
145 Fairphone aims for full traceability of all the materials used, and "fair" working conditions for people involved in manufacturing their phone. Additionally, they work on making phones as modular as possible to be able to replace only parts that fail, rather than changing the whole phone. And their phone is cheaper than those of some very famous brands.

https://www.fairphone.com/en/ Note that I don't work for this company and this is just an example to show that some people really have the common good in mind, while still earning money.

146 The Guardian says Fairtrade is an unjust movement that serves the rich: https://www.theguardian.com/global-development/2014/sep/05/fairtrade-unjust-movement-serves-rich The Economist wonders if Fairtrade is "good or bad": https://www.economist.com/news/business-books-quarterly/21606248-easing-consciences-good-thing-or-bad Others also wonder about it: https://ssir.org/articles/entry/the_problem_with_fair_trade_coffee

147 "We need to nationalize Google, Facebook and Amazon": https://www.theguardian.com/commentisfree/2017/aug/30/nationalise-google-facebook-amazon-data-monopoly-platform-public-interest

148 See for instance this http://www.inclusionexclusion.eu/site/wp-content/uploads/2010/03/Paper-Joras-Ferwerda.pdf and that https://www.theguardian.com/global/2009/dec/13/drug-money-banks-saved-un-cfief-claims. A French investigator also wrote a book about this where he exposes the schemes used by the mafias to benefit from the crisis (in French): "La Grande Fraude: Crime, subprimes et crises financières", by Jean-François Gayraud

149 The Dispute Settlement Body: https://en.wikipedia.org/wiki/Dispute_Settlement_Body

150 There is a very disturbing book about this, not to be put into sensitive hands: "50 Years is Enough : the Case Against the World Bank and the International Monetary Fund, by Kevin Danaher.

151 In an article in the Wall Street Journal, Milton Friedman wrote: "The IMF is ineffective, unnecessary, and obsolete". See for instance on this page: http://www.wright.edu/~tdung/imf_wb.htm (article titled "Markets to the Rescue").

152 Congo struggles to pay bills to maintain dams that power mines: http://www.bbc.com/news/world-africa-24856000

153 Greece is dismantled: http://www.independent.co.uk/voices/comment/greece-is-about-to-be-completely-dismantled-and-fed-to-profit-hungry-corporations-10452068.html

154 It is easy to check this. The Wikipedia page informs us that the state sold on June then October 2013: https://en.wikipedia.org/wiki/OPAP You simply need to navigate to some sites giving the historical rates for OPAP, such as http://www.4-traders.com/GREEK-ORGANISATION-OF-FOO-1408787/charts-historical/ While you are at it, you will observe the frenzy on the market the exact day of the last sale, on October 11, 2013.

155 Greece privatization chief resigns after being accused of corruption: http://www.nytimes.com/2013/08/20/business/global/missteps-in-big-asset-sales-plague-greece-as-privatization-chief-resigns.html

156 In Europe, the "expert" Jacques Attali is a specialist of this kind of propaganda. In 2012, he was promising that 2014 and 2015 would be marvelous, thanks to the budget cuts performed in Europe (in French): http://www.lefigaro.fr/conjoncture/2012/12/31/20002-

20121231ARTFIG00331-merkel-predit-une-annee-2013-encore-plus-dure-que-2012.php
157 Portugal bets on anti-austerity measures and succeeds (so far): https://www.theguardian.com/commentisfree/2017/aug/24/austerity-lie-deep-cuts-economy-portugal-socialist
158 Turkey pays back to IMF thanks to privatizations: http://www.hurriyetdailynews.com/turkeys-imf-debt-to-be-paid-off-foreign-debt-stock-still-on-increase.aspx?pageID=238&nid=46647
159 To go directly to the page with the graph: https://tradingeconomics.com/turkey/external-debt then click on the "MAX" button under the histogram
160 You can actually use the exact same site, by simply replacing "turkey" in the URL by "iceland". Otherwise, you can click here and then click on "MAX" under the graph to see the full history: https://tradingeconomics.com/iceland/external-debt
161 In the early 1990s, people were already very well aware of the problems caused by intense privatizations, as shown by this very interesting article published in no less that the Harvard Business Review: https://hbr.org/1991/11/does-privatization-serve-the-public-interest
162 It is called "Price Fixing": https://en.wikipedia.org/wiki/Price_fixing
163 See for instance: https://www.theguardian.com/business/economics-blog/2012/aug/22/russia-entry-world-trade-organisation
164 Brazil, Russia, India, China, and South Africa are uniting together to create alternatives to the WTO: https://en.wikipedia.org/wiki/BRICS
165 China-Congo deal meets the IMF: http://af.reuters.com/article/topNews/idAFJOE57908C20090810
166 Russia invites Greece to join the BRICS: http://www.ibtimes.co.uk/russia-invites-greece-join-brics-new-development-bank-1500901
167 The "New Development Bank": https://en.wikipedia.org/wiki/New_Development_Bank
168 This information is of course not really on the front page of the mainstream media, but one small team of investigators dug a little and compiled a good summary from public information (in French): https://www.youtube.com/watch?v=41lAe0mgjjU
169 In the great French "democracy", we could take the example of Natacha Polony who was evicted from Europe 1, but this hasn't been on the front page of any mainstream media. What about the eviction of Jean-Pierre Canet (in French): http://www.20minutes.fr/medias/2100507-20170706-envoye-special-journalistes-protestent-contre-eviction-redacteur-chef
170 In French: https://youtu.be/6Ns-i1FoO7o?t=14m50s
171 If you have no idea what the Bilderberg is, please close your TV immediately. You can start with Wikipedia: https://fr.wikipedia.org/wiki/Groupe_Bilderberg
172 Fourty economists support Macron (in French): http://fr.reuters.com/article/topNews/idFRKBN17E1L4-OFRTP
173 Securitization, a very bad name for a very risky practice: https://en.wikipedia.org/wiki/Securitization

References

174 Subprimes are back and kicking: https://dealbook.nytimes.com/2014/07/19/in-a-subprime-bubble-for-used-cars-unfit-borrowers-pay-sky-high-rates/?_php=true&_type=blogs&_r=0

175 In fact, they may not be "that mad", and may perfectly know what they are doing. A very interesting documentary that shows how that crisis was actually "planned" and taken advantage of by some is "Inside Job", by Charles Ferguson.

176 The ECB is expected to gradually end its QE program: https://www.reuters.com/article/us-ecb-policy-idUSKBN19Z0UW

177 The President of the Ifo recommends ending the ECB QE program, the publication itself titled "Inflation is Back" is in German and can be downloaded on the page of the Press Release in English: http://www.cesifo-group.de/ifoHome/presse/Pressemitteilungen/Pressemitteilungen-Archiv/2017/Q1/press_20170309-EZB

178 Banco Popular on Wikipedia: https://en.wikipedia.org/wiki/Banco_Popular_Espa%C3%B1ol

179 Banco Popular bought 1€ by Santander: http://money.cnn.com/2017/06/07/investing/santander-banco-popular-spain-banks/index.html

180 Italian bail-outs: http://fortune.com/2017/06/26/italy-bank-bailout-eu-intesa-sanpaolo/

181 Reuters wondering if "100,000" will be enough: http://www.reuters.com/article/us-global-markets-selloff-idUSKBN1AR1RW

182 Bank accounts in Europe are guaranteed... up to 100,000 Euros: https://en.wikipedia.org/wiki/Deposit_insurance#European_Union

183 Blocking indiscriminately all accounts in case of a systemic failure: https://www.reuters.com/article/us-eu-banks-deposits-idUSKBN1AD1RS

184 Ben Laden's bank scheme: http://www.thenewsminute.com/article/hsbc-accounts-and-golden-chain-osama-bin-laden-23183

185 Deutsche Bank CEO predicts cash will be gone in a decade: http://www.reuters.com/article/us-davos-meeting-banks-technology-idUSKCN0UY259

186 Denmark plans to become a cashless country: http://www.telegraph.co.uk/finance/economics/11586778/Denmark-moves-step-closer-to-being-a-cashless-country.html

187 Korea can offer roadmap to cashless Asia: https://www.reuters.com/article/us-south-korea-cash-breakingviews-idUSKBN13R0OT

188 Confusion prevails even four months after demonetization: http://www.hindustantimes.com/delhi-news/confusion-prevails-at-rbi-even-four-months-after-demonetisation/story-Vgw8OVPZAInfnVGF7IM0AP.html

189 Visa offers restaurants $10,000 to go cashless: http://www.nbcnews.com/business/consumer/war-cash-intensifies-visa-offers-restaurants-10-000-go-cashless-n782276

190 The Economist on the failed demonetization in India: https://www.economist.com/news/finance-and-economics/21727909-thats-bad-news-government-hoping-windfall-indian-banknotes-cancelled

191 Venezuela withdraws 100 bolivars: http://www.bbc.com/news/world-latin-america-38339479
192 Someone is learning how to take down the Internet: https://www.schneier.com/blog/archives/2016/09/someone_is_lear.html
193 Forbes' take is that the Russian Central Bank is "forced to buy its own gold": https://www.forbes.com/sites/timworstall/2014/11/22/russias-central-bank-buying-gold-isnt-quite-what-you-think-it-is/#ccde11379123 Nevertheless, it's a good excuse to stockpile gold, and I don't believe the Russians are so desperate to sell their gold abroad anyway.
194 Forbes acknowledges that China does buy gold, and the excuse is this time the considerable growth of China's economy in the past decades. Well, why buy gold then, rather than anything else? https://www.forbes.com/sites/greatspeculations/2015/02/19/china-buys-more-gold-than-the-world-produces/#2bc494ef587a
195 Sarkozy sells one fifth of the Bank of France's gold (in French): http://www.lepoint.fr/economie/cour-des-comptes-quand-sarkozy-liquidait-un-cinquieme-du-stock-d-or-de-la-france-08-02-2012-1428657_28.php
196 The German Bundesbank is getting its gold back into its own vaults rather than abroad: https://www.cnbc.com/2017/02/14/germany-has-got-its-gold-back--they-must-know-something-we-dont.html
197 Unprecedented economy: http://www.telegraph.co.uk/finance/comment/ambroseevans_pritchard/4177664/Europes-economy-contracts-at-rates-not-seen-since-1930s.html
198 Two months before the burst of the subprimes crisis, Olivier Blanchard, lead economist, writes "The State of Macro (Ecomony) is Good". Better not imagine what would have happened if it had been "bad": http://www.nber.org/papers/w14259
199 Janet Yellen believes there won't be a new crisis in our lifetime: https://www.reuters.com/article/us-usa-fed-yellen/feds-yellen-expects-no-new-financial-crisis-in-our-lifetimes-idUSKBN19I2I5
200 Christine Lagarde is held "negligent" of giving a rogue businessman more than 400 million Euro, but not condemned: http://www.reuters.com/article/us-france-lagarde-idUSKBN1481HE
201 In his book "The Natural Economic Order", Silvio Gessell explains that he was lucky not to have known Proudhon's theories when he developed his own. Thanks to this, he was uninfluenced and had a brand new vision of things.
202 Bracteates: https://en.wikipedia.org/wiki/Bracteate#Early_medieval_bracteates
203 It is impressive to see the number of "inactive" local currencies in Wikipedia on this page for instance: https://en.wikipedia.org/wiki/List_of_community_currencies_in_the_United_States Note that even the ones that are not marked as "inactive" are sometimes only projects that never took off (such as the Ukiah Hours, for instance).
204 BerkShares could be indexed on a basket of goods rather than the USD:

https://en.wikipedia.org/wiki/BerkShares
205 Second Life economy: https://en.wikipedia.org/wiki/Second_Life
206 See for instance the incredible story of Andre Pires: https://www.pcgamesn.com/second-life/the-story-of-a-second-life-furniture-magnate
207 M-Pesa on Wikipedia: https://en.wikipedia.org/wiki/M-Pesa Note that this page has very incorrect numbers especially regarding the fees on transactions. To get an idea of these fees, you can check for instance this other page, which shows that small transactions between M-Pesa users have no fees at all: https://kenyaprice.com/mpesa-charges-rates-costs-fees/
208 To follow in real-time the total market capitalization of Bitcoin: https://coinmarketcap.com/currencies/bitcoin/
209 Sweden is considering making its own cryptocurrency: http://www.reuters.com/article/sweden-cenbank-ecurrency/swedish-central-bank-eyeing-e-currency-idUSL8N1DH3MM
210 China is building its own cryptocurrency: https://www.bloomberg.com/news/articles/2017-02-23/pboc-is-going-digital-as-mobile-payments-boom-transforms-economy
211 Russia to build its own cryptocurrency: http://tass.com/economy/949263
212 Bundesbank works on blockchain-based settlements: https://www.cryptocoinsnews.com/deutsche-bundesbank-cites-progress-blockchain-based-settlement/
213 Japan wants to launch its own cryptocurrency, the J-Coin: https://www.cnbc.com/2017/09/27/japanese-banks-cryptocurrency-j-coin.html
214 USC to be used by major banks to do their transactions: http://fortune.com/2017/08/31/banks-ubs-blockchain-settlements/
215 IBM is building a blockchain for European banks to finance SMBs: https://www.cnbc.com/2017/06/26/ibm-building-blockchain-for-seven-major-banks-trade-finance.html
216 Naxitis and Trafigura are already trading crude oil on a blockchain: http://www-03.ibm.com/press/us/en/pressrelease/51951.wss
217 The food industry looks into blockchains: http://uk.businessinsider.com/ibm-and-walmart-are-using-blockchain-in-the-food-supply-chain-2017-8?r=US&IR=T
218 Blockchain technology in French banks: http://iex.ec/blockchain-france-primer-emerging-market-alexandre-stachtchenko/
219 Nasdaq to develop blockchain technologies in Estonia: https://www.reuters.com/article/us-nasdaq-blockchain-estonia-idUSKCN0T301H20151114
220 Blockchains disrupt the energy sector: https://rmi.org/news/blockchain-reimagining-rules-game-energy-sector/
221 Blockchain technology in mobility services: https://www.reuters.com/article/us-autos-blockchain/blockchain-technology-moves-into-car-sharing-mobility-services-idUSKCN1BA1PH
222 If you like detective stories, this is a must read: https://www.coindesk.com/information/who-is-satoshi-nakamoto/

223 How Blockchain technology could change the world: https://www.forbes.com/sites/bernardmarr/2016/05/27/how-blockchain-technology-could-change-the-world/#6aa67380725b
224 In fact, he was probably inspired by the works of Friedrich Hayek, who was advocating deflation, advising austerity measures against crises, and an extremely liberal economy: no more institutions, and cities competing all over the world in an open and free market that would regulate itself without any interference from the states. He also imagined currencies not managed by the states, and in competition with each other, without regulations, the market regulating them through offer and demand. Cryptocurrencies are exactly that. It is interesting that the very people who run institutions actually supported Bitcoin, like Ben Bernanke in 2013: http://blogs.reuters.com/nicholas-wapshott/2013/11/21/the-strange-convergence-of-bernanke-hayek-and-bitcoin/
225 It is very difficult to estimate who own how much, and these estimations are based on individual Bitcoin addresses. However, anyone can split their Bitcoins on many addresses, especially to avoid losing everything if one of their addresses is compromised. It is thus very probable that this graph shows a much lower estimate than reality. The origin is probably here: http://tech.eu/features/926/Bitcoin-ecosystem/
226 Chinese miners support the "New York Agreement": https://asia.nikkei.com/Politics-Economy/Economy/Bitcoin-secessionists-fate-hinges-on-Chinese-miners
227 "Bitcoin is now useless for micropayments": https://bitcoinmagazine.com/articles/bitcoin-now-useless-micropayments-solutions-are-coming1/
228 Bitcoin and Quantum Computers: https://en.bitcoin.it/wiki/Quantum_computing_and_Bitcoin
229 Denmark and Bitcoins : http://www.coindesk.com/danish-police-claim-breakthrough-Bitcoin-tracking/
230 In the US, people who want to escape the law are turning their backs to Bitcoin, in the meantime Government Agencies repeatedly admit that they can easily trace Bitcoins: https://www.cnbc.com/2017/08/29/dark-web-finds-bitcoin-increasingly-more-of-a-problem-than-a-help-tries-other-digital-currencies.html
231 MtGox case investigated, with a very nice graph of the flow of the stolen Bitcoins: https://www.ethnews.com/new-developments-surface-in-mtgox-hacking-case-after-arrest-in-greece
232 MtGox owner Mark Karpeles arrested and charged, the investigation is still going on: http://www.japantimes.co.jp/news/2017/08/05/national/media-national/bitcoin-exchange-operator-arrested-amid-new-questions-mt-gox-theft/#.WZDLyidLfRY
233 Cryptsy's owner Vernon in China: https://news.bitcoin.com/vanished-cryptsy-ceo-big-vern-ordered-to-pay-8m-in-class-action-lawsuit/
234 Bitcoin legality: https://en.wikipedia.org/wiki/Legality_of_Bitcoin_by_country_or_territory

References

235 Australia looking to regulate Bitcoin exchanges: https://news.bitcoin.com/australia-introduces-bill-regulates-bitcoin-exchanges/
236 The banks such as Goldman Sachs don't stop telling us that the blockchain is the technology of the future: http://www.goldmansachs.com/our-thinking/pages/blockchain/
237 Check for instance this site to have a glimpse on what is going on: https://coinmarketcap.com/
238 ICO for Tezos at more than 200 million dollars, and probably not the last of that scale: https://www.forbes.com/sites/omribarzilay/2017/07/15/tezos-232-million-ico-may-just-be-the-beginning/#2abfc86b4c52
239 The European Institutions are under extreme pressure by lobbyists: http://www.independent.co.uk/voices/if-youre-not-concerned-about-behind-the-scenes-lobbying-you-should-be-it-affects-everything-from-the-a6697056.html
240 At the end of the 6th paragraph of chapter 1.2, "The Natural Economic Order".
241 At the end of the 4th paragraph of chapter 1.2, "The Natural Economic Order".
242 Loss Aversion on Wikipedia: https://en.wikipedia.org/wiki/Loss_aversion
243 OkCupid plays with its users and discovers disturbing facts about human biases: https://www.nytimes.com/2014/07/29/technology/okcupid-publishes-findings-of-user-experiments.html?_r=0
244 MtGox's bots bought millions in the last days: https://www.theguardian.com/technology/2014/may/29/bitcoin-bots-bought-millions-in-the-last-days-of-mt-gox
245 The Galileo Module by Éloïs (in French): https://librelois.fr/2017/06/11/module-galilee/
246 This was just speculation in the first edition, then a, few weeks later, I came across the following article: https://www.quantamagazine.org/a-brain-built-from-atomic-switches-can-learn-20170920/
247 The RTM: http://www.creationmonetaire.info/2012/11/theorie-relative-de-la-monnaie-2-718.html A translation is currently under way: https://github.com/libre-money-projects/theorie-relative-de-la-monnaie
248 The Universal Basic Income seen by a trade union in Finland: http://www.independent.co.uk/news/business/news/universal-basic-income-finland-useless-says-trade-union-a7571966.html
249 I'm not the only one thinking that way. Here is an interesting study on the Universal Basic Income: https://www.scientificamerican.com/article/is-guaranteed-income-for-all-the-answer-to-joblessness-and-poverty/
250 Guy Standing at the Bilderberg (just search in the page with Ctrl-F, you'll find his name): https://en.wikipedia.org/wiki/2016_Bilderberg_Conference#Delegates_.28alphabetical.29
251 For an explanation of what the ğ stands for, have a look there (in French – you can use the English flag on the right to translate the site with Google Translate): http://www.glibre.org/
252 Both are still centered on French exchanges at the time of this writing. The

first marketplace: https://gannonce.duniter.org/. The second marketplace: https://www.gchange.fr

253 Read this post before creating your account: https://forum.duniter.org/t/security-recommendations-read-this-before-creating-your-g1-account/2246

254 The Ringelmann Effect: https://en.wikipedia.org/wiki/Ringelmann_effect

255 Social Loafing: https://en.wikipedia.org/wiki/Social_loafing

256 Here is an interesting article about the struggles of big companies: https://www.forbes.com/sites/georgedeeb/2014/01/08/the-five-reasons-big-companies-struggle-with-innovation/#57c8e85d2958

257 I will give only one of the most famous examples here, although they are all over the place: DeepMind, from "Google" which is now "Alphabet", was actually the result of buying the UK-based company called "DeepMind": https://www.theguardian.com/technology/2014/jan/27/google-acquires-uk-artificial-intelligence-startup-deepmind

258 Multinational corporations turn to places where secrecy is the norm, especially to avoid taxes: https://www.economist.com/blogs/economist-explains/2013/12/economist-explains-5

259 See the chapter "Solutions" in the RTM.

260 This is not just a random example. Some people claim that the "first man who will live 1000 years is already born": http://www.dailymail.co.uk/health/article-3285537/Has-person-ll-live-1-000-born-s-experts-believe-new-book-professor-reveals-s-good-news-rest-us.html But when confronted with skeptics, Laurent Alexandre is less affirmative (in French): http://future.arte.tv/fr/face-a-lavenir-testart-alexandre

261 The Ğ1 license : https://duniter.org/en/get-g1/

262 Note that the money mass of Monero grows at an extremely slow pace compared to free currencies. Monero, "omg infinte moneros! scam!": https://www.reddit.com/r/Monero/comments/3z527f/does_monero_have_a_maximum_cap_like_bitcoin_21/cyjpue5/

www.ingramcontent.com/pod-product-compliance
Lightning Source LLC
Chambersburg PA
CBHW071205240526
45470CB00018B/1508